AF600692

Blocking and Complementarity in Phonological Theory

Advances in Optimality Theory

Series Editors: Vieri Samek-Lodovici, University College London and
Armin Mester, University of California, Santa Cruz

Optimality Theory is an exciting new approach to linguistic analysis that originated in phonology but was soon taken up in syntax, morphology, and other fields of linguistics. Optimality Theory presents a clear vision of the universal properties underlying the vast surface typological variety in the world's languages. Cross-linguistic differences once relegated to idiosyncratic language-specific rules can now be understood as the result of different priority rankings among universal, but violable constraints on grammar.

Advances in Optimality Theory is designed to stimulate and promote research in this provocative new framework. It provides a central outlet for the best new work by both established and younger scholars in this rapidly moving field. The series includes studies with a broad typological focus, studies dedicated to the detailed analysis of individual languages, and studies on the nature of Optimality Theory itself. The series publishes theoretical work in the form of monographs and coherent edited collections as well as pedagogical texts and reference texts that promote the dissemination of Optimality Theory.

Consultant Board

Published

Blocking and Complementarity in Phonological Theory
Eric Baković

Conflicts in Interpretation
Petra Hendriks, Helen de Hoop, Irene Krämer, Henriëtte de Swart and Joost Zwarts

Hidden Generalizations: Phonological Opacity in Optimality Theory
John J. McCarthy

Modeling Ungrammaticality in Optimality Theory
Edited by Curt Rice

Optimality Theory, Phonological Acquisition and Disorders
Edited by Daniel A. Dinnsen and Judith A. Gierut

Phonological Argumentation: Essays in Evidence and Motivation
Edited by Steve Parker

The Phonology of Contrast
Anna Łubowicz

Prosody Matters: Essays in Honor of Elisabeth Selkirk
Edited by Toni Borowsky, Shigeto Kawahara, Takahito Shinya and Mariko Sugahara

Forthcoming

Faithfulness in Phonological Theory
Marc van Oostendorp

Understanding Allomorphy: Perspectives from Optimality Theory
Edited by Bernard Tranel

Blocking and Complementarity in Phonological Theory

Eric Baković

Published by Equinox Publishing Ltd.

UK: Unit S3, Kelham House, 3 Lancaster Street, Sheffield, S3 8AF
USA: ISD, 70 Enterprise Drive, Bristol, CT 06010

www.equinoxpub.com

First published 2013

ISBN 978-1-84553-336-6 (hardback)

British Library Cataloguing-in-Publication Data

A catalogue record for this book is available from the British Library.

Library of Congress Cataloging-in-Publication Data

Bakovic, Eric, 1971-
Blocking and complementarity in phonological theory / Eric Bakovic.
p. cm. -- (Advances in Optimality Theory)
Includes bibliographical references and index.
ISBN 978-1-84553-336-6 (hardcover)
1. Grammar, Comparative and general--Phonology. 2. Optimality theory (Linguistics) I. Title.
P158.42.B35 2012
414--dc23

2012003528

Printed and bound in Great Britain by Lightning Source UK Ltd, Milton Keynes

Contents

Preface

THIS WORK BEGAN as a presentation at a Rutgers Linguistics Lunch gathering on November 25, 1996. A very early and entirely insufficient draft was not-so-widely circulated in 1998 as "Elsewhere effects in Optimality Theory", and a more comprehensive (but still insufficient) paper with the same title appeared as Baković (2006). Much of the core substance of that latter paper remains intact here, but much more of it is rewritten, expanded, and corrected. I realize that a truly exhaustive treatment of a topic as rich as the present one cannot possibly be achieved, but I nevertheless endeavor to do so in these pages.

Well, not *only* in these pages. If there's one thing I've learned from working on a project like this for as long as I have (off and on, but still), it's that it can all too easily spread itself around and spin off into other projects, big and small. I've been tempted at various times to attempt to consolidate all of this work here, thereby delaying this manuscript's completion even longer (perhaps perpetually). The restraint I've managed to muster means that there's a lot more left unsaid here than I might otherwise have intended, but I've tried to make reference to the other related work that I've been doing on the side whenever it's relevant.

Alan Prince has offered incredibly helpful remarks touching on most if not all aspects of this work, much of these solicited by random email messages punctuated throughout the years since I left Rutgers in 1998. I foolishly embarked on this project when I was supposed to be coming up with a dissertation topic, and Alan had the wisdom to encourage me just enough to put my thoughts at the time down on paper and to steer me toward something more worthy (and manageable) for the thesis. If I've managed to maintain an interest in this topic over these many years, it's because I've thought that at least Alan would appreciate it.

Given such a long gestation period, there are lots of other people to thank for helpful comments, suggestions, and discussion along the way: Farrell Ackerman, Strang Burton, Jane Grimshaw, Morris Halle, Gunnar Hansson, Bruce Hayes, Bill Idsardi, Ed Keer, Paul de Lacy, Greg Lamontagne, Rob Malouf, John McCarthy, Andrew Nevins, Joe Pater, Doug Pulleyblank, Sharon Rose, Hotze Rullman, Roger Schwarzschild, Paul Smolensky, Bruce Tesar, Hubert Truckenbrodt, Bert Vaux, Colin Wilson, Martina Wiltschko, Kie Zuraw, and all of the folks at a Rutgers Optimality Research Group (RORG) meeting held on November 10, 2006. I of course assume full responsibility for any errors that may have nevertheless found their way into these pages (and there are surely lots of them).

Thanks also to Janet Joyce, Valerie Hall, and Kate Williams at Equinox Publishing for shepherding the manuscript along, especially at the final stages. For crucial LaTeX tips and assistance at various points, big thanks are due to Sylvia Blaho, Andy Kehler, and Bożena Pająk; to William Adams, Alan Munn, and Herbert Schulz (via the MacOSX-TeX mailing list), to Nathan Sanders for `OTtablx`, and to all the good folks on the Internets who post and answer queries in ways that I could relatively easily find within a few Google searches. And to my Google+ agraphia group friends (Lauren Hall-Lew, Ben Tucker, Jen Nycz, Jackie Jia Lou, and Sandra Jansen): thanks for seeing me to the finish and may you all experience the joy of finishing many times over (structural ambiguity intended).

I must also acknowledge the *Advances in Optimality Theory* editors: Armin Mester, for his encouragement and patience as I sort of slowly moved things along on my end, and to both Armin and Vieri Samek-Lodivici for very helpful comments and suggestions on the near-final manuscript. I should also thank Armin as well as Junko Ito here for first introducing me to phonological theory, some 20 years ago now. My continued enthusiasm about the questions we ask and attempt to answer in this field can be traced back to their instruction and encouragement of my early pursuits. It's no mistake that the topics that have held my interest are the ones I found most difficult to wrap my head around as an undergraduate; Armin and Junko gave me the confidence to enjoy the challenge and keep at it.

A more indirect but nevertheless significant intellectual debt is due here to Stephen Anderson and to Paul Kiparsky. Anderson's early work was the first I remember reading as an undergraduate with any discernible degree of awareness, understanding, and appreciation. By contrast, an inordinate amount of my time has been spent reading and re-reading Kiparsky's work, struggling to understand it as thoroughly as possible — but, of course, it's always been worth the effort.

Finally, I must thank some friends and family. To my friend Antony Lyon, for working-at-a-coffeeshop companionship and for always reminding me that I had only intended to write a monograph-length work. To my daughter Katya Aurelia, for being so worth the constant distraction. To my mother-in-law Linda Carter, for visiting for long enough stretches of time to allow me to really focus on writing. And to my wife Karen Shelby, who has had to endure me working on this for so long. This book is for her, though I really don't recommend that she try to read any of it lest she be convinced that it really *was* a collosal waste of time.

Eric Baković
San Diego

Chapter 1

Introduction

> [T]he principle of linear ordering must in fact be qualified, since in certain cases it is untrue that a linear ordering can be imposed on phonological rules.
>
> *Chomsky (1967: 118)*

BASIC GENERALIZATIONS in generative phonology are typically expressed in the form of MAPPINGS from input representations to output representations. To the extent that a given phonological theory individualizes these mappings, the otherwise expected application of a given mapping is sometimes observed to be prevented or BLOCKED under systematic circumstances attributable to other, independently motivated generalizations.

I take it as a given that an adequate phonological theory must accurately define the ways in which mappings interact such that one can block another and the conditions under which blocking of a mapping is expected. (These are of course not the only conditions on an adequate phonological theory; they are simply the ones on which I choose to focus attention here.) The relative adequacy of competing theories can be measured in part by the extent to which these manners of interaction and conditions of blocking follow from more basic assumptions.

A blocked mapping is a generalization about the phonology of a language that sometimes does not hold due to its systematic INTERACTION with some other generalization. Blocking shares this definition with certain types of OPACITY (Kiparsky 1971, 1973a), about which much ink has been spilled over the past decade and a half or so. Blocking and opacity are both examples of OBSCURED GENERALIZATIONS (Baković 2007, 2011), which have been the lynchpins of arguments between proponents of Optimality Theory (henceforth OT; Prince and Smolensky 1993) and proponents of Chomsky and Halle's (1968) original theory of generative phonology (henceforth *SPE*, after the title of that landmark text).

In the broadest possible terms, the argument in favor of OT comes from blocking and the argument in favor of *SPE* comes from opacity. (Though there are significant wrinkles in both arguments; see Chapter 7 for specific discussion.) The latest and perhaps most comprehensive rehearsal of the argument from opacity can be found in this series (McCarthy 2007b); my overall aim in this book is to provide a comparably comprehensive treatment of blocking.

1.1 Disjunctive application

I focus on a particular type of blocking that I refer to in this book as DISJUNCTIVE APPLICATION, for three reasons. First, because disjunctive application was the first type of blocking identified in generative phonology and it has thus received recurring special attention in the literature. Second, because key phenomena in other domains of linguistics (morphology and morphosyntax in particular) have been argued to be best described in terms that are virtually identical to those that define disjunctive application; phonologists and nonphonologists alike may thus benefit from the focused attention that this topic receives here. And third, because some serious work advocating *SPE* over OT has somewhat mysteriously invoked disjunctive application as a key argument (Halle 1995; Halle and Idsardi 1997, 1998); my hope is that this book will put such arguments to rest, regardless of the ultimate verdict on which of *SPE* and OT is the superior theory.

Briefly, schematically, and mercilessly glossing over the many and varied details that are investigated in depth in later chapters, disjunctive application refers to the following type of situation. Suppose there are two mappings, δ and Δ, such that their individually predicted outputs are *incompatible* in some specifiable set of contexts σ. Suppose further that σ is the only set of contexts in which δ is applicable, while Δ is applicable in a larger set of contexts Σ that *properly includes* σ. Under these conditions, only δ actually applies in σ; Δ is blocked from applying in σ, and thus only applies in the complementary set of contexts σ' in Σ. This is illustrated in (1.1) below, where arrows indicate mapping applicability and '$\otimes$' indicates blocking of an otherwise applicable mapping.

(1.1) The complementarity of disjunctive application

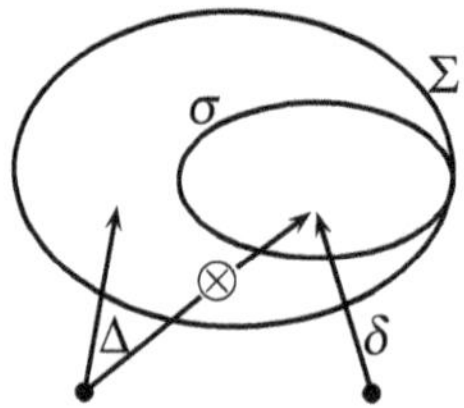

COMPLEMENTARITY is thus at the heart of disjunctive application. The same is of course true of the one kind of phonological analysis that is all but guaranteed to be covered in an introductory linguistics textbook, the COMPLEMENTARY DISTRIBUTION of allophones in basic phonemic analysis. Complementary distribution problems invite the same descriptive language — one allophone occurs in one specific context, another occurs elsewhere — but, curiously, this is as far as the connection with disjunctive application usually goes. Complementarity is widely held to be an irreducible part of the statement of a principle that is responsible for the imposition of disjunctive application as a special mode of interaction between mappings while at the same time being equally widely held to be *derived* from analytical devices particular to complementary distribution.

A central argument of this book is that the complementarity observed in cases of disjunctive application is an epiphenomenon of the formal relationship that happens to hold between the basic analytical elements responsible for the interacting mappings defined as δ and Δ are above; complementarity is thus just as much a derived property of disjunctive application as it is of complementary distribution. An important consequence of this argument is that disjunctive application does not deserve the special attention that it has received in the literature, though I of course hope that the current book is the exception that proves this rule. Disjunctive application is nothing more than a subspecies of a more inclusive type of blocking, following directly from the most basic assumptions of OT and highlighting the inherent limitations of the most basic assumptions of *SPE*.

1.2 Basic assumptions

So what *are* these 'most basic assumptions' of OT and *SPE*? In OT, they are CONSTRAINT RANKING and CANDIDATE COMPARISON. When two candidates being compared bring two constraints into conflict, the higher-ranked constraint $\mathbb{C}_1$ trumps the lower-ranked constraint $\mathbb{C}_2$ such that the winner is the candidate that fares better on $\mathbb{C}_1$. If this winner wins all candidate comparisons, and if $\mathbb{C}_2$ defines the structural description of an otherwise motivated mapping, then that mapping is effectively blocked in this scenario. Ranking thus settles the conflict between the constraints that define the inputs to the mappings δ and Δ in the abstract situation described above: if $[\![\mathbb{C}_\delta \gg \mathbb{C}_\Delta]\!]$, then δ will prevail in σ and Δ will carry the day in σ' (that is, elsewhere in Σ); if on the other hand $[\![\mathbb{C}_\Delta \gg \mathbb{C}_\delta]\!]$, then Δ will hold sway everywhere in Σ, as if δ didn't even exist.

In the case of *SPE*, the most basic assumptions are RULE ORDERING and SERIAL DERIVATION. Whether a rule applies is determined strictly by whether its structural description is met by the representation delivered by the immediately preceding rule in the ordering. This method is referred to as CONJUNCTIVE APPLICATION, a term of art that appropriately highlights the contrast with disjunctive application. It is not that Chomsky and Halle (1968) did not countenance disjunctive application; indeed, it is this work and Chomsky (1967) that first brought the significance of disjunctive application to the attention of phonologists and other linguists. However, the proposals made for determining disjunctive application in these works involved special interpretive conventions on rule abbreviation notations that were specifically designed to *circumvent* what would otherwise be conjunctive application of rules (see §2.2 for details).

1.3 The Elsewhere Condition

Interpretive conventions on rule notations were eventually abandoned in favor of a more general principle referred to as the ELSEWHERE CONDITION (henceforth the EC) by Kiparsky (1973b), adopted in some form in much subsequent work in phonology as well as in other domains of linguistics. Individual definitions of the EC vary in their details, but the core of the principle lies in a required formal relationship between two rules, stated in two parts. Two rules that are formally related by these twin criteria apply disjunctively, with the properly included (= 'more specific') rule blocking the properly including (= 'more general') rule.

(1.2) The EC's core criteria for disjunctive application

a. **Proper inclusion of contexts.** The contexts of applicability of one rule are properly included in those of the other.

b. **Incompatibility of changes.** The structural changes of the rules are incompatible with each other.

These core criteria do not necessarily originate with Kiparsky (1973b), but for a variety of reasons this one article seems to have had more influence than any other work — prior, contemporaneous, or since — on subsequent research pertaining to the topic of disjunctive application. Indeed, Kiparsky (1973b) is regarded by some as being "among the most important contributions to phonology" (Halle and Idsardi 1997: 344), and this significance appears also to be appreciated by some of our colleagues in other subfields of linguistic theory. But for all its promise of greater empirical coverage than the notational conventions of Chomsky and Halle (1968), the EC does not rise above the theoretical exigency of those conventions. The EC exists purely because the normal mode of interaction between rules in *SPE*, conjunctive application, must be circumvented in certain cases.

It is useful at this point to consider an example of the kind of case about which the EC has something to say. In English, two rules are applicable to the head vowels of branching main stress feet (Kenstowicz 1994b; Halle 1995; see §3.3 for more extensive discussion): one rule aims to lengthen the head vowel of a branching foot if it is [–high] and if the nonhead of the foot is an *i* followed immediately by another vowel, and another rule aims to shorten the head vowel of all branching feet. The structural changes of these rules are clearly incompatible, and the contexts of applicability of the lengthening rule are properly included in those of the shortening rule. The more general shortening rule is thus blocked by the EC from applying just to those heads of branching feet meeting the more specific conditions of the lengthening rule, as illustrated in (1.3).

(1.3) An example of disjunctive application

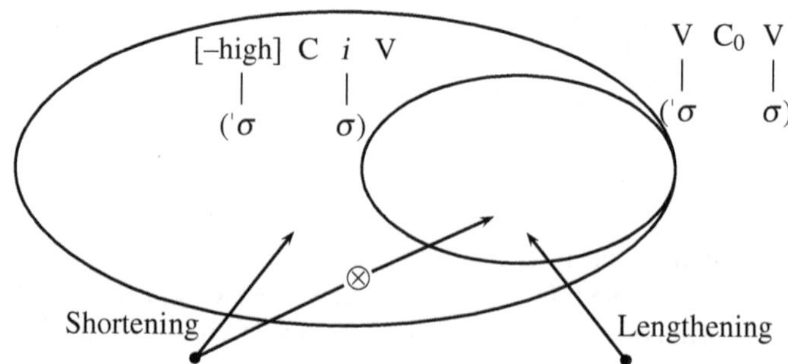

But note that the same rules applying conjunctively can achieve the same result: if the more general shortening rule applies before the more specific lengthening rule, then those vowels that are 'incorrectly' shortened in contexts of lengthening are simply (re-)lengthened later (Chomsky and Halle 1968; Kiparsky 1982; Prince 1997a).[1] Proponents of the EC point to the fact that this kind of conjunctive analysis results in so-called DUKE OF YORK DERIVATIONS (Pullum 1976), whereby e.g. an underlying long vowel is shortened only to be re-lengthened, and that these types of derivations are in principle undesirable (Halle and Idsardi 1998). Other work has demonstrated that Duke of York derivations are undesirable in fact (McCarthy 1999b, 2003c; Norton 2003); see §3.3.5 for discussion.

There is undoubtedly something right about the spirit of the EC, but as I explain in Chapter 5, the letter of this principle is riddled with stipulations; disjunctive application is not so much predicted as it is depicted by the EC. This is due to the very fact that the EC must be stated in the first place: its statement is necessary because no part of it follows from the most basic assumptions of *SPE*. The EC is a completely separate, normative principle grafted on to the architectural framework of *SPE*, dictating how certain very particular rule pairs must interact: disjunctively, rather than conjunctively. The EC can as such be refined and redefined, as it has in fact been several times in the literature, to accommodate this or that particular empirical example of (what looks like) an 'elsewhere effect'.

Even the core criteria in (1.2) have been tweaked from definition to definition, as we'll see, although there appears to be an implicit understanding that these are the least negotiable of the EC's terms — but again the very fact that these terms have to be stated at all belies this understanding. For example, why shouldn't incompatible rules with merely *overlapping* contexts of applicability apply disjunctively in those shared contexts? After all, conjunctive application of some such rules can and does also lead to undesirable Duke of York derivations (McCarthy 1999b, 2003c, 2007a, b); see §5.3. The apparent key to proper inclusion is that it is *asymmetrical*, allowing a unique determination of which rule blocks the other. The symmetry of overlap makes this determination impossible on these grounds alone, and so countenancing blocking in such cases requires that the EC be complicated even more than it already is.

1.4 OT logic

As I explain in Chapters 4 and 6, the foundational logic of OT directly predicts the disjunctive application of mappings in an elsewhere relationship without the need for a separate principle like the EC and its attendant problems of formulation. The various details of an empirically adequate formulation of the EC, each of which must be stipulated within *SPE*, fall out as necessary consequences of the same OT logic responsible for all mappings and their interactions, including other types of blocking. We can lead up to the more detailed discussion of this OT logic in later chapters with the following. Paraphrasing Grimshaw's (1997) compact statement, the relative harmony of any two competing candidates is measured by the

1. There are other cases for which a conjunctive analysis is not so readily available; see §2.4.

highest-ranked constraint on which those candidates conflict. Now consider two constraints $\mathbb{C}_1$ and $\mathbb{C}_2$ that conflict over the choice between an optimal `winner` candidate and a suboptimal `loser` candidate from some `input`, and suppose that $\mathbb{C}_1$ is the highest-ranked constraint on which `winner` and `loser` conflict. $\mathbb{C}_1$ must prefer `winner` and $\mathbb{C}_2$ must prefer `loser` in order to correctly resolve the conflict between the constraints' assessments of the candidates.

(1.4) Conflict resolution in OT

input	$\mathbb{C}_1$	$\mathbb{C}_2$
☞ winner		*
loser	* !	

All mappings and their interactions are defined by this one mechanism in OT, the particular differences among them being due to different logical relationships that arise naturally from different definitions of $\mathbb{C}_1$ and $\mathbb{C}_2$ and their expected interactions with other constraints. All that is peculiar about disjunctive application is that the constraints $\mathbb{C}_\delta$ and $\mathbb{C}_\Delta$ conflict only over a proper subset of the comparisons in which $\mathbb{C}_\Delta$ prefers `loser`; in other words — and simplifying somewhat — $\mathbb{C}_\Delta$ is violated whenever $\mathbb{C}_\delta$ is satisfied, but not vice versa. Such situations satisfy the twin criteria in (1.2). Given this logical relationship between the constraints, the independent coexistence of two mappings defined by $\mathbb{C}_\delta$ and $\mathbb{C}_\Delta$ in the same grammar requires the ranking $[\![\mathbb{C}_\delta \gg \mathbb{C}_\Delta]\!]$, and the disjunctivity of their application is entailed; the opposite ranking $[\![\mathbb{C}_\Delta \gg \mathbb{C}_\delta]\!]$, on the other hand, renders the mapping defined by $\mathbb{C}_\delta$ completely inoperative.

This last point follows from the result that Prince and Smolensky (1993) call PĀṆINI'S THEOREM ON CONSTRAINT-RANKING (henceforth PTC), which is often mischaracterized in the literature as the OT counterpart of the EC. There is a very important difference between the EC and PTC, however. PTC is a *theorem*, a provable proposition following from the most basic assumptions of OT. Unlike the EC, PTC is *not* a separate, normative principle grafted on to the independent architectural framework of OT, dictating how particular constraint pairs must interact; PTC instead descriptively identifies certain conditions under which the more specific of two constraints is expected to be INACTIVE — unable to participate in the selection of an optimal candidate from some input.[2]

But Prince and Smolensky's (1993) proof of PTC is incomplete, both in a way that Prince and Smolensky themselves note and in a way that emerges particularly clearly from the present study. The incomplete proof of PTC is nevertheless used in Chapter 6 as a necessary jumping off point for a more complete proof of another theorem that identifies the relevant set of conditions guaranteeing the inactivity of *the more specific of two constraint rankings that correspond to mappings* and from which elsewhere interactions between mappings meeting the criteria for disjunctive application in (1.2) follow. To distinguish it from PTC, I call this theorem the ELSEWHERE THEOREM ON CONSTRAINT-RANKING (ETC).

2. This point, made clearly enough by Prince and Smolensky (1993), has been lost on many linguists, perhaps due to a general unfamiliarity with the distinction between theorems and principles.

Much of the argument in this book thus amplifies and refines the following statement by Prince and Smolensky (1993), made in their brief but significant discussion of the "obvious affinities" between the EC and PTC.

> There is an important difference: PTC is merely a point of logic, but the [EC] is thought of as a principle specific to UG, responsible for empirical results which could very well be otherwise. ... [The EC] folds together a point of logic (PTC) with additional claims about what linguistic phenomena are incompatible. With the incompatibility claims properly factored out into substantive constraints of various types, what's left is PTC; that is to say, nothing. (Prince and Smolensky 1993: 119–120)

The difference is that the EC *must be stated* in order to guarantee blocking of a more general rule by a more specific incompatible rule in *SPE*; blocking of a more general constraint by a more specific conflicting constraint is *already guaranteed* by the logic of OT, and so PTC and the ETC needn't be stated at all.

1.5 Organization

The remainder of the book is organized as follows.

Chapter 2: A brief history of blocking, where I lay the groundwork for understanding — and for justifying — the provenance and privileged place of disjunctive application and other types of blocking in phonological theory.

Chapter 3: Elsewhere in *SPE*, where I distinguish two types of elsewhere interactions, named UNBOUNDED COMPLEMENTARY DISTRIBUTION (UCD) and BOUNDED COMPLEMENTARY DISTRIBUTION (BCD). I illustrate the ways in which both types can be analyzed in *SPE*, and I demonstrate that the need for disjunctive application analysis in *SPE* is restricted to a particular class of cases of BCD, which I refer to thereafter as DISJUNCTIVE BCD.

Chapter 4: Elsewhere in OT, where I present the OT analysis of UCD and disjunctive BCD and demonstrate how their basic sameness is captured in OT by the use of the same fundamental analytical elements.

Chapter 5: The Elsewhere Condition, where I discuss in detail various stipulations that have been and must be made in the statement of the EC in order to properly describe purported examples of disjunctive application.

Chapter 6: The Elsewhere guarantee, where I take on the task of demonstrating how elsewhere interactions follow from the most basic assumptions of OT, building on Prince and Smolensky's (1993) incomplete proof of PTC.

Chapter 7: Conclusion, where I conclude with summary remarks as well as discussions of other uses of disjunctive application in linguistic theory, other instances of apparently elsewhere-like interactions, and the weaknesses of the opacity argument for *SPE* and of the blocking argument for OT.

Chapter 2

A brief history of blocking

> Conjunctive ordering is wrong ... because it represents the generalization in the wrong way, namely, by requiring a stage in phonological derivations which ... has no psychological reality.
>
> *Kiparsky (1973b: 100)*

THE PHONOLOGY of a language, according to *SPE*, consists of an ordered list of n rules $\langle \mathcal{R}_1, \mathcal{R}_2, \ldots, \mathcal{R}_n \rangle$ and the derivation of a phonological form Φ consists of an ordered set of $n+1$ representations $\langle \phi_0, \phi_1, \ldots, \phi_n \rangle$: ϕ_0 is the underlying representation submitted as input to the first rule of the list, $\mathcal{R}_1$, which delivers as output the intermediate representation ϕ_1, which is submitted as input to $\mathcal{R}_2$, ... and so on, until the final rule of the list, $\mathcal{R}_n$, delivers the surface representation ϕ_n as its output.[1] The derivation of Φ is thus like an assembly line, with each rule $\mathcal{R}_i$ only having access to the nonsurface representation ϕ_{i-1}.

(2.1) Derivation of a form Φ in *SPE*

Ordered list of rules: $\langle \quad \mathcal{R}_1 \quad \mathcal{R}_2 \quad \ldots \quad \mathcal{R}_n \rangle$

Ordered set of representations: $\langle \phi_0 \quad \phi_1 \quad \ldots \quad \phi_{n-1} \quad \phi_n \rangle$

Whether a given rule $\mathcal{R}$ actually *applies* in the derivation of a form depends strictly on whether the nonsurface representation that is input to $\mathcal{R}$ meets the structural description of $\mathcal{R}$; stated differently but equivalently, it depends on whether a nonsurface representation that meets the structural description of $\mathcal{R}$ is input to $\mathcal{R}$. If so, $\mathcal{R}$ applies to the form; if not, $\mathcal{R}$ does not apply to the form. More formally:

(2.2) Basic condition for rule application in *SPE*

A rule $\mathcal{R}$ applies in the derivation of a form Φ iff the derivation of Φ contains a nonsurface representation ϕ such that (a) ϕ meets the structural description of $\mathcal{R}$ and (b) ϕ is the input representation to $\mathcal{R}$.

1. What I say about underlying and surface representations in the text holds equally, *mutatis mutandis*, of the first and last representations of a cycle or level.

When $\mathcal{R}$ doesn't apply, the result is that the representation that was input to $\mathcal{R}$ is unchanged; an exact copy of this representation is thus input to the next rule in the list. For clarity, this fact about nonapplication of a rule $\mathcal{R}$ will be illustrated in derivations by resubmitting $\mathcal{R}$'s input representation to the next rule in the list.

When $\mathcal{R}$ *does* apply, $\mathcal{R}$'s output may or may not be distinct from its input. This is because $\mathcal{R}$ may apply *vacuously* to some ϕ. The important distinction between vacuous and nonvacuous rule application will be addressed in detail later (see §5.6 in particular); unless the distinction is directly relevant, we proceed for now under the simplifying assumption that all rule application is nonvacuous and thus that application of $\mathcal{R}$ to input ϕ always results in a distinct output ϕ'.

2.1 Blocking by ordering

A particular rule $\mathcal{R}$ fails to apply to a particular form Φ when $\mathcal{R}$ fails the basic condition for rule application with respect to Φ as defined in (2.2). Naturally, $\mathcal{R}$ can be prevented from applying to Φ purely for reasons of formulation; that is, because no ϕ at all meets $\mathcal{R}$'s structural description. We are only interested here in the more interesting types of situations in which $\mathcal{R}$ fails to apply to Φ even though $\mathcal{R}$'s formulation is such that there is indeed some ϕ that meets $\mathcal{R}$'s structural description — situations in which $\mathcal{R}$ is *blocked* from applying to Φ.

Armed only with rule ordering, $\mathcal{R}$ can be blocked from applying to Φ in either of two ways.[2] One way is to crucially order $\mathcal{R}$ such that any ϕ that meets the structural description of $\mathcal{R}$ only arises in the course of the derivation *prior* to $\mathcal{R}$'s turn in the ordering. These potential prior representations are indicated as '*prior to* $\mathcal{R}$' in the diagram in (2.3) below. The other way is to crucially order $\mathcal{R}$ such that any ϕ that meets the structural description of $\mathcal{R}$ only arises in the course of the derivation *subsequent* to $\mathcal{R}$'s turn in the ordering. These potential subsequent representations are indicated as '*subsequent to* $\mathcal{R}$' in (2.3), where blocking of $\mathcal{R}$ is indicated by a '⊗' between $\mathcal{R}$ and its input representation.

(2.3) Blocking by ordering in *SPE*

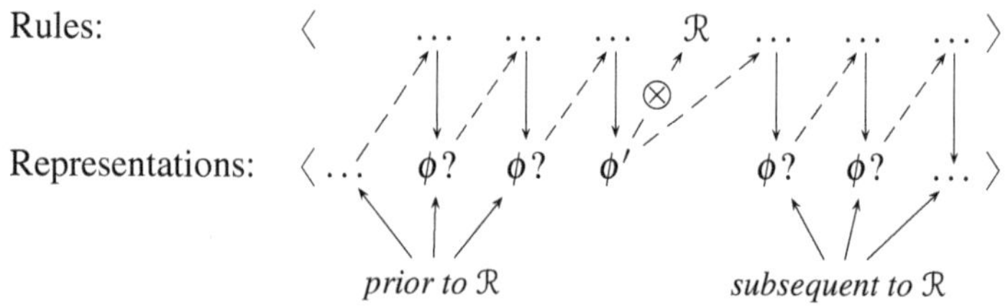

If the ϕ that meets $\mathcal{R}$'s structural description crucially appears only prior to $\mathcal{R}$'s turn in the ordering, then some rule (or combination of rules) crucially ordered *before* $\mathcal{R}$ must be responsible for changing ϕ to a distinct ϕ' that is input to $\mathcal{R}$ but that does not meet $\mathcal{R}$'s structural description. This amounts to what phonologists generally call a BLEEDING interaction, discussed in detail in §2.1.1 below.

2. If there are multiple potential loci of application of $\mathcal{R}$ in Φ, $\mathcal{R}$ may be blocked in some loci but not others. We assume only one potential locus in Φ for now, but return to this important point in §5.5.

If the ϕ that meets $\mathcal{R}$'s structural description crucially appears only subsequent to $\mathcal{R}$'s turn in the ordering, then some rule (or combination of rules) crucially ordered *after* $\mathcal{R}$ must be responsible for creating ϕ from a distinct ϕ' that was input to $\mathcal{R}$ but that did not meet $\mathcal{R}$'s structural description. This amounts to what phonologists call a COUNTERFEEDING interaction, discussed in detail in §2.1.2.

2.1.1 Bleeding

In a bleeding interaction, the application of a rule $\mathcal{R}$ is blocked by the application of another rule $\mathcal{P}$ in the derivation of a form Φ if (i) $\mathcal{P}$ precedes $\mathcal{R}$ in the rule order, (ii) $\mathcal{P}$ applies to a representation ϕ that also meets the structural description of $\mathcal{R}$, (iii) application of $\mathcal{P}$ to ϕ results in a distinct representation ϕ' which does not meet the structural description of $\mathcal{R}$, and (iv) there is no rule $\mathcal{Q}$, crucially ordered between $\mathcal{P}$ and $\mathcal{R}$, such that application of $\mathcal{Q}$ effectively changes ϕ' back to a ϕ-like representation that meets $\mathcal{R}$'s structural description. Under these conditions, $\mathcal{P}$ is said to bleed $\mathcal{R}$.[3] Consider, for example, the bleeding interaction between the following two rules of Lamba (Doke 1938; Kenstowicz and Kisseberth 1979).

(2.4) Lowering and Palatalization in Lamba

a. Lowering

$$[-\text{back}] \longrightarrow [-\text{high}] \;/\; [-\text{high}]\ C_0 \;\text{—} \qquad = \mathcal{P}$$

b. Palatalization

$$\text{k, s} \longrightarrow \text{ʧ, ʃ} \;/\; \text{—} \begin{bmatrix}+\text{high}\\ -\text{back}\end{bmatrix} \qquad = \mathcal{R}$$

Given the underlying representation */kos+ik+a/* 'be strong', either Lowering or Palatalization could in principle apply nonvacuously: application of Lowering would change the representation to |*koseka*|, and application of Palatalization would change it to |*koʃika*|. But Palatalization is not applicable to the output of Lowering, |*koseka*|, because Palatalization requires the vowel following the s to be [+high]. If Lowering applies first, then, Palatalization is blocked from applying to this kind of form. This is what happens in Lamba: the correct surface representation is *koseka*. Lowering thus bleeds Palatalization in the derivation of this kind of form, by crucially changing a ϕ (*kosika*) that meets the structural descriptions of both rules to a distinct ϕ' (*koseka*) that does not meet the structural description of Palatalization. This bleeding interaction is illustrated in (2.5).

(2.5) Blocking by bleeding in Lamba

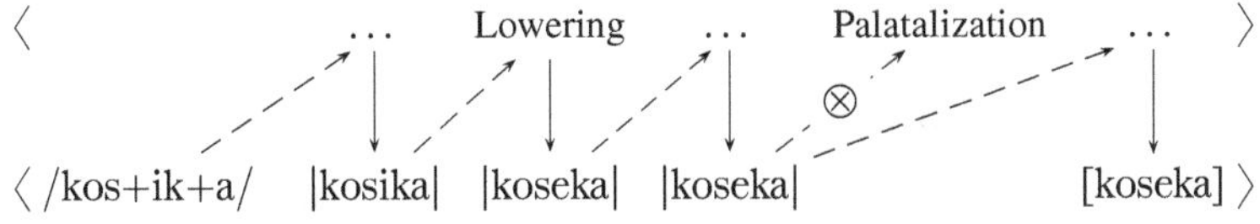

3. The fact that ϕ' does not meet the structural description of $\mathcal{R}$ could in principle be due to the crucially combined application of two or more rules. Suppose, for example, that $\mathcal{P}$ is crucially fed by a prior rule $\mathcal{O}$; if $\mathcal{O}$ doesn't apply, then neither does $\mathcal{P}$ and thus $\mathcal{R}$ is not blocked. In such a situation, we would have to say that $\mathcal{R}$ is blocked by the ordered set $\langle \mathcal{O}, \mathcal{P} \rangle$. Whether this should be called 'bleeding' or something else is a terminological question of little import here. Interesting though such caveats may be, they are set aside here for the sake of clarity.

If these rules applied in the opposite order, Lowering would successfully apply to the output of Palatalization in what is called a COUNTERBLEEDING order:

(2.6) Hypothetical counterbleeding, assuming the rules in (2.4)

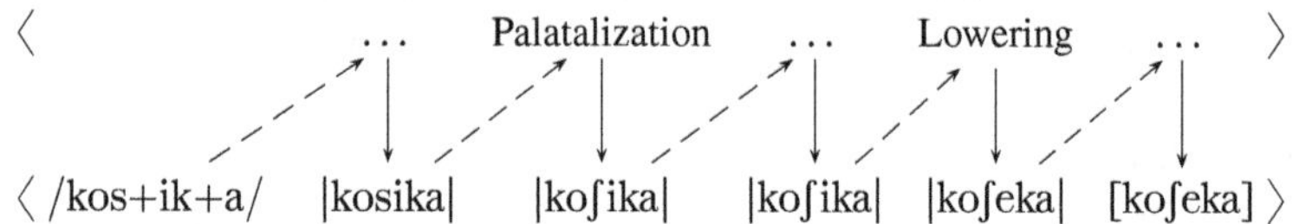

Note that there is no blocking in this hypothetical derivation: the structural description of Palatalization is met by its input representation and so Palatalization applies; this result does not affect the fact that Lowering is applicable and so Lowering also applies. Counterbleeding can thus be characterized as a *failure to bleed*: Lowering bleeds Palatalization in (2.5), but fails to bleed it in (2.6).[4]

2.1.2 Counterfeeding

In a counterfeeding interaction, the application of a rule $\mathcal{R}$ is blocked in the derivation of a form Φ if (i) another rule $\mathcal{S}$ follows $\mathcal{R}$ in the rule order, (ii) $\mathcal{S}$ applies to a representation ϕ' that does not also meet the structural description of $\mathcal{R}$, and (iii) application of $\mathcal{S}$ to ϕ' results in a distinct representation ϕ that does meet the structural description of $\mathcal{R}$.[5] Under these conditions, $\mathcal{S}$ is said to counterfeed $\mathcal{R}$. Consider, for example, the counterfeeding interaction between the following two rules of Lomongo (Hulstaert 1961; Odden 2005).

(2.7) Gliding and Deletion in Lomongo

a. Gliding

$[\text{–low}] \longrightarrow [\text{–syll}]\ /\ \underline{\quad}\ \text{V} \qquad = \mathcal{R}$

b. Deletion

$\begin{bmatrix}\text{+voi}\\ \text{–son}\end{bmatrix} \longrightarrow \varnothing\ /\ \text{V}\ \underline{\quad} \qquad = \mathcal{S}$

Given the underlying representation /*o+bina*/ 'you (sg.) dance', only Deletion (= $\mathcal{S}$) can apply nonvacuously; its application changes the representation to |*oina*|. Gliding (= $\mathcal{R}$) is now applicable to this new representation, because Gliding requires that there be a sequence of two adjacent vowels. If Gliding is ordered before Deletion, then, Gliding is blocked from applying to this kind of form. This is indeed what happens in Lomongo: the correct surface representation for this

4. The characterization of counterbleeding as a failure to bleed is adapted from Kenstowicz (1994b: 97); thanks to Lev Blumenfeld for originally bringing this characterization to my attention.

5. A fourth condition holds of many proposed cases of counterfeeding: that there is no rule $\mathcal{T}$, crucially ordered after $\mathcal{S}$, such that application of $\mathcal{T}$ effectively changes ϕ back to a ϕ'-like representation that does not meet $\mathcal{R}$'s structural description. This condition ensures that counterfeeding crucially results in $\mathcal{R}$ being *opaque* (Kiparsky 1971, 1973a) or more specifically *non-surface-true* (McCarthy 1999b); see §4.1.6 for further discussion. The definition in the text more broadly defines situations where application of $\mathcal{R}$ is blocked in the derivation of Φ due to its ordering with respect to another rule $\mathcal{S}$, regardless of what any other rules like $\mathcal{T}$ might do in the derivation of Φ.

form is *oina*. Deletion thus counterfeeds Gliding in the derivation of this kind of form, by crucially changing a ϕ' that does not meet the structural description of Gliding to a distinct ϕ that does, but too late for Gliding to apply to that ϕ. The counterfeeding interaction between these two rules is illustrated in (2.8).

(2.8) Blocking by counterfeeding in Lomongo

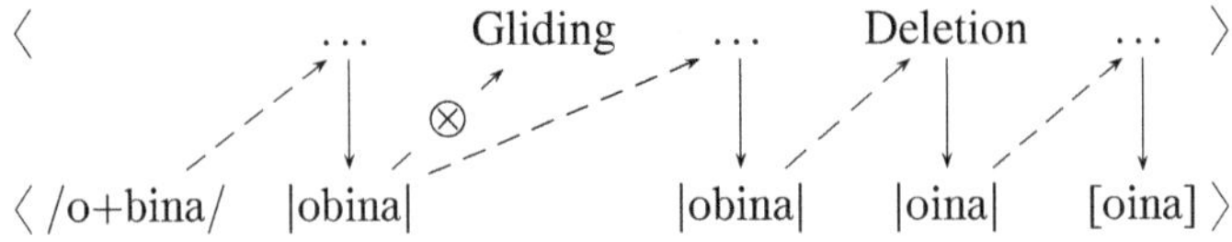

If these rules applied in the opposite order, Gliding would successfully apply to the output of Deletion in what is called a FEEDING order:

(2.9) Hypothetical feeding, assuming the rules in (2.7)

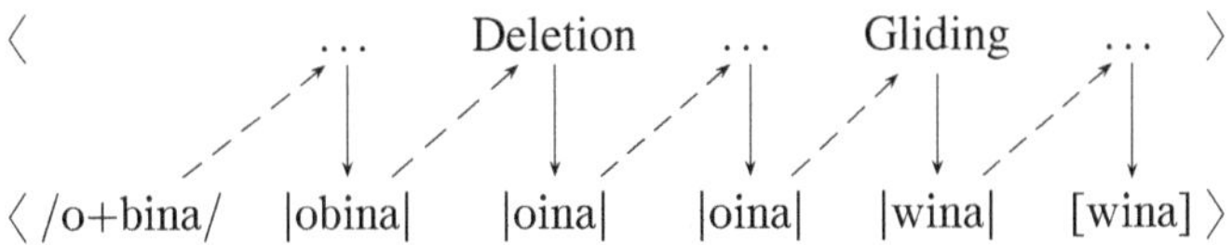

Note again that there is no blocking in this hypothetical derivation: the structural description of Deletion is met by its input representation and so Deletion applies; the result of this application crucially enables the applicability of Gliding and so Gliding also applies. Counterfeeding can thus be characterized as a *failure to feed*: Deletion feeds Gliding in (2.9), but fails to feed it in (2.8).

2.1.3 Summary

Cases of bleeding and counterfeeding show that the applicability of a rule $\mathcal{R}$ crucially depends on the ordering of $\mathcal{R}$ with respect to other rules. If a representation ϕ of a form Φ meets the structural descriptions of two rules $\mathcal{P}$ and $\mathcal{R}$, and application of $\mathcal{P}$ to ϕ results in a distinct representation ϕ' that does not meet $\mathcal{R}$'s structural description, then the order $\langle \mathcal{P} > \mathcal{R} \rangle$ ('$\mathcal{P}$ precedes $\mathcal{R}$') entails that $\mathcal{R}$ will be bled and not apply to Φ (the potential intervention of other rules aside). Similarly, if a representation ϕ' of a form Φ meets the structural description of $\mathcal{S}$, and application of $\mathcal{S}$ to ϕ' results in a distinct representation ϕ that does meet $\mathcal{R}$'s structural description, then the order $\langle \mathcal{R} > \mathcal{S} \rangle$ entails that $\mathcal{R}$ will be counterfed and not apply to Φ (again, the potential intervention of other rules aside).

2.2 Ordering is not enough

There has been general agreement since the earliest days of generative phonology that bleeding and counterfeeding are insufficient to account for all known types of blocking. There are also cases in which a rule $\mathcal{R}$ is blocked in the derivation of a form Φ due to a kind of interaction with another rule $\mathcal{R}'$ that cannot be characterized in terms of bleeding or counterfeeding. Examples of this type involve *disjunctive application* of $\mathcal{R}$ and $\mathcal{R}'$: $\mathcal{R}$ is blocked from applying in the derivation of Φ simply due to the fact that $\mathcal{R}'$ applies to some ϕ in the derivation of Φ. (There are still other types of blocking, as discussed in §2.5 below.)

The special status of disjunctive application with respect to the basic condition for rule application in (2.2) has led to the proposal of several 'interpretive conventions' for some of *SPE*'s various notational devices. The hypothesis underlying this kind of move is that if neither $\mathcal{R}$'s structural description nor $\mathcal{R}$'s position in the order can be held responsible for the failure of $\mathcal{R}$ to apply, then blocking of $\mathcal{R}$ must be due to some other formal relationship between $\mathcal{R}$ and another rule $\mathcal{R}'$, and that relationship must be expressible in terms of some notational device.

2.2.1 The parenthesis notation

The best known of the interpretive conventions proposed to handle disjunctive application is the convention for the interpretation of the parenthesis notation (Chomsky et al. 1956; Chomsky 1967; Chomsky and Halle 1968; Halle and Keyser 1971). Consider the Latin stress rules in (2.10), after Anderson (1974: 97).

(2.10) Latin stress rules

a. $\mathrm{V} \longrightarrow [\text{+stress}] \,/\, \text{—}\, \mathrm{C_0 \breve{V} C_0^1 V C_0 \#}$

b. $\mathrm{V} \longrightarrow [\text{+stress}] \,/\, \text{—}\, \mathrm{C_0 V C_0 \#}$

c. $\mathrm{V} \longrightarrow [\text{+stress}] \,/\, \text{—}\, \mathrm{C_0 \#}$

Any form meeting the structural description of one of the longer rules in (2.10) also meets the structural description of any shorter rule in (2.10). Conjunctive application to any form that meets the structural descriptions of more than one of the rules will thus result in multiple stresses on the form, regardless of the order in which the rules apply. This is illustrated by the various derivations in (2.11) of a form meeting the structural descriptions of all three of the rules in (2.10).

(2.11) Conjunctive application of (2.10)

a. /patricia/ $\underset{(2.10a)}{\longrightarrow}$ |pa'tricia| $\underset{(2.10b)}{\longrightarrow}$ |pa'tri'cia| $\underset{(2.10c)}{\longrightarrow}$ *[pa'tri'ci'a]

b. /patricia/ $\underset{(2.10b)}{\longrightarrow}$ |patri'cia| $\underset{(2.10a)}{\longrightarrow}$ |pa'tri'cia| $\underset{(2.10c)}{\longrightarrow}$ *[pa'tri'ci'a]

c. /patricia/ $\underset{(2.10b)}{\longrightarrow}$ |patri'cia| $\underset{(2.10c)}{\longrightarrow}$ |patri'ci'a| $\underset{(2.10a)}{\longrightarrow}$ *[pa'tri'ci'a]

d. /patricia/ $\underset{(2.10a)}{\longrightarrow}$ |pa'tricia| $\underset{(2.10c)}{\longrightarrow}$ |pa'trici'a| $\underset{(2.10b)}{\longrightarrow}$ *[pa'tri'ci'a]

e. /patricia/ $\underset{(2.10c)}{\longrightarrow}$ |patrici'a| $\underset{(2.10a)}{\longrightarrow}$ |pa'trici'a| $\underset{(2.10b)}{\longrightarrow}$ *[pa'tri'ci'a]

f. /patricia/ $\underset{(2.10c)}{\longrightarrow}$ |patrici'a| $\underset{(2.10b)}{\longrightarrow}$ |patri'ci'a| $\underset{(2.10a)}{\longrightarrow}$ *[pa'tri'ci'a]

The intended result, of course, is for only one of the rules in (2.10) to apply to any given form. Forms that meet the structural description of (2.10a) — trisyllabic or longer forms with short open penults — are also guaranteed to meet the structural descriptions of (2.10b, c), but only (2.10a) applies to them (*pa'tricia*, *'reficit*). Forms that do not meet the structural description of (2.10a) but that do meet the structural description of (2.10b) — bisyllabic forms and forms with long or closed penults — are also guaranteed to fit the structural description of (2.10c), but only (2.10b) applies to them (*re'fectus, re'fēcit, 'aqua, 'amō*). Finally, (2.10c) applies elsewhere; i.e., only to forms that fit its structural description and not the structural descriptions of (2.10a, b) — monosyllabic forms (*'mens, 'cor, 'rē*).

Application of either of the longer rules must thus somehow block application of the shorter rules, even though application of these longer rules cannot possibly bleed nor counterfeed application of the shorter ones. Chomsky and Halle (1968: 77) propose that the complementarity of application among stress rules like these is a result of the formal overlap among the strings they describe, abbreviable via parentheses as in (2.12) (after Anderson 1974: 100).

(2.12) Collapse of (2.10) with parentheses

$$\mathrm{V} \longrightarrow [+\mathrm{stress}] \,/\, \text{—}\, \mathrm{C}_0\big(\big(\breve{\mathrm{V}}\mathrm{C}_0^1\big)\mathrm{V}\mathrm{C}_0\big)\#$$

By convention, the parenthesis notation in a rule $\mathcal{R}$ is interpreted as follows. First, the longest subrule $\mathcal{L}$ of $\mathcal{R}$ — the subrule including all parenthesized material — is considered for application to the nonsurface representation ϕ of Φ that is input to $\mathcal{R}$. If ϕ meets the structural description of $\mathcal{L}$, then $\mathcal{L}$ applies to ϕ and application of all remaining subrules of $\mathcal{R}$ is blocked. Otherwise, the material enclosed within the innermost pair of parentheses is removed to yield the next subrule $\mathcal{N}$ of $\mathcal{R}$, which is then considered for application to ϕ. If ϕ meets the structural description of $\mathcal{N}$, then $\mathcal{N}$ applies to ϕ and application of any remaining subrules is blocked. Otherwise, the innermost parenthesized material (if any remains) is removed, yielding the next subrule ... and so on down the line.

In the case of the Latin stress rule in (2.12), the longest subrule is (2.10a), the next longest subrule is (2.10b), and the shortest subrule is (2.10c). Each subrule is given an opportunity to apply to the ϕ that is input to (2.12) in this order, with the proviso that once one of the subrules actually applies the remaining subrules are blocked. This is illustrated by the derivations in (2.13), where '⊗' indicates a blocked subrule (because a longer, earlier subrule has applied) and '⊙' indicates a subrule that is not applicable (thus allowing a shorter, later subrule to apply).

(2.13) Application of (2.10) to different forms

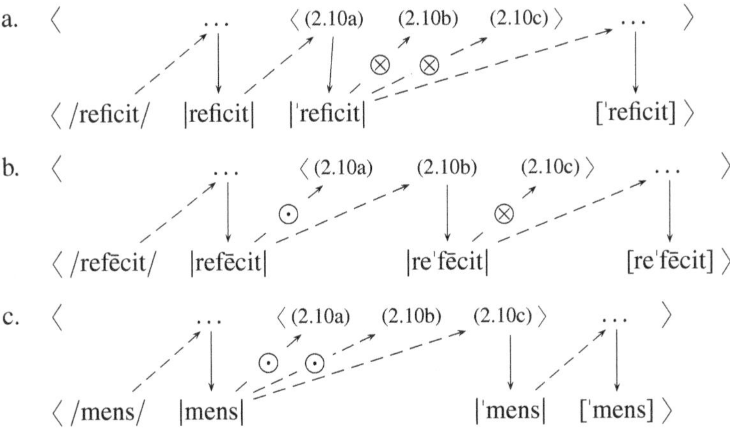

The form derived in (2.13a) represents the class of forms that meet the structural descriptions of all three subrules of (2.12). Because the longest subrule has a chance to apply first, it does in fact apply, crucially blocking the remaining two subrules. The form derived in (2.13b) represents the class of forms that do not meet the structural description of the longest subrule of (2.12), but that do meet the structural descriptions of the other two subrules. The longest subrule has a chance to apply first but is not applicable, and thus the input representation is passed on to the second longest subrule. This subrule applies, crucially blocking the remaining subrule. The form derived in (2.13c) represents the class of forms that only meet the structural description of the shortest subrule of (2.12). The first two, longer subrules have a chance to apply first but are not applicable, and thus the input representation is passed on to the shortest subrule, which then applies.

The generalization expressed by (2.12) can be summarized as in (2.14). The '*otherwise*' introducing both (2.14b) and (2.14c) expresses the crucial complementarity that follows from the interpretive convention of the parenthesis notation: (2.14a) applies if its structural description is met, (2.14b) only applies if its structural description is met and (2.14a) does not apply, and (2.14c) only applies if its structural description is met and neither (2.14a) nor (2.14b) apply.

(2.14) Generalization expressed by (2.12)

a. Stress the antepenultimate vowel followed by a short penultimate vowel and at most one consonant (if there is one);
b. *otherwise*, stress the penultimate vowel (if there is one);
c. *otherwise*, stress the final vowel.

Though basically effective, there are some significant limitations to the parenthesis notation. First, the parenthesis notation can only be used to abbreviate rules that are already adjacent in the ordering, but there is nothing in principle that guarantees that a set of rules abbreviable via parentheses will be adjacently ordered. (See §5.1 for discussion of rule adjacency and related disjunctivity requirements.)

Second, the parenthesis notation can only be used to abbreviate rules that specify the same structural change — in the case of the Latin stress rule, applying stress to a vowel — but there are also examples of rules that make *different* structural changes that must also be predicted to apply in similarly complementary fashion. (See §2.2.3, §2.3.1, and §3.3 for examples, and §5.4 for discussion.)

Third, there is the empirically curious fact that only stress rules appear to necessitate the interpretive convention of parentheses outlined above. In nonstress rules, parentheses simply indicate optionality of material intervening between the trigger and the target of, say, an assimilation rule. (See §2.3.3 for discussion.)

Finally, while the parenthesis notation requires that the contexts of application of the subrules it abbreviates *overlap* in a significant way, examples that have been argued to involve disjunctive application are consistent with a more restrictive requirement: that the contexts of application of the subrules it abbreviates be in a *proper inclusion* relationship, each subrule being strictly less inclusive in its contexts of application than the next. (See §5.3 for further discussion of the distinction between proper inclusion and overlap.)

2.2.2 Other notations

Several authors have claimed that other notational devices also abbreviate disjunctively ordered sets of rules. Four specific examples of such claims that I am aware of are listed below, with relevant references and brief comments highlighting either the relative insignificance of or the controversy surrounding the claim.

- *Subscript notation* (Howard 1972: 93)
  The subscript notation "is definable in terms of the parenthesis notation" (Chomsky and Halle 1968: 62; see also Johnson 1972: 114).

- *Angled brackets* (Chomsky and Halle 1968: 76–77)
  It is only necessary for longer expansions to be ordered before shorter ones; bleeding takes care of the blocking (Kenstowicz and Kisseberth 1979: 355).

- *Greek-letter variables* (Chomsky and Halle 1968: 357)
  Blocking is only necessary to account for the complementarity of 'polarity' (or 'exchange') rules, on which see now Anderson and Browne (1973), Alderete (2001), Moreton (2004), and Bye (2006), *inter alia.*

- *Mirror-image rules* (Anderson 1969: 122ff; 1974: 110ff)
  But: "other examples argue with equal force for the conjunctive application of mirror-image schemata" (Anderson 1974: 118).

2.2.3 Notations are not enough

Discussion of the insufficiency of all of the interpretive conventions noted above begins with Anderson's (1969: 139ff; 1974: 102ff) analysis of some Middle English facts apparently involving disjunctive application between a vowel shortening rule and a somewhat complex rule accomplishing both open-syllable lengthening and (stepwise) lowering. Anderson states these two rules as follows.[6]

(2.15) Disjunctively ordered rules in Middle English

a. Trisyllabic Shortening (TSS) — *'sɔ̄ri* ∼ *'sɔ̆riə* 'sorry (sg., pl.)'

$$\begin{bmatrix} \text{+syll} \\ \text{+stress} \end{bmatrix} \longrightarrow [\text{–long}] \;/\; \_\_\, \text{CVC}_0\text{V}$$

b. Open Syllable Lengthening (OSL) — *'wĭk* ∼ *'wēkes* 'week (sg., pl.)'

$$\begin{bmatrix} \text{+syll} \\ \text{+stress} \\ \langle\text{–high}\rangle \end{bmatrix} \longrightarrow \begin{bmatrix} \text{+long} \\ \text{–high} \\ \langle\text{+low}\rangle \end{bmatrix} \;/\; \_\_\, \text{CV}$$

Trisyllabic Shortening (TSS, 2.15a) shortens stressed vowels in open syllables that are followed by at least two other syllables, while Open Syllable Lengthening (OSL, 2.15b) lengthens and lowers stressed vowels in open syllables that are followed by at least one other syllable. The structural description of TSS is thus met

6. See also Wright and Wright (1923) and Lahiri and Fikkert (1999), among others. See §2.4.2 for discussion of the possibility that the lengthening and lowering changes of OSL might be separated.

by a proper subset of strings that meet the structural description of OSL, and the two rules impose partially conflicting requirements on the strings that meet both structural descriptions: TSS shortens and OSL lengthens (and lowers).

When the structural descriptions of both rules are met, only TSS applies. Anderson thus proposes that TSS disjunctively blocks both the lengthening and lowering subparts of OSL. This is shown by the following derivations of *ˈbēsi* ‘busy’ (2.16a), *ˈbĭsines* (2.16b), ‘business’, *ˈsōmer* ‘summer’ (2.16c), and *ˈsŭmeres* ‘summers’ (2.16d). As before, ⊗ indicates blocking of OSL (because TSS applies) and ⊙ indicates that TSS is not applicable (thus allowing OSL to apply).

(2.16) Application of TSS (2.15a) and OSL (2.15b) to different forms

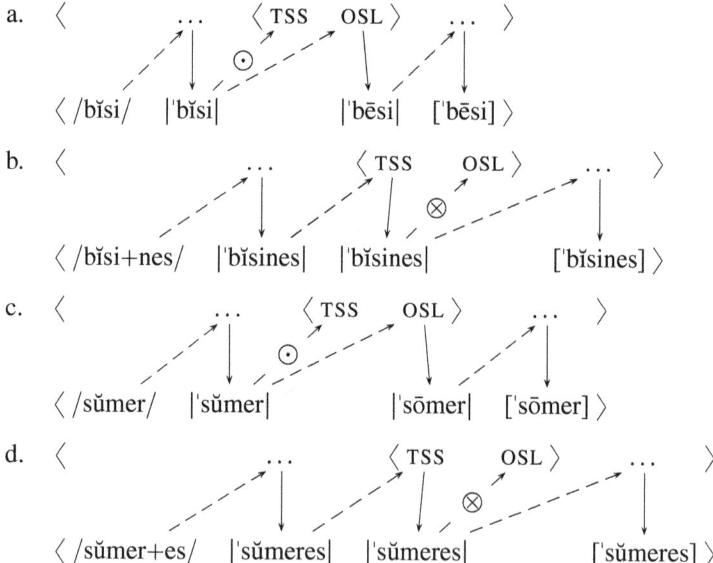

TSS is not applicable in (2.16a, c), since the stressed vowel is only followed by one syllable; OSL thus gets to apply in these cases, lengthening and lowering the underlyingly short high vowel. The addition of a suffix to these two forms in (2.16b, d), on the other hand, means that TSS is applicable; it thus applies — albeit vacuously, since the vowel is already short in both cases — and blocks OSL.

Note that these two rules are not abbreviable via any notational devices associated with disjunctive application. The options are thus either to allow disjunctive application to be stipulated *ad hoc* or to modify the conditions for disjunctive application. Anderson (1969: 141–143; 1974: 105) pursues the latter route, noting that the external contexts of the two rules (not structural descriptions; see §5.3) can be abbreviated parenthetically as — $CV(C_0V)$ and that

> while the structural changes performed by the two rules are not identical ... both serve primarily to specify the value of the feature of length. ... [T]he parentheses notation could be modified, so as not to require total identity of strings ... but rather that (a) the structural changes of the two rules be ‘related’; and (b) the [external contexts] be collapsable by the present convention for the use of parentheses. (Anderson 1974: 105)

Although Anderson does not explain how the complex change specified by OSL is "primarily" about length as opposed to height, his point is nevertheless clear: whatever else they may do, OSL and TSS demand opposite values of [±long] in the set of contexts in which both rules apply, and thus their structural changes are 'related' in a sense that requires weakening the identity requirement met by the structural changes of stress rules like those of Latin in (2.10).

Anderson (1974: 105ff) also discusses a case involving the disjunctive application of stress rules that further highlights the insufficiency of notational devices. In Indonesian, main stress is penultimate unless the penultimate vowel is schwa; failing that, stress is antepenultimate if there is an antepenultimate vowel that is not schwa; failing that, stress is final (and schwa is independently disallowed in final syllables). The rules are as given in (2.17), adapted from Anderson (1974: 106). Anderson only makes reference to the complementarity of penultimate and final stress to make his point, but this more complete description (from Cohn 1989: 173ff) only strengthens Anderson's argument.

(2.17) Indonesian stress rules

a. $V \longrightarrow [\text{+stress}] \,/\, \left\{ \begin{matrix} \# \\ \text{ə} \end{matrix} \right\} C_0\text{ə}C_0 \,\_\_\, C_0\# \quad \begin{matrix} \text{(i)} \\ \text{(ii)} \end{matrix}$

b. $V \longrightarrow [\text{+stress}] \,/\, \_\_\, C_0\text{ə}C_0VC_0\#$

c. $V \longrightarrow [\text{+stress}] \,/\, \_\_\, C_0VC_0\#$

The complex disjunctive interaction among the rules in (2.17) is perhaps best illustrated with the set of representative derivations shown in (2.18) below. (I revert to the standard vertical representation of derivations for conciseness here.)

(2.18) Disjunctive application of the rules in (2.17)

	a.	b.	c.	d.
UR	/bəri/	/sətəlah/	/gaməlan/	/bicara/
(2.17a.i)	|bə'ri|	⊙	⊙	⊙
(2.17a.ii)	⊙	|sətə'lah|	⊙	⊙
(2.17b)	⊙	⊗	|'gaməlan|	⊙
(2.17c)	⊗	⊗	⊗	|bi'cara|
SR	[bə'ri]	[sətə'lah]	['gaməlan]	[bi'cara]
gloss	'give'	'after'	'Indo. orchestra'	'speak'

The derivation in (2.18a) illustrates that (2.17a.i) assigns final stress to bisyllables with initial schwa, blocking application of the otherwise applicable (2.17c). The derivation in (2.18b) illustrates that (2.17a.ii) assigns final stress to longer words with both antepenultimate and penultimate schwas, blocking application of the otherwise applicable (2.17b) and (2.17c). The derivation in (2.18c) illustrates that (2.17b) assigns antepenultimate stress to words with penultimate schwa, blocking application of the otherwise applicable (2.17c). Finally, the derivation in (2.18d) illustrates that (2.17c) assigns penultimate stress in all remaining cases.

The parenthesis notation, even in the extended sense Anderson proposes for the Middle English case discussed further above, is clearly of limited use here.

Only (2.17b, c) can be collapsed with parentheses, resulting in $—(C_0ə)C_0VC_0\#$ and correctly capturing the disjunctive interaction between these two rules. The problem is with how the two subrules assigning final stress in (2.17a) block either of the other two rules in (2.17b, c): neither of the contexts in (2.17a) overlaps in any significant way with either of the contexts in (2.17b, c), and significant overlap is required in order to use the parenthesis notation for disjunctive application.

2.3 Enter the Elsewhere Condition

Anderson (1969, 1974) proposes a principle for determining disjunctive application that accounts for all of the examples discussed above: Latin stress, Middle English TSS and OSL, and Indonesian stress. The key, of course, is to extract from these examples what they have in common and to ensure that this commonality is not shared by other pairs of rules that do *not* apply disjunctively. Anderson's later statement of the principle is most worth quoting here.

> Given two rules, if the domain of one is a proper subset of the set of forms to which the other can apply, we can refer to the former as the 'more specific' rule. We can then say that if two rules are adjacent, and specify changes that are related, then for any given form, if the more specific of the two is applicable, this precludes the application of the other. (Anderson 1974: 107)

This principle is a clear precursor to the Elsewhere Condition (henceforth the EC), later proposed by Kiparsky (1973b: 94) and stated in (2.19).

(2.19) The Elsewhere Condition (EC)

Two adjacent rules of the form

$A \longrightarrow B \,/\, P — Q$
$C \longrightarrow D \,/\, R — S$

are disjunctively ordered if and only if:

a. the set of strings that fit *PAQ* is a subset of the set of strings that fit *RCS*, and
b. the structural changes of the two rules are either identical or incompatible.

According to both the EC and Anderson's earlier statement of the principle, two rules are disjunctively ordered if and only if they are related in two specific ways.[7] The first way is in terms of the rules' structural descriptions (2.19a): one rule must be applicable to a proper subset of the set of strings to which the other rule is applicable. This means that every string meeting the structural description of one rule also meets the structural description of the other, but not vice versa.

The other way is in terms of the rules' structural changes (2.19b). In Anderson's terms, the changes must be "related" (1974: 107) or, more precisely,

7. Technically three, since both require that the rules be adjacent in the ordering (which is formally presupposed by the parenthesis notation, as noted in §2.2.1). This is discussed in detail in §5.1.

"specifying the value of the same feature" (1969: 142). The corresponding condition of Kiparsky's EC is stated somewhat differently: the changes must be "either identical or incompatible". The "identical" case is intended to cover stress rules, which all assign stress to a vowel. The "incompatible" case covers rules like those in Middle English which specify opposite values of the same feature.

2.3.1 Diola Fogny

Kiparsky's condition on structural changes is somewhat more inclusive than Anderson's because two rules can be 'incompatible' in the relevant sense without affecting the same feature. Kiparsky (1973b: 96–97) argues that this captures the complementary interaction between two rules of Diola Fogny (Sapir 1965). The relevant facts can be described as follows: nasals assimilate in place to following noncontinuants (2.20a); otherwise, preconsonantal consonants delete (2.20b).

(2.20) Diola Fogny assimilation (a) and deletion (b)

a.	/ni+gam+gam/	⟶	[nigaŋgam]	'I judge'
	/ku+bɔn+bɔn/	⟶	[kubɔmbɔn]	'they sent'
	/na+tiːŋ+tiːŋ/	⟶	[natiːntiːŋ]	'he cut (it) through'
	/na+miːn+miːn/	⟶	[namiːmmiːn]	'he cut (with a knife)'
b.	/na+laɲ+laɲ/	⟶	[nalalaɲ]	'he returned'
	/na+jɔkɛn+jɔkɛn/	⟶	[najɔkɛjɔkɛn]	'he tires'
	/na+waɲ+aːm+waɲ/	⟶	[nawaɲaːwaɲ]	'he cultivated for me'
	/let+ku+ʤaw/	⟶	[lekuʤaw]	'they won't go'

This description is adequately captured by the rules in (2.21), adapted from Kiparsky (1973b: 98), applied disjunctively. Assimilation applies to a proper subset of strings to which Deletion applies, and the very general Deletion rule effectively deletes only unassimilated consonants.[8]

(2.21) Assimilation and Deletion in Diola Fogny

a. Assimilation

$$\begin{bmatrix} \text{C} \\ \text{+nasal} \end{bmatrix} \longrightarrow [\alpha\text{place}] \;/\; \text{—} \begin{bmatrix} -\text{cont} \\ \alpha\text{place} \end{bmatrix}$$

b. Deletion

$$\text{C} \longrightarrow \varnothing \;/\; \text{—}\,\text{C}$$

Notational devices such as parentheses are of no use here, but the EC correctly captures the complementary interaction between these two rules. First, Deletion is applicable to all preconsonantal consonants while Assimilation is applicable to only a proper subset of preconsonantal consonants: nasals followed by non-

8. Kiparsky refers to the disjoint set of nasals and obstruents in the context of Assimilation (2.21a) — but there are no post-nasal fricatives in the data cited, hence the possibility of the more inclusive 'noncontinuants' classification here. But Kiparsky's classification also serves another purpose: word-final nasals assimilate to word-initial obstruents and delete before word-initial nasals. This is coded into Kiparsky's rule so that word-final nasals correctly delete before word-initial nasals.

continuants. This satisfies the condition in (2.19a). Second, the structural changes of the two rules are ‘incompatible’, satisfying the condition in (2.19b): a consonant can either be assimilated or deleted, but not both — at least, not discernibly (see §5.4). Assimilation thus correctly blocks Deletion when both are applicable.

2.3.2 Previous cases

Here I briefly summarize the applicability of the EC to each of the other cases of disjunctive application discussed thus far: Latin, Middle English, and Indonesian.

Latin

The Latin stress rules in (2.10) are repeated in (2.22), and the derivations in (2.13) illustrating their disjunctive application are repeated in (2.23).

(2.22) Latin stress rules, repeated from (2.10)

a. $V \longrightarrow [+\text{stress}] \,/\, \_\_\, C_0\breve{V}C_0^1VC_0\#$

b. $V \longrightarrow [+\text{stress}] \,/\, \_\_\, C_0VC_0\#$

c. $V \longrightarrow [+\text{stress}] \,/\, \_\_\, C_0\#$

(2.23) Application of (2.22) to different forms, repeated from (2.13)

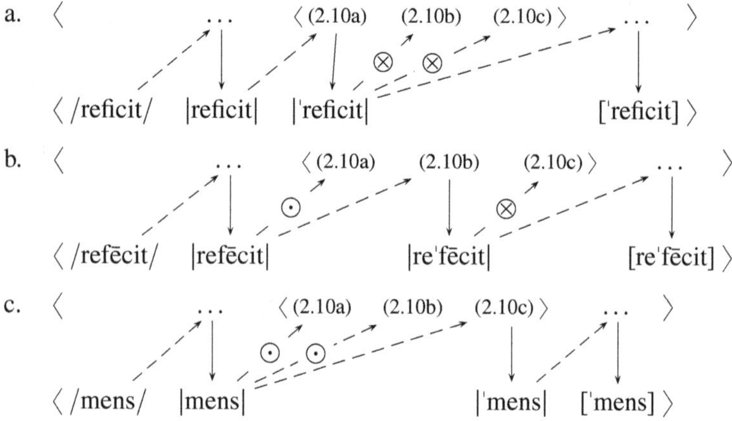

The disjunctive application of these rules is correctly predicted by the EC. The structural changes of all three rules are ‘identical’ in that they all assign stress to vowels. The structural description of (2.22a) is $VC_0\breve{V}C_0^1VC_0\#$, which describes a proper subset of the strings described by both the structural descriptions of (2.22b) and (2.22c), $VC_0VC_0\#$ and $VC_0\#$, respectively. The former rule thus correctly blocks the latter two in the derivation of forms like *ˈreficit* (2.23a). The structural description of (2.22b) also describes a proper subset of the set of strings that fit the structural description of (2.22c), so the former rule correctly blocks the latter in the derivation of forms like *reˈfēcit* (2.23b).

Middle English

The Middle English rules in (2.15) are repeated in (2.24), and the derivations in (2.16) illustrating their disjunctive application are repeated in (2.25).

(2.24) Disjunctively ordered rules in Middle English, repeated from (2.15)

a. Trisyllabic Shortening (TSS) *ˈsōri* ~ *ˈsŏriə* ‘sorry (sg., pl.)’

$$\begin{bmatrix} +\text{syll} \\ +\text{stress} \end{bmatrix} \longrightarrow [-\text{long}] \;/\; \text{—}\, \text{CVC}_0\text{V}$$

b. Open Syllable Lengthening (OSL) *ˈwĭk* ~ *ˈwēkes* ‘week (sg., pl.)’

$$\begin{bmatrix} +\text{syll} \\ +\text{stress} \\ \langle -\text{high} \rangle \end{bmatrix} \longrightarrow \begin{bmatrix} +\text{long} \\ -\text{high} \\ \langle +\text{low} \rangle \end{bmatrix} \;/\; \text{—}\, \text{CV}$$

(2.25) Application of TSS and OSL to different forms, repeated from (2.16)

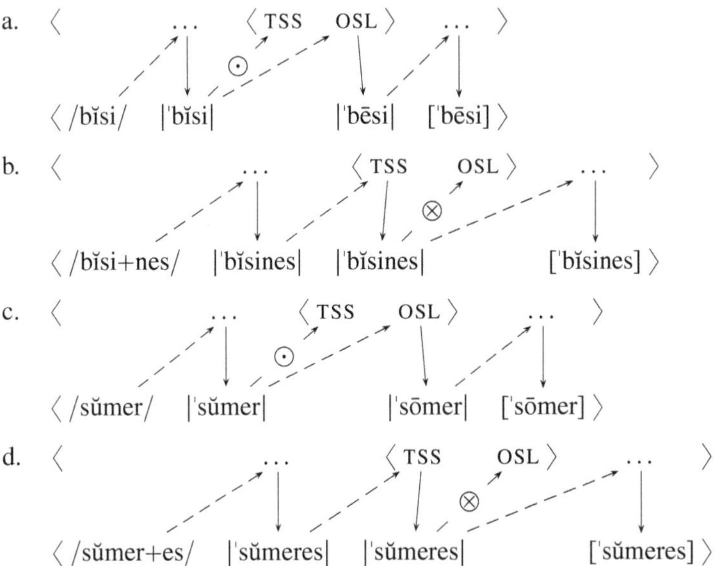

The disjunctive application of these rules is again correctly predicted by the EC. The structural changes of TSS and OSL are ‘incompatible’ in that they specify different values of the [±long] feature. The set of substrings described by the structural description of TSS (2.24a), which is ˈVCVC_0V, is a proper subset of the set of substrings described by the structural description of OSL (2.24b), which is ˈVCV, so TSS correctly blocks OSL in the derivation of forms like *ˈbĭsines* ‘business’ (2.25b) and *ˈsŭmeres* ‘summers’ (2.25d).

Indonesian

The Indonesian stress rules in (2.17) are repeated in (2.26), and the derivations in (2.18) illustrating their disjunctive application are repeated in (2.27).

(2.26) Indonesian stress rules, repeated from (2.17)

a. $\text{V} \longrightarrow [+\text{stress}] \;/\; \left\{ \begin{matrix} \# \\ ə \end{matrix} \right\} \text{C}_0ə\text{C}_0 \text{ — } \text{C}_0\# \quad \begin{matrix} \text{(i)} \\ \text{(ii)} \end{matrix}$

b. $\text{V} \longrightarrow [+\text{stress}] \;/\; \text{—}\, \text{C}_0ə\text{C}_0\text{VC}_0\#$

c. $\text{V} \longrightarrow [+\text{stress}] \;/\; \text{—}\, \text{C}_0\text{VC}_0\#$

(2.27) Disjunctive application of the rules in (2.26), repeated from (2.18)

	a.	b.	c.	d.
UR	/bəri/	/sətəlah/	/gaməlan/	/bicara/
(2.26a.i)	|bə'ri|	⊙	⊙	⊙
(2.26a.ii)	⊙	|sətə'lah|	⊙	⊙
(2.26b)	⊙	⊗	|'gaməlan|	⊙
(2.26c)	⊗	⊗	⊗	|bi'cara|
SR	[bə'ri]	[sətə'lah]	['gaməlan]	[bi'cara]
gloss	'give'	'after'	'Indo. orchestra'	'speak'

The disjunctive application of these rules is also correctly predicted by the EC. The structural changes of all of these rules are 'identical' in that they all assign stress to vowels. The structural description of (2.26a.i) is $\# C_0əC_0VC_0\#$, which describes a proper subset of the set of substrings described by the structural description of (2.26c), $VC_0VC_0\#$. The former rule thus correctly blocks the latter in the derivation of forms like *bə'ri* 'give' (2.27a): (2.26a.i) applies, blocking (2.26c). The structural description of (2.26a.ii) is $əC_0əC_0VC_0\#$, which describes a proper subset of the set of substrings described by the structural descriptions of both (2.26b) and (2.26c), which are $VC_0əC_0VC_0\#$ and $VC_0VC_0\#$, respectively. So, the former rule correctly blocks these latter two in the derivation of forms like *sətə'lah* 'after' (2.27b): (2.26a.ii) applies, blocking both (2.26b) and (2.26c). Finally, the set of substrings described by the structural description of (2.26b) is a proper subset of the set of substrings described by the structural description of (2.26c), so the former rule correctly blocks the latter in the derivation of forms like *'gaməlan* 'Indonesian orchestra' (2.27c): (2.26b) applies, blocking (2.26c).

2.3.3 Parenthetical release

Not only does the EC account for disjunctive application in a wider range of cases than the interpretive convention for the parenthesis notation, it also allows parentheses to be used simply to indicate the optionality of certain elements in the structural description of a rule. Kiparsky (1973b: 95) offers the following argument for the desirability of this move: in Karok (Bright 1957), a rule palatalizing coronal fricatives after front vocoids applies whether (2.28b) or not (2.28a) a consonant intervenes (data from Kenstowicz and Kisseberth 1979: 342).

(2.28) Karok palatalization

a.	/skak/	[ʔuskak]	[niʃkak]	'jump' (3sg, 1sg)
	/suprih/	[ʔusuprih]	[niʃuprih]	'measure' (3sg, 1sg)
b.	/ksah/	[ʔuksah]	[nikʃah]	'laugh' (3sg, 1sg)
	/ksup/	[ʔuksup]	[nikʃup]	'point' (3sg, 1sg)

The palatalization rule can be stated as in (2.29), with the optionality of the intervening consonant indicated by parentheses.

(2.29) Palatalization

$$\begin{bmatrix}+\text{cor}\\+\text{cont}\end{bmatrix} \longrightarrow [-\text{ant}] \;/\; \begin{bmatrix}-\text{cons}\\-\text{back}\end{bmatrix}(\text{C}) \;\_\_$$

This rule abbreviates two expansions: one with the intervening consonant, applying to the forms in (2.28b), and the other without the intervening consonant, applying to the forms in (2.28a). Since only one expansion is applicable to either set of forms, their structural descriptions are not in a proper inclusion relation and so the EC predicts that their application is conjunctive. The interpretive convention for the parenthesis notation of *SPE* of course predicts that their application should be disjunctive: in cases where both rules are applicable, the longer expansion (with the intervening consonant) should apply and block application of the shorter expansion (without the consonant). The question can thus be settled empirically by a form that meets the structural descriptions of both expansions.

Kiparsky argues that the form *ʔiʃʃaha* 'water' settles the question in favor of conjunctive application and thus in favor of the EC. Under the assumption that all instances of surface *ʃ* are derived from underlying *s*, the underlying representation of this form is /*ʔissaha*/. Both instances of *s* in this form are in palatalization contexts: the first is immediately preceded by *i* and the second is preceded by the same *i* but with a consonant intervening (to wit, the first *s*). If the two expansions of (2.29) were to apply disjunctively, the prediction is that the longer expansion should block the shorter and thus that the surface representation of this form should be **ʔisʃaha*, contrary to fact. Applying the two expansions conjunctively, on the other hand — and in either order — makes the correct prediction.

Kenstowicz and Kisseberth (1979: 349) point out a problem with this argument.[9] Because the distribution of geminates is predictable in Karok ("[t]hey occur intervocalically after a short accented vowel"), the correct result can be obtained if Gemination applies after Palatalization (2.29), as shown in (2.30).

(2.30) Gemination follows Palatalization

/ʔisaha/ $\xrightarrow[\text{PAL}]{}$ |ʔiʃaha| $\xrightarrow[\text{GEM}]{}$ [ʔiʃʃaha]

This defeats the empirical relevance of this example to the question of whether parentheses abbreviate disjunctively ordered rule expansions. But even if the distribution of geminates were not predictable in Karok, we now know from research on the phonology of geminates that they behave as a melodic unit and are rarely if ever 'split' by rules that affect them (Kenstowicz and Pyle 1973; Guerssel 1978; Hayes 1986; Schein and Steriade 1986). Besides, Kenstowicz and Kisseberth continue, disjunctive application of the rule expansions abbreviated in (2.29) "make[s] the phonetically implausible prediction that palatalization would only affect the *s* that is furthest removed from the high front vowel. But in general such assimilation rules will affect consonants that are closer to the vowel" (1979: 349). This valid point (albeit now hypothetical) holds regardless of the fact that in this particular example the segments involved are the two halves of a geminate.

2.3.4 Summary

Notational devices such as parentheses can only go so far in abbreviating sets of disjunctively ordered rules. There are examples for which the parenthesis nota-

9. See also Howard (1975: 114, n. 8).

tion works (Latin), but there are also examples that do not submit to parenthetical abbreviation, either very well (Middle English) or at all (Indonesian, Diola Fogny). Kiparsky's argument based on Karok that the parenthesis notation *should not* abbreviate disjunctively ordered rules may be incomplete, but his argument that the EC correctly accounts for all previously known cases of disjunctive application appears to hold — leaving parentheses free to be used to simply indicate the optionality of elements in the structural description of a rule.

There are two key differences between the EC and the parenthesis notation. First, the requirement of the parenthesis notation that the structural changes specified by the rules be identical is broadened in the EC to also include incompatible structural changes. Second, the requirement of the parenthesis notation that the structural descriptions of the rules overlap is narrowed in the EC to include only rules the structural descriptions of which are in a proper inclusion relationship. There is no notational device that can relate all and only those rules that meet these two key requirements of the EC, hence the need for a separate principle.

2.4 Insufficiency of conjunctive alternatives

What would it take to construct workable conjunctive analyses of examples like those discussed in the previous three sections? One way is to somehow reformulate the structural descriptions of the more general rule(s) so that they exclude the contexts in which the more specific rule(s) apply, thus ensuring their complementarity of application — albeit more or less accidentally. Other alternatives are also possible, depending on particularities of each example.

2.4.1 Diola Fogny

We begin by considering what it would take to construct a workable conjunctive analysis of the Diola Fogny case. I repeat the rules for ease of reference.

(2.31) Diola Fogny rules, repeated from (2.21)

a. Assimilation

$$\begin{bmatrix} \text{C} \\ \text{+nasal} \end{bmatrix} \longrightarrow [\alpha\text{place}] \;/\; \text{—} \begin{bmatrix} \text{–cont} \\ \alpha\text{place} \end{bmatrix}$$

b. Deletion

$$\text{C} \longrightarrow \varnothing \;/\; \text{—}\,\text{C}$$

Conjunctively, either order of these rules simply results in deletion of all preconsonantal consonants by (2.31b), including all nasals — whether they were previously assimilated by (2.31a) or not. This is obviously not the desired result. There is a workable conjunctive analysis, however, with the rules in (2.32) ordered as shown (adapted from Kiparsky 1973b: 97).

(2.32) Conjunctive Diola Fogny rules

a. Deletion′

$$\begin{bmatrix} \text{C} \\ \langle\text{+nasal}\rangle \end{bmatrix} \longrightarrow \varnothing \,/\, \text{—} \begin{bmatrix} \text{C} \\ \langle\text{+cont}\rangle \end{bmatrix}$$

b. Assimilation′

$$\text{C} \longrightarrow [\alpha\text{place}] \,/\, \text{—} \begin{bmatrix} \text{C} \\ \alpha\text{place} \end{bmatrix}$$

There is still a necessarily disjunctive element to this analysis, of course, as indicated by the angled brackets in Deletion′ (2.32a). This rule deletes all preconsonantal consonants except nasals followed by noncontinuants. This residue of Deletion′ is then passed on conjunctively to Assimilation′ (2.32b). Assimilation′ thus needn't specify that the consonant being assimilated to is [–cont], because Deletion′ will have already removed all other relevant strings from consideration.[10] The [±cont] value of the following consonant is thus a condition on Deletion′ under the conjunctive analysis in (2.32), as opposed to the condition on Assimilation that it is under the disjunctive analysis in (2.31).

And herein lies the problem with this conjunctive alternative. That the following consonant must be [–cont] in (2.31a) is a common and natural condition on nasal place assimilation rules; see Padgett (1991, 1994) for extensive discussion of this fact. By contrast, the complex condition on Deletion′ (2.32a) — that the following consonant should be [+cont] if the consonant-to-be-deleted is [+nasal] — is not similarly justified; it appears to get the generalization backwards.

2.4.2 Middle English

Consider now what it would take to construct a workable conjunctive analysis of the Middle English case. I again repeat the rules for ease of reference here.

(2.33) Middle English rules, repeated from (2.15) and (2.24)

a. Trisyllabic Shortening (TSS) *ˈsɔ̄ri* ~ *ˈsɔ̆riə* 'sorry (sg., pl.)'

$$\begin{bmatrix} \text{+syll} \\ \text{+stress} \end{bmatrix} \longrightarrow [\text{–long}] \,/\, \text{—}\, \text{CVC}_0\text{V}$$

b. Open Syllable Lengthening (OSL) *ˈwĭk* ~ *ˈwēkes* 'week (sg., pl.)'

$$\begin{bmatrix} \text{+syll} \\ \text{+stress} \\ \langle\text{–high}\rangle \end{bmatrix} \longrightarrow \begin{bmatrix} \text{+long} \\ \text{–high} \\ \langle\text{+low}\rangle \end{bmatrix} \,/\, \text{—}\, \text{CV}$$

As noted by Anderson (1969: 141; 1974: 104), conjunctive application of these rules as stated leads to incorrectly lowered stressed vowels, whether long

10. Assimilation′ also needn't specify that the focus of the rule is [+nasal], *pace* Kiparsky's (1973b: 97) claim that both (2.32a, b) "must mention the feature of nasality on the left of the arrow".

(2.34a, b, where ⟨TSS > OSL⟩) or short (2.34c, d, where ⟨OSL > TSS⟩). Disjunctive application is thus required in this case because TSS must block not only the 'related' lengthening change but also the 'unrelated' lowering change of OSL.[11]

(2.34) Conjunctive application of (2.33)

a. /ˈbĭsi+nes/ $\xrightarrow[\text{TSS}]{}$ |ˈbĭsines| $\xrightarrow[\text{OSL}]{}$ *[ˈbēsines]
b. /ˈsŭmer+es/ $\xrightarrow[\text{TSS}]{}$ |ˈsŭmeres| $\xrightarrow[\text{OSL}]{}$ *[ˈsōmeres]
c. /ˈbĭsi+nes/ $\xrightarrow[\text{OSL}]{}$ |ˈbēsines| $\xrightarrow[\text{TSS}]{}$ *[ˈbĕsines]
d. /ˈsŭmer+es/ $\xrightarrow[\text{OSL}]{}$ |ˈsōmeres| $\xrightarrow[\text{TSS}]{}$ *[ˈsŏmeres]

But a conjunctive analysis of these Middle English facts is not impossible to construct; there are in fact two ways one might think of to do so. One way is to decouple the two different changes of OSL, lengthening and lowering. The lengthening change (LNG) can apply before TSS, and the lowering change (LOW) afterwards. Those critical vowels that are shortened by TSS after being temporarily lengthened by LNG are thus correctly not lowered by LOW, as shown in (2.35).

(2.35) Conjunctive application with split OSL

a. /ˈbĭsi+nes/ $\xrightarrow[\text{LNG}]{}$ |ˈbī sines| $\xrightarrow[\text{TSS}]{}$ |ˈbĭsines| $\xrightarrow[\text{LOW}]{}$ [ˈbĭsines]
b. /ˈsŭmer+es/ $\xrightarrow[\text{LNG}]{}$ |ˈsūmeres| $\xrightarrow[\text{TSS}]{}$ |ˈsŭmeres| $\xrightarrow[\text{LOW}]{}$ [ˈsŭmeres]

Anderson anticipates this alternative, noting that "[t]his quality shift [i.e., lowering] is confined to long vowels produced by [OSL], and it must be incorporated into the formulation of the rule" (1974: 103). But the only evidence offered in support of this claim is that there are "numerous forms in which an underlying long vowel is not affected by [lowering]", which could just as well be interpreted to mean that this is a case of nonderived environment blocking (on which see §2.5 below). In any event, there are potential empirical consequences to splitting the 'related' lengthening and 'unrelated' lowering changes of OSL.[12]

The other way to construct a workable conjunctive analysis of the Middle English facts is to reformulate the structural description of OSL so that it just so happens to exclude those contexts where TSS applies. This type of reanalysis is considered in more detail in the case of Latin below.

2.4.3 Latin

Finally, consider what it takes to construct a workable conjunctive analysis of Latin stress. (Similar considerations apply to the analysis of Indonesian stress, which will therefore not be discussed separately here.) Once again I repeat the rules from the disjunctive analysis of Latin stress for ease of reference.

11. I know of only one other proposal for blocking of a rule due to 'relatedness' with only one of its two changes: Harris's (1974) analysis of Brazilian Portuguese, discussed in §5.1, §5.3, and §5.6.
12. For arguments that the lowering change is *not* a subcomponent of OSL, see Dobson (1962), Luick (1964), Lieber (1979), and Stockwell and Minkova (2002).

(2.36) Latin stress rules, repeated from (2.10) and (2.22)

a. $V \longrightarrow [+\text{stress}] \,/\, \text{—}\, C_0\breve{V}C_0^1VC_0\#$

b. $V \longrightarrow [+\text{stress}] \,/\, \text{—}\, C_0VC_0\#$

c. $V \longrightarrow [+\text{stress}] \,/\, \text{—}\, C_0\#$

As was shown in (2.11), simple conjunctive application of these rules (in any order) incorrectly results in multiply stressed forms. One way to ensure complementarity in this case is to reformulate the penultimate (2.36b) and final (2.36c) stress rules as in (2.37b, c) — where '$\breve{V}$' crucially denotes an *unstressed* vowel — and to apply the rules in the order shown.

(2.37) Conjunctive Latin stress rules

a. $V \longrightarrow [+\text{stress}] \,/\, \text{—}\, C_0\breve{V}C_0^1VC_0\#$

b. $V \longrightarrow [+\text{stress}] \,/ \left\{ \begin{matrix} \# \\ \breve{V} \end{matrix} \right\} C_0 \,\text{—}\, C_0VC_0\#$

c. $V \longrightarrow [+\text{stress}] \,/ \left\{ \begin{matrix} \# \\ \breve{V}\,C_0\,\breve{V} \end{matrix} \right\} C_0 \,\text{—}\, C_0\#$

The penultimate stress rule in (2.37b) now requires that the antepenultimate vowel be unstressed — i.e., for the antepenultimate stress rule in (2.37a) to have not applied — and the final stress rule in (2.37c) now requires that both the antepenultimate and penultimate vowels be unstressed — i.e., for neither of the rules in (2.37a, b) to have applied. The first two rules would thus correctly block the second two rules, but via ordinary bleeding. However, as Anderson (1974: 106) points out regarding a similar alternative approach to the Indonesian case, "this is obviously nothing but a way of coding disjunctive application". Moreover, there is nothing to ensure the crucial bleeding order of the rules in (2.37); any reordering of the rules would lead to the same kind of problem we observed in (2.11), with multiple stresses per form.[13]

Other rule reformulations that make no reference to other vowels being crucially unstressed are possible, but they are likewise obvious hacks. Consider the most general of these rules, (2.36c). Since this rule is only needed to apply to monosyllables — all longer forms are stressed by (2.36a) or (2.36b) — the external context can simply be stated as $\#C_0\text{—}C_0\#$, successfully excluding the longer forms to which the other two rules (2.36a, b) apply. This reformulated external context is slightly more specific (and thus more complex) than the original external context $\text{—}C_0\#$ of (2.36c), and there is no longer any sense in which this reformulated rule applies 'otherwise' — it simply applies directly to monosyllables, with no interaction whatsoever with the other stress rules.

Things get a bit more complicated in the case of (2.36b). This rule must stress the penultimate vowel not only in bisyllables but also in longer forms; specifically, those in which the penultimate vowel is long or followed by two or more

13. Of course the rules in (2.37) could be coded even further: if all vowels mentioned in structural descriptions are required to be stressless, then only the bleeding order of the rules shown in (2.37) would ensure that each rule applies nonvacuously to some subset of forms in the first place.

consonants. In the disjunctive analysis, these longer forms are simply the residue of (2.36a), which stresses the antepenultimate vowel when the penultimate vowel is short and followed by at most one consonant. But the idea of a 'residue' cannot be counted on in a conjunctive analysis (*pace* the 'coded' bleeding analysis in (2.37)), and so it is instead necessary to split (2.36b) into the three rules in (2.38).

(2.38) Latin penultimate stress rules

a. V $\longrightarrow$ [+stress] / $\#C_0 — C_0VC_0\#$ (penults of bisyllables)
b. $\bar{V}$ $\longrightarrow$ [+stress] / $— C_0VC_0\#$ (long penults)
c. V $\longrightarrow$ [+stress] / $— C_2VC_0\#$ (closed penults)

The problem of coded complementarity comes into even sharper focus here. The rule in (2.38b) stresses penultimate *long* vowels ($\bar{V}$), and the rule in (2.38c) stresses penultimate vowels followed by *two or more* consonants (C_2) — together, the precise complement of the contexts already specified by (2.36a), which stresses antepenultimate vowels if the penultimate vowel is *short* ($\breve{V}$) and followed by *at most one* consonant (C_0^1). Complementarity is correctly achieved here, but only because the rules just so happen to apply to complementary sets of forms.

Long vowels and vowels followed by two or more consonants arguably form the natural class of 'heavy syllables' in Latin, and so an appropriate notation in terms of syllables and their subconstituents could be used to collapse the two rules (2.38b, c) into one rule — and the antepenultimate stress rule in (2.36a) could similarly be written such that the penultimate syllable is required to be 'light'. Still, some distinction between (2.38a) and (2.38b, c) is required: the penultimate vowel is stressed if (a) the word is bisyllabic or (b, c) the penultimate syllable is heavy. And, of course, the complementarity between (2.36a) and (2.38b, c) is no less accidental under this revised construal of the relevant context.

This highlights an independent issue with the antepenultimate stress rule in (2.36a), which assigns stress to the antepenult if the penult is light. This arguably gets the generalization backwards: light syllables don't repel stress; rather, heavy syllables attract it (see e.g. Prince 1991 and references therein). The generalization behind Latin stress might thus be better stated as in (2.39).[14]

(2.39) Alternative Latin stress generalization (cf. (2.14))

a. Stress the penult if it is heavy (and if there is one);
b. *otherwise*, stress the antepenult (if there is one);
c. *otherwise*, stress the initial syllable.

As with the Indonesian rules in (2.17), the parenthesis notation would not be able to abbreviate rules stated in accord with the generalization in (2.39). The EC would not be of much help in this case either: the structural description of (2.39a) is met by heavy penults whether or not there is an antepenult, and such strings do

14. Note how (2.39c) mentions the *initial* syllable rather than the *final* vowel mentioned in (2.14c); this is so that bisyllabic words with light penults, which are missed by (2.39a), are correctly stressed. Monosyllables are correctly stressed either way, their only syllable being both initial and final.

not constitute a proper subset of the set of strings that meet the structural description of (2.39b). One could simply reformulate (2.39a) such that an antepenult is required to be present, given that (2.39c) will correctly stress all bisyllables regardless of penult weight — but this move would of course be entirely *ad hoc*, motivated only by the desire to meet the strict conditions imposed by the EC.

Somewhat ironically, the disjunctive vs. conjunctive distinction is no longer much of an issue in the very empirical domain — the distribution of stress — that uniquely motivated disjunctive analyses in the first place. This is due to the availability of metrical stress theory (Liberman and Prince 1977; Hayes 1980; Hayes 1995) and other 'nonlinear' approaches to the analysis of stress. The development of these alternatives to the 'linear' rules and representations of *SPE* has played a key role in the protracted turf war between ordered rules on the one hand and conditions on representations on the other; the overall success of these alternatives is now widely and openly acknowledged on both sides of the continuing conflict.

Under the metrical approach, stress is not assigned to individual vowels but rather to the heads of metrical feet, the placement of which must satisfy various conditions. In Latin, the main stress foot (a) is bimoraic (= two light syllables or a single heavy syllable), (b) is a trochee (= left-headed), and (c) stands at the right edge of the word, not including the final syllable (Hayes 1980; Mester 1994). This set of conditions correctly distributes main stress in Latin without the need for disjunctive application of multiple rules of stress assignment. (But there remains a residue of blocking even in this metrical analysis, as discussed in §4.1.6.)

2.5 Other types of blocking

Since at least the pioneering works of Kisseberth (1970a) and Kiparsky (1973a), it has become generally acknowledged that there are types of blocking beyond bleeding, counterfeeding, and disjunctive application of the type that is predicted by the EC.[15] I briefly discuss two such types of blocking in this section. The first is NONDERIVED ENVIRONMENT BLOCKING (§2.5.1), in which a rule is blocked unless some part of its structural description is derived. The second is DO-SOMETHING-EXCEPT-WHEN BLOCKING (§2.5.2), in which a rule is blocked from creating structures that for independent reasons are not allowed to surface. Each of these well-established types of blocking has required the postulation of some principle or other beyond rule ordering in order to account for it.

2.5.1 Nonderived environment blocking

The best-known and most-cited example of nonderived environment blocking is found in Finnish (Kiparsky 1973a, 1993). Consider the two rules stated in (2.40).

(2.40) Raising and Assibilation in Finnish

a. Assibilation: t ⟶ s / — i

b. Raising: e ⟶ i / — #

15. This section borrows liberally from parts of Baković (2011).

Assibilation (2.40a) only applies if its environment is *derived* in one of two ways: (i) by morpheme concatenation (i.e., a *t*-final morpheme concatenated with an *i*-initial morpheme) or (ii) by application of another phonological rule (such as Raising in (2.40b), which can crucially change an *e* to an *i* after a *t*). An example where the environment of Assibilation is phonologically derived is illustrated in (2.41a), alongside an example in (2.41b) in which the *ti* sequence that matches the structural description of Assibilation is underlying, not derived.

(2.41) Nonderived environment blocking in Finnish

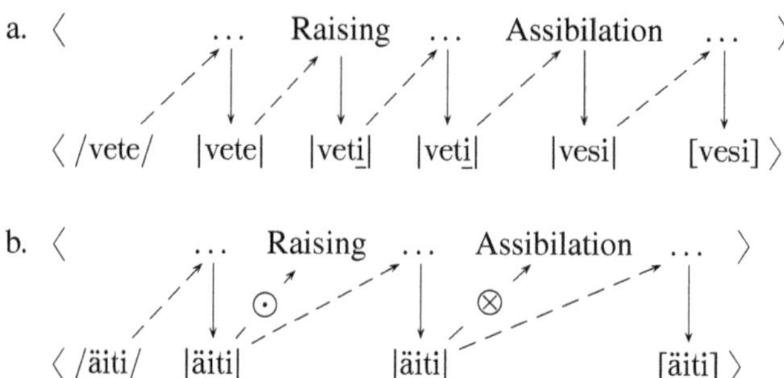

The crucial difference between these two derivations is that the *ti* sequence of *äiti* 'mother' (2.41b), although it matches the structural description of Assibilation, is present in the underlying representation; by contrast, the same sequence in the derivation of *vesi* 'water' (2.41a) is crucially derived by Raising, which creates the *i*.[16] This is indicated by underlining to highlight the fact that information about the *i*'s derived status must persist long enough in the derivation to give Assibilation license to apply in (2.41a) as opposed to being blocked in (2.41b).

Note that the conditions that hold of nonderived environment blocking are essentially the opposite of those that hold of counterfeeding (§2.1.2). In cases of counterfeeding, earlier-derived strings undergo a rule that later-derived strings do not; ordering this rule earlier than another rule that is responsible for those later-derived strings is thus possible. In cases of nonderived environment blocking, on the other hand, later-derived strings (whether by morpheme concatenation or by phonological rule) undergo a rule that earlier-derived strings do not. Rule ordering is clearly insufficient to the task: early ordering of Assibilation (2.41b) can only hope to achieve counterfeeding, and late ordering will if anything only increase the set of forms to which Assibilation might apply.

As the ample literature on the topic attests, some additional principle ensuring blocking of relevant rules in nonderived environments (or their application only in derived environments) is necessary within *SPE* in the form of either the Revised Alternation Condition (Kiparsky 1973a), the Strict Cycle Condition (Kean 1974; Mascaró 1976), a combination of lexical identity rules and the Elsewhere Condition (Kiparsky 1982; cf. Giegerich 1988), or the judicious use of underspecification and feature-filling rule application (Kiparsky 1993; cf. Poser 1993).

16. Presumably, the most general possible statement of Raising would have it apply vacuously to word-final *i* as well as nonvacuously to word-final *e*, but only the latter, nonvacuous application must count as 'deriving' the environment of Assibilation. See Kiparsky (1993) for discussion.

A notable problem with these proposals is that they often aim to be more general than the facts end up bearing out. Earlier work (Kiparsky 1973a, 1982; Kean 1974; Mascaró 1976) attempted to identify the class of rules subject to nonderived environment blocking with the set of cyclic rules, but this identification has been shown to be mistaken (Hualde 1989; Kiparsky 1993). Kiparsky's (1993) alternative does not arbitrarily assign nonderived environment blocking properties to individual rules, but it moves closer to that end of the continuum of possibilities; this appears to be roughly true of most if not all subsequent proposals (e.g. Inkelas 1999; Burzio 2000, 2011; Łubowicz 2002; McCarthy 2003a; Kula 2006, 2008; van Oostendorp 2007a).

2.5.2 Do-something-except-when blocking

Do-something-except-when blocking encompasses a wide range of cases in which a rule is blocked from creating certain structures for independently motivated reasons. It is usually motivated by the *general absence* of a particular structure in a language, one that is otherwise expected to be created by the rule in question. It differs from disjunctive application in that application of another rule (formally related or otherwise) is generally not necessary, and it differs from nonderived environment blocking in that the relevant structures are generally blocked from being created across the board, not only in nonderived environments.

The earliest argument for do-something-except-when blocking was made by Kisseberth (1970a, 1972). In Yawelmani Yokuts (Newman 1944; Kuroda 1967; Kisseberth 1969), word-final monosyllabic suffix vowels are deleted *except when* such deletion would result in a final consonant cluster. One way to achieve this result is to build the blocking condition into the environment of the deletion rule, by stating it as *V+C—#*. The vowel preceding the morpheme boundary is crucial, as it describes all but those contexts in which a final consonant cluster is in danger of being created by deletion of a word-final monosyllabic suffix vowel. Kisseberth argues that this solution misses a significant functional generalization — a 'conspiracy' — uniting a suite of processes in Yawelmani phonology that are blocked by the avoidance of tautosyllabic consonant clusters.[17] He proposes that the environment of deletion should instead be simplified to *+C—#*, with the preceding vowel of the more complex *V+C—#* environment being a derivative property of a 'derivational constraint' against tautosyllabic consonant clusters.

There are also cases of rules that are blocked for other do-something-except-when reasons. For example, assimilation rules are often subject to the same conditions as the underlying segment inventory itself, such that the product of assimilation cannot be a segment outside the inventory. In the vowel inventory of the Fante variety of Akan (Stewart 1967; Clements 1981; O'Keefe 2003), all vowels have a [±ATR] counterpart (*i∼ɪ, e∼ɛ, u∼ʊ, o∼ɔ*) except the low, [–ATR] vowel *a*; as a result, [ATR] harmony is blocked from applying to *a*. This blocking condition can be built in to the statement of the focus of the vowel harmony rule by stipulating that it only applies to [–low] vowels, but this sort of move has been

17. Kisseberth also argues that some rules participating in this conspiracy are crucially *triggered* to avoid tautosyllabic consonant clusters. I ignore triggering here, given that our focus is on blocking.

argued since at least Kiparsky (1981b) to miss a significant generalization about the relationship between conditions on harmony and conditions on the inventory.

In the case of conspiracies, rule ordering quite obviously cannot do the necessary work; the phonology of a language must include some set of constraints that is somehow linked to the set of rules in order to achieve blocking. Despite a concerted effort by Kiparsky (1973a), among others, to dismiss the notion, it is now generally accepted that there exist 'derivational constraints' (or 'output conditions') that block rule application.[18] This acceptance is reflected by the substantial and influential body of work arguing for — and in some cases spelling out — the interaction between rules and constraints; see e.g. Haiman (1972), Sommerstein (1974), Kiparsky (1981b), Singh (1987), Paradis (1988), Calabrese (1988, 1995, 2005), Myers (1991a), Archangeli and Pulleyblank (1994).[19]

Kenstowicz and Kisseberth (1977: 136ff) discuss some examples like the one in Akan described above under the rubric of the 'duplication problem'. They explain that, as with conspiracies, a model armed with rule ordering alone is forced to view the relationship between the segment inventory and the output of some phonological rules as a coincidence. Later work addressed the duplication problem with the Structure Preservation principle (Kiparsky 1981b, 1982, 1985), but of course this principle cannot hold of the phonological component of any language as a whole given that there always exist at least some rules that create nonphonemic allophones. Kiparsky's hypothesis, then, was that constraints on the segment inventory hold "throughout the lexical phonology" (1985: 92), thus relegating allophonic rules to postlexical status (uncontroversially). But even this hypothesis is too strong (Myers 1991b): there are both lexical rules that create nonphonemes and postlexical rules that must be prevented from creating them. Myers suggests subjecting Structure Preservation to the Strong Domain Hypothesis (Kiparsky 1984, 1985; Borowsky 1986), meaning that it would be deactivated at some language-particular point along the way through the entire phonological component, but this idea seems to have never been pursued further.

The literature on output conditions more generally tells much the same story. Many of the most striking examples of do-something-except-when blocking are ones that are motivated by conditions holding very generally of the language in question, but there are also examples in which a given constraint only holds of a proper subset of eligible rules of a language. It is of course possible that an apparent condition on the output of some but not all eligible rules is just a coincidence that can simply be factored into the structural descriptions of the affected rules, but significant similarities have long been observed between output conditions that apply very generally in some languages but apparently only in a limited fashion in others. The question is thus not *whether* to employ output conditions in such cases, but *how* to employ them in some maximally explanatory fashion.

18. To be fair, Kiparsky's (1973a) intent was to delimit the behavior of these also-called 'global rules' (Lakoff 1970; Kisseberth 1973) and to have this behavior follow from more general principles.

19. It is nowhere near my intention to be thorough with the very short list of relevant citations here. See Prince and Smolensky (1993: 1–2) for a much longer but similarly nonexhaustive list; as those authors note, the relevant "body of work is so large and various as to defy concise citation".

2.6 Summary remarks

Blocking interactions, whereby a rule $\mathcal{R}$ fails to apply in the derivation of a form Φ that includes a representation ϕ that meets $\mathcal{R}$'s structural description, have deservedly been the focus of much work in generative phonology. Two types of blocking fall within the scope of the basic rule ordering and serial derivation assumptions of *SPE*: bleeding and counterfeeding. Indeed, the term 'blocking' is rarely if ever defined broadly enough to include bleeding and counterfeeding precisely because they are entirely unremarkable from the vantage point of *SPE*.

Disjunctive application has received particular attention from the very beginnings of generative phonology (Chomsky and Halle 1968; Anderson 1969, 1974; Kiparsky 1973b), but the fact that the authors of these foundational documents took the relevant phenomena into account should not be mistaken for anything more than what it was: insightful recognition of the problem disjunctive application poses for rule ordering and serial derivation, plus a series of essentially *ad hoc* theoretical proposals — from special interpretations of an assortment of notational conventions to various versions of an EC-like principle — specifically designed to address the problem.

The treatment that the remaining two types of blocking have received in the *SPE* literature has been interestingly mixed, given that both types are equally beyond the reach of *SPE*. Kiparsky (1973a) recognized nonderived environment blocking as problematic for *SPE*, and proposed solutions to these problems have been generally welcomed in large part because they were argued to also provide solutions to other, apparently unrelated problems such as the potential for excessively abstract analysis. Kisseberth (1970a, 1972) and others also recognized conspiracies — one of the two subspecies of do-something-except-when blocking — as problematic for *SPE*, but in this case proposed solutions were not so generally welcomed and the very existence of conspiracies and the problems they pose have even been denied (see e.g. Kiparsky 1973a: 75ff; Vaux 2008: 57ff). The other subspecies of do-something-except-when blocking — rules blocked by inventory conditions — has had comparatively better support, but in this case the proposed solutions are as *ad hoc* as those proposed for disjunctive application.

As the motivation for blocking interactions of various sorts accumulated, the foundation of phonological theory gradually shifted from rule ordering to constraints on derivations and representations, and eventually away from serial derivation altogether. OT is one of several endpoints of this shift; the OT approaches to the various types of blocking addressed in this chapter — disjunctive application in particular, of course — will be discussed in detail in Chapter 4.

Chapter 3

Elsewhere in *SPE*

THE PHONOLOGICAL COMPONENT of a language is primarily tasked with delimiting the distribution of elements of speech sounds and structures, defining the contexts in which these phonological elements are found and where they are not found. The concept of 'elsewhere' is intimately tied to this task of delimitation. The distribution of any contextually restricted phonological element — one that is not found in every possible context — can always be stated in elsewhere language: 'Phonological element *x* is found in context *C*; elsewhere, *x* is not found' — where 'elsewhere' means 'in contexts other than *C*'.

Analytically more interesting are those cases in which *x* is found in context *C* and some other, closely related element *y* is found elsewhere; that is, where *x* and *y* are in COMPLEMENTARY DISTRIBUTION. The complementary distribution of the allophones of a phoneme is of course a special case of this type. Typically, the distribution of one allophone (the BASIC one) is predictable only when juxtaposed with the independently predictable distribution of the other (the DERIVED one).[1] The contexts in which the basic allophone is found in these typical cases are too varied to be stated in anything like a unified way, and thus the best one can say, once one has defined the context(s) *C* in which the derived allophone occurs, is that the basic allophone is found 'elsewhere' — again, 'in contexts other than *C*'.

It is useful at this point to make a distinction between what I will henceforth refer to as UNBOUNDED and BOUNDED cases of complementary distribution. Unbounded cases are those that can be described relative to *all possible contexts*. The complementary distribution of the allophones of a phoneme is unbounded in this sense; in the statement of the distribution of the basic allophone, 'elsewhere' means, at least in principle, '*everywhere* else'.[2] The unboundedness of allophony is due to the fact that the allophones of a phoneme do not contrast in any context; this lack of contrast is part and parcel of the definition of allophony.

1. There may of course be multiple derived allophones; I simplify here for the sake of exposition.
2. This is often not literally true, of course, due to independent distributional facts. Unaspirated stops in English are not found in *every single context* in which aspirated stops are not found; for example, they are not found word-initially before other obstruents nor word-finally after other obstruents. But this is obviously not a fact about the allophonic distribution of aspirated and unaspirated stops; rather, it is due to independent restrictions on the distribution of stops in English more generally.

Cases of bounded complementary distribution, on the other hand, are ones that must be described relative to *some proper subset* of all possible contexts. In other words, the elements in question *do* contrast in (some of) the remaining contexts; complementary distribution only holds within the proper subset.

In the remainder of this chapter I discuss in detail the analytical properties of unbounded (§3.1) and bounded (§§3.2–3.4) complementary distribution, presupposing common assumptions of work stemming — and in some cases diverging — from the fundamental assumptions of *SPE*. There are five distinct, viable analytical options for unbounded complementary distribution that are possible within these assumptions, while only three of these are also possible analytical options for bounded complementary distribution. This means that there is potential for a unified account of complementary distribution in *SPE*, but for reasons that I speculate on in §3.5 this potential has not been realized.

3.1 Unbounded complementary distribution

The distinguishing property of unbounded complementary distribution (UCD) is that the elements in question do *not* contrast in *any* context. Allophony is a paradigm case of UCD, and so for the purposes of illustration here we will use the following elementary case of allophonic complementary distribution, adapted in vastly simplified form from the well-known case of voiced stop ~ spirant alternations in Spanish (see e.g. Harris 1969; Lozano 1979; Baković 1994): voiced obstruents are [+cont] between vowels, and [–cont] elsewhere.

According to this simple descriptive statement, the incompatible feature values [+cont] and [–cont] are in complementary distribution in voiced obstruents. A proper subset of voiced obstruents — those found between vowels — surface with the [+cont] value, and the complement of that proper subset — those found elsewhere — surface with the [–cont] value. In the rules and derivations illustrated in this section, [+cont] voiced obstruents are represented as β, [–cont] ones are represented as *b*, the intervocalic context conditioning the [+cont] variants is represented as *V* — *V*, and the nonintervocalic context conditioning the [–cont] variants is represented as *N* — (the post-nasal context being a prototypical one for the [–cont] variants of voiced obstruents in the actual Spanish case).

There are five ways in which such a distributionally complementary situation can be analyzed under standard assumptions of work in the *SPE* tradition.

3.1.1 Prior underlying specification

The first and most familiar sort of analysis of allophonic complementary distribution is that the basic (elsewhere) allophone underlies all instances of the phoneme, and a single rule changes a proper subset of these to the derived allophone. In the case at hand, all voiced obstruents are underlyingly specified as [–cont] and a lone, feature-changing Spirantization rule spirantizes the proper subset of voiced obstruents that occur intervocalically. This is illustrated in (3.1).

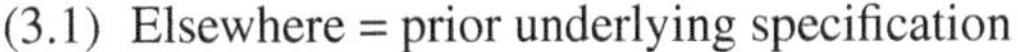

(3.1) Elsewhere = prior underlying specification

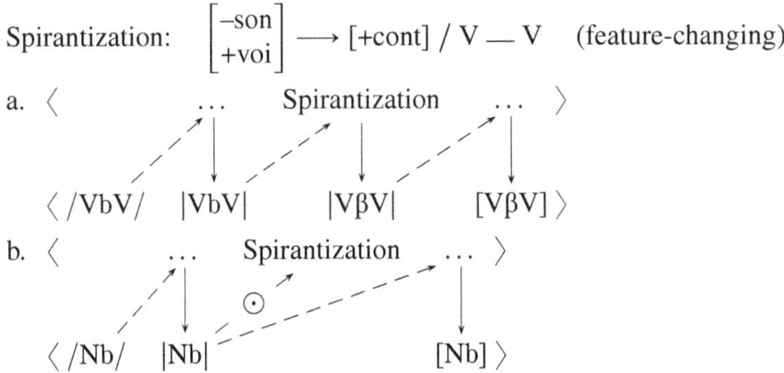

Under this analysis, the distribution of the elsewhere allophone is nothing more than the epiphenomenal outcome of all voiced obstruents being specified underlyingly as [–cont]. Because Spirantization only affects a proper subset of these obstruents, the remaining ones all surface with their underlying [–cont] specification. No additional rule is necessary to accomplish this.

The main empirical challenge to analyzing some cases of UCD in terms of prior underlying specification is that it can be unclear which allophone is basic. This lack of clarity could be due to the fact that the contexts in which every one of the allophones of the phoneme occur can be stated in some unified way; for example, one allophone may be found only syllable-initially and the other only syllable-finally. In such a case, the basic allophone can only be decided upon based on some other, nondistributional reasons (or simply arbitrarily).

The distributional reasons for choosing one allophone as basic may also conflict with some nondistributional reasons for choosing another allophone as basic. This is arguably the case in the actual example of voiced stop ~ spirant alternations is Spanish. Harris (1969: 37ff), for example, proposes a rule spirantizing underlyingly [–cont] voiced obstruents even though the distribution of the [–cont] alternants in Spanish is simpler to state, as Harris (1969: 39) makes clear: they occur "initially and after homorganic noncontinuant sonorants" while the [+cont] alternants occur elsewhere.[3] (See fn. 10, p. 46 for more relevant discussion.)

The near-ubiquity of the prior underlying specification analysis of UCD is hardly surprising given the relative complexity of the alternative analyses to be discussed below. If and when one of these more complex analyses is proposed, it is typically because there are auxiliary reasons (such as prior theoretical or analytical commitments made by the analyst) that render the prior underlying specification analysis more costly. For example, having to specify an underlying value for the relevant feature on all instances of a phoneme is incompatible with standard theories of underspecification (see e.g. Steriade 1987; Archangeli 1988); indeed, underspecification opens up another option for the analysis of UCD.[4]

3. Harris (1969) does not clarify why he does not follow the distributional facts, but we can reasonably speculate that he was instead simply following the traditional descriptions by Spanish grammarians which reflect the historical provenance of these alternations (see e.g. Penny 2002: 72ff).
4. Having to specify a particular value of a feature on all instances of a phoneme is also incompatible with the Richness of the Base hypothesis of OT (Prince and Smolensky 1993; Smolensky 1996).

3.1.2 Underspecification + feature-filling rule application

Under this analysis, all voiced obstruents are underlyingly unspecified for the feature [±cont] and there are two rules applying in a strictly feature-filling fashion. A Spirantization rule affects the subset of underspecified intervocalic voiced obstruents, followed by a context-free Fortition rule that affects only the remaining, still underspecified voiced obstruents elsewhere.[5] The elsewhere case is the combined result of underspecification and feature-filling rule application, which together force the rules to operate in complementary environments: if (and only if) Spirantization applies, Fortition is blocked. This is illustrated in (3.2), where *B* represents a voiced obstruent that is underspecified for the feature [±cont].[6]

(3.2) Elsewhere = underspecification + feature-filling rule application

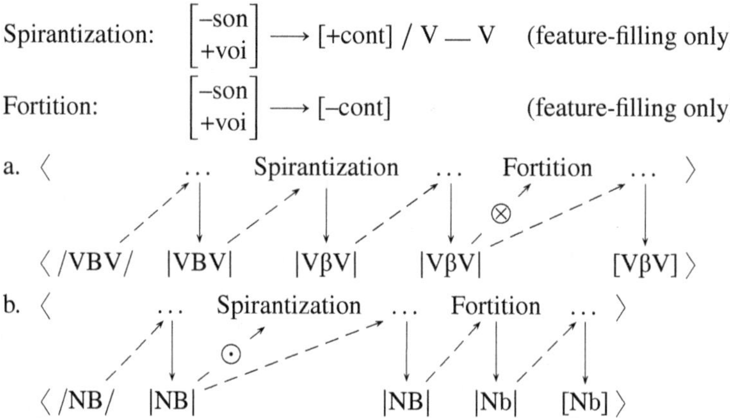

The blocking of Fortition by Spirantization in the derivation in (3.2a) is of course due to bleeding, but unlike the example of bleeding discussed in §2.1.1, the opposite order of the two rules in (3.2) would also result in bleeding. Indeed, it would simply render Spirantization inapplicable in all contexts: once all voiced obstruents are made [–cont] by the context-free (and thus more general) Fortition rule, they have been specified for the feature and the context-sensitive (and thus more specific) Spirantization rule is blocked from applying to them.

These two rules are thus in what is sometimes called a MUTUAL BLEEDING relationship (Kiparsky 1971: 600), given the direct incompatibility between their structural changes. Recall that structural change incompatibility is one of the two conditions that needs to be met in order to invoke Kiparsky's (1973b) EC in (2.19); the other is structural description inclusion, which is also met by the rules in (3.2). The EC could thus be held responsible for the blocking of Fortition by

5. Lozano (1979) ultimately proposes an analysis of this sort for the stop ~ spirant alternation in actual Spanish, except that the context-free, elsewhere rule in Lozano's analysis is Spirantization.

6. If we instead assume a privative feature [cont] — the mere absence of which is equivalent to [–cont] — then this analysis is in all relevant respects reduced to the prior underlying specification analysis in (3.1) because no context-free Fortition rule is required. However, if spirants are analyzed as the elsewhere allophones (as in Lozano's (1979) analysis; see fn. 5 just above), then either two rules and a binary [±cont] feature or one Fortition rule and a privative [stop] feature are required.

Spirantization in (3.2a), but this is strictly unnecessary in this case because the bleeding interaction already achieves the necessary blocking.

Koutsoudas et al. (1974: 8ff) discuss cases of this type, where two rules are in a mutual bleeding relationship and the structural description of one rule properly includes the structural description of the other. The examples they discuss do not involve underspecification or feature-filling rules, but nevertheless they have exactly the same character as the rules and their interaction in (3.2). One of their examples involves "the following pair of rules for Latin American Spanish discussed by Saporta [(1965: 222)]" (adapted from Koutsoudas et al. 1974: 8).

(3.3) Latin American Spanish rules

a. Depalatalization: ʎ ⟶ l / — #
b. Delateralization: ʎ ⟶ j

Because both rules in (3.3) are stated such that they apply strictly to the palatal lateral ʎ, and not to palatals or laterals more generally, application of one is guaranteed to bleed application of the other much like the rules in (3.2). The order observed in Latin American Spanish is ⟨Depalatalization > Delateralization⟩, resulting in depalatalization of word-final palatal laterals and delateralization of palatal laterals elsewhere. This is illustrated by the derivations of *akel* 'that' and *akejos* 'those' in (3.4), which are assumed to share the stem *akeʎ*.

(3.4) Blocking by bleeding in Latin American Spanish

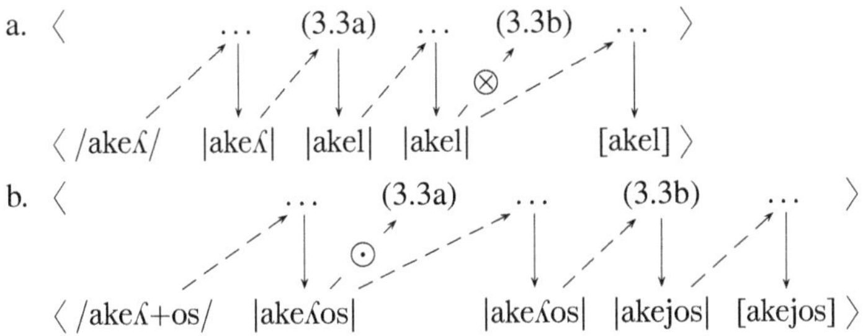

The structural description of Depalatalization is properly included in that of Delateralization, so the order ⟨Delateralization > Depalatalization⟩ would render Depalatalization inapplicable in all contexts — just as in the case of the alternative order to (3.2), ⟨Fortition > Spirantization⟩. Following Sanders (1974), Koutsoudas et al. (1974: 8) invoke a "universal principle of proper inclusion precedence" to fix the order of rules in such cases to the (only apparently sensible) order observed in (3.2) and (3.4) and state the principle as in (3.5).

(3.5) Proper Inclusion Precedence Principle (PIPP)

For any representation R, which meets the structural description of each of two rules A and B, A takes applicational precedence over B with respect to R if and only if the structural description of A properly includes the structural description of B.

The similarity between the PIPP and the EC is fairly obvious. There are two notable differences, however. One difference is that the PIPP imposes an order between two rules that make unrelated structural changes so long as their structural descriptions are in a proper inclusion relationship, while the EC also requires that the structural changes of the two rules be "identical or incompatible" (2.19b). Kiparsky's argument for this requirement of the EC is relevant here:

> [S]uppose that obstruents are voiced in the environment V—V and palatalized in the environment i—i. Clearly, we expect /iki/ → [ig,i], with both rules applying. Here the subset relation holds, but the structural changes are neither identical nor incompatible and therefore one rule is still not a "special case" relative to the other. (Kiparsky 1973b: 94, fn. 2)

The consequences of the PIPP's lack of this kind of requirement appear to be limited to the possibility of rule ordering paradoxes. Building on Kiparsky's hypothetical example, consider the rules and derivations illustrated in (3.6).

(3.6) Hypothetical rule ordering paradox induced by the PIPP (3.5)

		a.	b.	c.	d.
		/aka/	/iki/	/anak/	/anik/
Voicing	[−son] ⟶ [+voi] / V — V	|aga|	|igi|	⊙	⊙
Devoicing	V ⟶ [−voi] / — [−voi]	⊗	⊗	|anḁk|	|ani̥k|
Epenthesis	∅ ⟶ i / C — #	⊙	⊙	|anḁki|	|ani̥ki|
Syncope	i̥ ⟶ ∅ / — CV	⊙	⊙	⊙	|anki|
Palatalization	[−son] ⟶ [+pal] / i — i	⊙	|ig,i|	⊙	⊗
		[aga]	[ig,i]	[anḁki]	[anki]

The first and last rules in (3.6), Voicing and Palatalization, are the rules as defined by Kiparsky, and the first two derivations (3.6a, b) illustrate their application. I've devised the three intervening rules such that several orderings are crucial. Devoicing devoices vowels before voiceless consonants, and is crucially bled by Voicing; this is why it is blocked in (3.6a, b) but applies in (3.6c, d). Epenthesis, which inserts an *i* after a word-final consonant, counterfeeds Voicing, as shown in (3.6c, d): if Epenthesis had applied first, the *k* in each of these forms would have been voiced. Syncope deletes the voiceless high vowel *i̥* when followed by CV; this rule is thus fed by the combined effects of Devoicing and Epenthesis, as shown in (3.6d). Finally, Palatalization is bled by Syncope as shown in (3.6d).

This complex, crucial ordering of rules entails, by the transitivity property of the ordering relation, that Voicing precedes Palatalization — but Palatalization must precede Voicing according to the PIPP, hence the rule ordering paradox. It may very well be, of course, that such paradoxes never arise because more specific rules like Palatalization must in fact always precede more general rules like Voicing (by the PIPP); that is, it may well be that hypothetical states of affairs such as the one illustrated in (3.6) are never instantiated in any language.

Another difference between the PIPP and the EC is that the EC imposes disjunctive application on rules that meet the relevant requirements, while the PIPP only imposes a conjunctive order. In the underspecification + feature-filling rule application (3.2) and Latin American Spanish (3.3) cases, the end result is the same; as Koutsoudas et al. (1974: 9, fn. 7) note, the rules in these kinds of cases "are intrinsically disjunctive, since application of either rule yields a representation that fails to satisfy the structural description of the other" — in other words, the rules are in a mutual bleeding relationship as described earlier. But Koutsoudas et al. (see also Sanders 1974: 373–374, fn. 9) go on to note that

> there is some evidence that ... there can be proper inclusion precedence between rules which do not destroy each other's contexts, but which must nevertheless be prevented from applying conjunctively ... It thus seems appropriate to consider disjunctive application as part of the meaning of proper inclusion precedence; this could be effected, e.g., by adding to [(3.5)] the condition that rule B cannot be applied to any (direct or indirect) product of the application of rule A. (Koutsoudas et al. 1974: 9, fn. 7)

If the PIPP is modified to impose disjunctive application in this way, then it is essentially reduced to the EC without the structural change requirement.[7] This of course has the direct consequence noted by Kiparsky: Palatalization between high vowels would block Voicing in the more general intervocalic context.

One final remark. As will be discussed at some length in §5.3, the precise formulation of rules can affect the applicability of any principle that, like the PIPP or the EC, relies on the form of the rules to determine their interaction. Consider Saporta's (1965: 222, fn. 11) suggestion that the Spanish Depalatalization rule in (3.3a) "is more general, applying to the palatalized nasals as well" — if this is indeed the case, then the proper inclusion relationship between Depalatalization and the supposedly more general Delateralization rule in (3.3b) is compromised (because the structural descriptions of the rules would merely *overlap*) and the PIPP would thus not achieve its intended result with these rules.[8]

3.1.3 Prior rule specification

A third possible analysis of UCD involves two feature-changing rules. Voiced obstruents in any context may be specified either as [+cont] or as [–cont] underlyingly, but the more general Fortition rule makes them all [–cont]. The more specific Spirantization rule then (re-)spirantizes the proper subset of intervocalic voiced obstruents. This analysis is illustrated in (3.7).

(3.7) Elsewhere = prior rule specification

$$\text{Fortition:} \quad \begin{bmatrix} -\text{son} \\ +\text{voi} \end{bmatrix} \longrightarrow [-\text{cont}] \qquad \text{(feature-changing)}$$

$$\text{Spirantization:} \quad \begin{bmatrix} -\text{son} \\ +\text{voi} \end{bmatrix} \longrightarrow [+\text{cont}] \,/\, \text{V} \_\_ \text{V} \qquad \text{(feature-changing)}$$

7. But note that Kiparsky's (1973b) version of the EC does not explicitly impose an order; this additional condition is not explicitly added to the EC until Kiparsky (1982). See §5.2 for discussion.
8. The validity of Depalatalization as an active synchonic alternation in Spanish is a matter of some debate in any event (see e.g. Alonso 1945; Harris 1983; Harris 1984; Harris 1999; Pensado 1997; Baković 2001; Lloret and Mascaró 2007). Only a handful of apparent alternations constitutes all of the evidence for the rules in (3.3); the alternation evidence for the extension of Depalatalization to nasals, while admittedly adding a bit of substantiation to the rule, is likewise very weak.

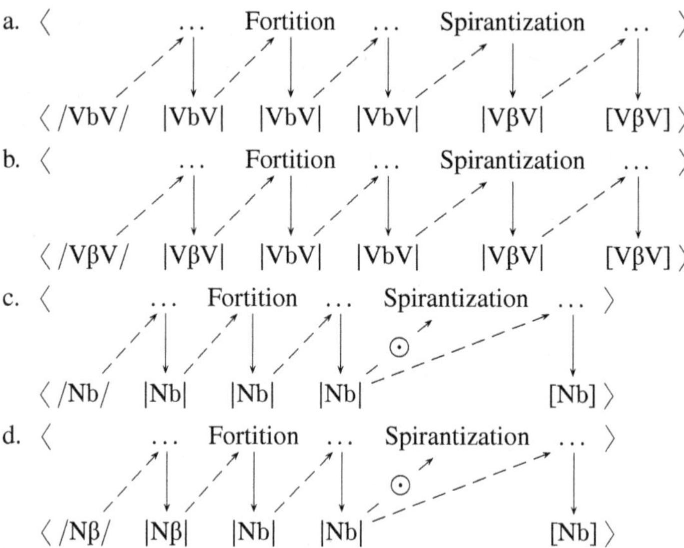

The elsewhere case is handled here in a manner very similar to the prior underlying specification analysis of (3.1). Although all voiced obstruents are underlyingly freely specified in (3.7), the prior application of context-free Fortition makes them all [–cont]. The inputs to context-sensitive Spirantization in (3.7) are thus specified just as they are underlyingly in (3.1), and the derivations thus proceed just as they did in the prior underlying specification analysis.

The big difference in (3.7), of course, is that there are two rules instead of just one. The key to this analysis is that Spirantization *fails to feed* Fortition, even though the result of Spirantization meets the structural description of Fortition. This failure to feed is, of course, ensured by ordering Spirantization after Fortition. This analysis is thus an instance of counterfeeding as defined and discussed in §2.1.2; the definition is repeated here (Fortition is $\mathcal{R}$ and Spirantization is $\mathcal{S}$).

> The application of $\mathcal{R}$ is blocked in the derivation of a form Φ if (i) another rule $\mathcal{S}$ follows $\mathcal{R}$ in the rule order, (ii) $\mathcal{S}$ applies to a representation ϕ' that does not also meet the structural description of $\mathcal{R}$, and (iii) application of $\mathcal{S}$ to ϕ' results in a distinct representation ϕ that does meet the structural description of $\mathcal{R}$. Under these conditions, $\mathcal{S}$ is said to counterfeed $\mathcal{R}$.

To be more precise, the relationship between the rules in (3.7) is an example of what Kavitskaya and Staroverov (2010) call FED COUNTERFEEDING. A fed counterfeeding interaction is one in which the first rule in the order feeds the second and the second rule counterfeeds the first. This is most obviously (i.e., nonvacuously) the case in the second derivation illustrated in (3.7a): the underlyingly [+cont] voiced obstruent is made [–cont] by Fortition and is then re-made [+cont] by Spirantization, which in turn makes the obstruent nonvacuously subject to Fortition again — though too late for Fortition to apply to it again, of course. Fortition thus feeds Spirantization, and Spirantization counterfeeds Fortition.

Even more precisely, this is a *fed counterfeeding on focus* order: the element affected by each of the two rules — each rule's *focus* — is the same. In derivations where both rules in a fed counterfeeding on focus relation apply, the second rule will simply undo the change effected by the first (assuming rules that make single changes along some binary dimension; here, [±cont]).[9] Pullum (1976) famously discusses derivations of this kind, specifically addressing "a tacitly held belief" that "[l]inguists very frequently seem to give evidence of", that there is

> something inept and risible about a linguistic analysis which determines that certain structures are assigned a derivation of the general form A → B → A, that is a derivation in which an underlying representation (or some nonultimate remote representation) is mapped on to an intermediate form distinct from it, and then on to a surface (or other superficial) representation which is identical with the earlier stage. (Pullum 1976: 83)

The putatively "inept and risible" nature of these sorts of derivations will be discussed at length in §3.3.5 further below. Pullum's (1976) conclusion is that they are, strictly speaking, mostly harmless; their potential opens the door, however, to other possible derivations that have been argued to be unattested.

3.1.4 Complementary contexts of application

A fourth possible analysis of UCD also involves two feature-changing rules, and voiced obstruents may again be specified either as [+cont] or as [–cont] underlyingly. Spirantization may also be the same as before, making all intervocalic voiced obstruents [+cont], but Fortition now makes all voiced obstruents [–cont] *except* those that are intervocalic. Both rules apply in precisely complementary contexts, so either order produces the same results. This is illustrated in (3.8).

(3.8) Elsewhere = rules with complementary contexts of application

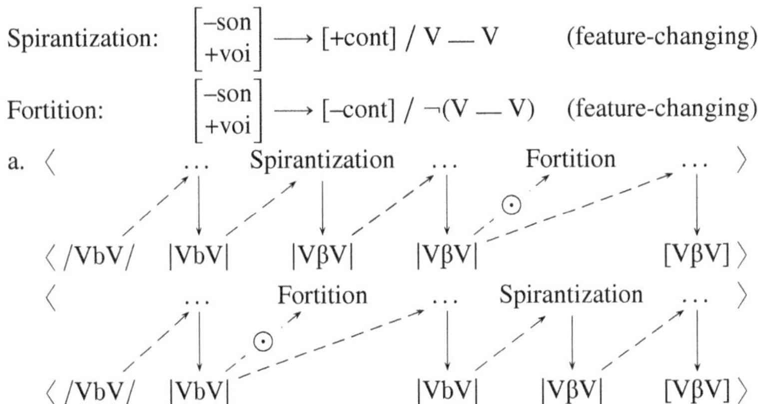

9. Kavitskaya and Staroverov's primary concern is with examples of *fed counterfeeding on environment* orders, where the focus of one rule is a crucial element in the environment of the other rule. The significance of the 'on focus' / 'on environment' distinction with respect to regular counterfeeding was first discussed by McCarthy (1999b); see now Baković (2011) for more specific discussion of the significance of this distinction with respect to fed counterfeeding.

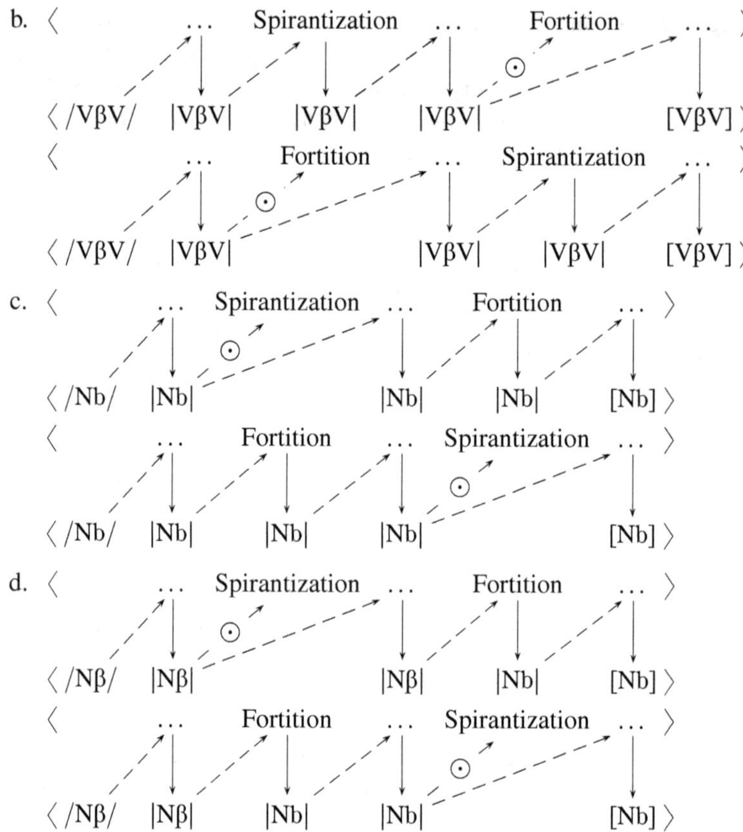

This analysis does little more than recapitulate the complementarity of the rules' effects by stipulating that complementarity in their contexts of application. There may be situations in which such stipulation is preferable or even necessary; for instance, when the distributions of the two allophones of a phoneme are equally predictable (e.g., one occurs syllable-initially and the other syllable-finally), or in situations like the one to be discussed in §3.4 further below. But the use of a negative context like the one in the Fortition rule in (3.8) is clearly suspect: its only justification is the need to stipulate complementarity.[10]

10. Recall from §3.1.1 that in actual Spanish, it is the distribution of the [–cont] voiced obstruents that is most directly predictable: they occur "initially and after homorganic noncontinuant sonorants", as Harris (1969: 39) puts it, while their [+cont] counterparts occur elsewhere. In proposing a rule spirantizing underlyingly [–cont] voiced obstruents, then, Harris (1969: 40) is forced to propose a negative context that is in all relevant respects just like the one under discussion here: voiced stops spirantize "EXCEPT" where they don't. For critiques of this move, see Lozano (1979) and Baković (1994). But note that rules with negative contexts like these can be easily replaced by two rules: in the case of Fortition in (3.8), one of the rules would be a context-free Fortition rule as in (3.7) and the other would be a prior rule that assigns a rule exception feature ('[–Fortition]') intervocalically, blocking the context-free Fortition rule there and only there (following Chomsky and Halle 1968: 175). For all intents and purposes, however, this alternative analysis reduces to the underspecification + feature-filling rule application analysis in (3.2): prior Spirantization assigns the 'rule exception feature' in the form of a feature value specification that blocks later Fortition.

3.1.5 Disjunctive application

The fifth and final possible analysis of UCD involves the same freely specified underlying representations and rules as in the prior rule specification analysis in (3.7), but with the added condition that the rules apply disjunctively. Recall that when two rules apply disjunctively, only the more specific of the rules is allowed to apply to representations that meet the structural descriptions of both rules; the more general rule is blocked from applying to those representations. In this case, Spirantization must disjunctively block Fortition as illustrated in (3.9).

(3.9) Elsewhere = disjunctive application

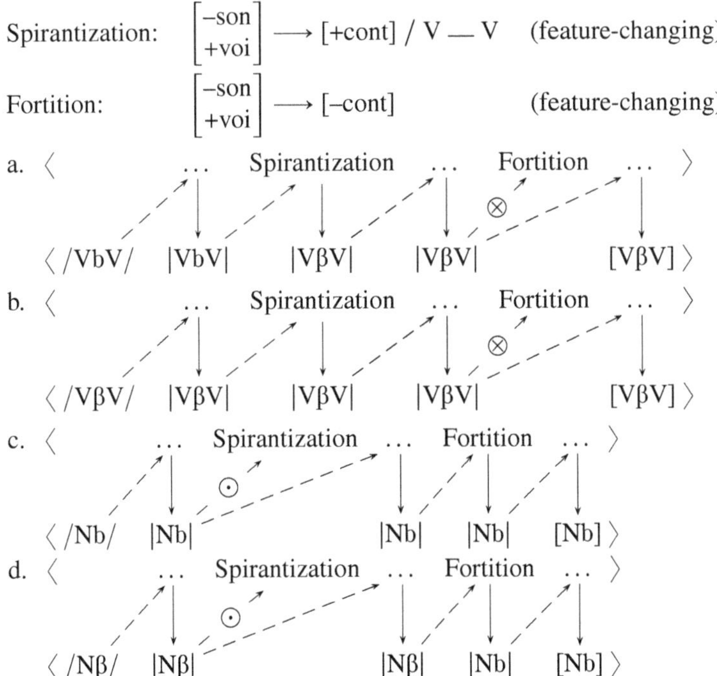

The rules in (3.9) cannot be abbreviated via any of the notations discussed in §2.2 that have been linked to disjunctive application, at least not in any meaningful way. Allowing subscripted angled brackets as in (3.10) might work, but the result borders on the preposterous. Essentially, this rule states that voiced obstruents take on the value specified in *a* ([+cont]) when in the *a* context (V — V) and the value specified in *b* ([−cont]) when in the *b* context (everywhere); the more specific *a* context disjunctively blocks the more general *b* context.

(3.10) Disjunctive application of (3.9) via subscripted angled brackets

$$\begin{bmatrix}-\text{son}\\+\text{voi}\end{bmatrix} \longrightarrow \begin{matrix}\langle[+\text{cont}]\rangle_a\\ \langle[-\text{cont}]\rangle_b\end{matrix} \Big/ \begin{matrix}\langle \text{V} \_\_ \text{V}\rangle_a\\ \langle \_\_ \rangle_b\end{matrix}$$

Disjunctive application in this case can of course be achieved with the EC (2.19): the structural description of Fortition properly includes that of Spirantization, and the structural changes of the two rules are directly incompatible. Because these rules are feature-changing, they are not in a mutual bleeding relationship like the rules in the underspecification + feature-filling rule analysis in (3.2) and thus the PIPP (3.5), unless modified so as to impose disjunctive application, will not suffice to achieve blocking in this case. The derivations that result, however, are the same in both analyses: intervocalic application of Spirantization either bleeds or disjunctively blocks Fortition, which thus only applies elsewhere.

Given the viability of any of the other analyses reviewed in this section — all of which are consistent with the generally conjunctive orientation of *SPE* — the disjunctive application analysis hardly seems worth the effort. The literature appears to be solidly in agreement: so far as I am aware, a disjunctive application analysis of UCD has never been proposed. This is in stark contrast with some types of bounded complementary distribution, as discussed in the next section.

3.2 Bounded complementary distribution

The distinguishing property of bounded complementary distribution (BCD) is that the elements in question *do* contrast in some contexts; they are only in complementary distribution in some proper subset of all possible contexts.

The fact that there is a contrast at all in cases of BCD means that underlying representations cannot be constrained one way or another, which rules out two of the five analytical possibilities reviewed in §3.1 above. The prior underlying specification analysis of §3.1.1 requires that only one member of the opposition be present in underlying representations, and the underspecification + feature-filling rule application analysis of §3.1.2 requires that the opposition be represented in underlying representations by an element that is underspecified for the feature defining the distinction between the members of the opposition. The only way to try and make either of these analyses work would be to demand prior underlying specification or underspecification just in those contexts where there is no contrast between the relevant elements, an assumption that is in fact a basis of some theories of underspecification (e.g. Steriade 1987; Archangeli 1988). Arguments against these theories aside (Mohanan 1991; Steriade 1995), this kind of solution is simply not available in cases where there are alternations between positions of contrast and positions of complementary distribution; it would be peculiar to assume that the same morpheme is underlyingly specified for one value of a feature in one context and for the other (or for neither) in another context.[11]

An analysis of BCD thus minimally requires that underlying representations be freely specified, as in the prior rule specification analysis of §3.1.3, the complementary contexts of application analysis of §3.1.4, or the disjunctive application analysis of §3.1.5. Given issues associated with the types of derivation entailed by the prior rule specification analysis (to be discussed in §3.3.5), the complementary contexts of application analysis and the disjunctive application analysis are the only two truly viable possibilities for the analysis of BCD.

11. Peculiar from the perspective of one of the most basic assumptions of generative phonological analysis, that every morpheme should have a single underlying representation and that any and all phonologically predictable alternations of that morpheme should be derived by rule.

I discuss two examples of BCD to make the case for this conclusion. The first concerns long and short vowels in (Modern) English. Complementary distribution in this case is limited to one context — heads of branching main stress feet — while a contrast is found in other contexts. Disjunctive application is the most appropriate analysis here, for reasons discussed in §3.3. The second example concerns tap and trill rhotics in Spanish. In this case, it is the contrast between the two that is limited to just one context — between vowels — while complementary distribution is found in all other contexts. The complementary contexts of application analysis turns out to be most appropriate here, as discussed in §3.4.

3.3 English vowel length

Long and short vowels in English are generally contrastive, but are in complementary distribution in the heads of branching main stress feet (Myers 1985, 1987; Halle and Vergnaud 1987; Prince 1991; Kenstowicz 1994b; Halle 1995; Hayes 1995; Lahiri and Fikkert 1999). Main stress feet are bimoraic trochees at the right edges of prosodic words, modulo extrametricality (Hayes 1982). Branching main stress feet contain two light syllables (denoted by $\breve{\sigma}$), as illustrated in (3.11a), while nonbranching main stress feet contain a single heavy syllable (denoted by $\bar{\sigma}$), as illustrated in (3.11b). Head syllables of branching feet, being stressed, are denoted by $'\sigma$; the post-podal syllable in angled brackets $\langle\sigma\rangle$ denotes the possible presence of a word-final extrametrical syllable.[12]

(3.11) Branching (a) and nonbranching (b) main stress feet in English

a. $\ldots(\,'\breve{\sigma}\;\breve{\sigma}\,)\,\langle\sigma\rangle\,\#$ b. $\ldots(\,'\bar{\sigma}\,)\,\langle\sigma\rangle\,\#$

The head of a branching main stress foot in English must be long if and only if the following three conditions are met. First: the head vowel in question must also be [–high]. Second: the nonhead vowel of the foot must be *i*. Third: the nonhead vowel *i* must be immediately followed by another vowel (i.e., it must be in hiatus). If any one of these conditions is not met — that is, elsewhere — then the head of a branching main stress foot must be short. These conditions can be appreciated by comparing the following near-minimal pairs.

First: compare ('*jōvi*)⟨*al*⟩, in which the head vowel is and must be long, with ('*trĭvi*)⟨*al*⟩, in which the head vowel is and must be short. In both cases, the nonhead vowel is *i* and it is in hiatus; the difference is that the head vowel is [–high] in the case of ('*jōvi*)⟨*al*⟩ whereas it is [+high] in the case of ('*trĭvi*)⟨*al*⟩. This difference is sufficient to account for the length distinction.

Second: compare ('*grādi*)⟨*ent*⟩, in which the head vowel is and must be long, with ('*grădu*)⟨*al*⟩, in which the head vowel is and must be short. In both cases, the head vowel is [–high] and the nonhead vowel is in hiatus; the difference is that the nonhead vowel is *i* in the case of ('*grādi*)⟨*ent*⟩ whereas it is *u* in the case of ('*grădu*)⟨*al*⟩, which is again sufficient to account for the length distinction.

Third: compare ('*rādi*)⟨*al*⟩, in which the head vowel is and must be long, with ('*rădi*)⟨*cal*⟩, in which the head vowel is and must be short. In both cases, the head

12. See Burzio (1993, 1994) for a somewhat different take on English metrification.

vowel is [–high] and the nonhead vowel is *i*; the difference is that the *i* is in hiatus in the case of (ˈ*rādi*)⟨*al*⟩ whereas it is not in hiatus in the case of (ˈ*rădi*)⟨*cal*⟩, once again a sufficient difference to account for the length distinction.

Given the boundedness of this distributional complementarity, simple alternations can generally be exploited in order to determine whether the head of a branching main stress foot is underlyingly long or short. For instance, the heads of the branching main stress feet in (ˈ*my̆thi*)⟨*cal*⟩, *hu*(ˈ*mĭdi*)⟨*ty*⟩, (ˈ*ty̆pi*)⟨*cal*⟩, and *di*(ˈ*vĭni*)⟨*ty*⟩ are obligatorily short, but the corresponding vowels in (ˈ*my̆th*) and (ˈ*hū*)⟨*mĭd*⟩ reveal an underlying short quantity while those in (ˈ*tȳpe*) and *di*(ˈ*vīne*) reveal an underlying long quantity. Likewise, the heads of the branching main stress feet in *re*(ˈ*mēdi*)⟨*al*⟩ and (ˌ*Shāke*)(ˈ*spe̅a̅ri*)⟨*an*⟩ are both obligatorily long while the corresponding vowels in (ˈ*rěmě*)⟨*dy*⟩ and (ˈ*Shāke*)(ˌ*spe̅a̅re*) contrast in length. Clearly, vowel length is underlyingly contrastive in English and neutralized one way or the other in the heads of branching feet.

Since there is a contrast between long and short vowels, there must be two feature-changing rules in an *SPE* analysis; these are formulated in (3.12) below, adapted from Kenstowicz (1994b: 218).[13] The rule in (3.12b) is the Modern English reflex of the Middle English Trisyllabic Shortening rule (TSS, 2.15a) and is more often than not referred to by the same name; the rule in (3.12a) is otherwise known as '*CiV*-Lengthening'. I refer to these rules simply as 'Shortening' and 'Lengthening' here to distinguish them from the Middle English rules.

(3.12) English Lengthening and Shortening rules

a. Lengthening

$$\begin{bmatrix} \text{V} \\ \text{-high} \end{bmatrix} \longrightarrow \bar{\text{V}} \; / \; \begin{array}{cccc} \_\_ & \text{C} & i & \text{V} \\ & | & & | \\ & ('\sigma & & \sigma) \end{array}$$

b. Shortening

$$\text{V} \longrightarrow \breve{\text{V}} \; / \; \begin{array}{ccc} \_\_ & \text{C}_0 & \text{V} \\ | & & | \\ ('\sigma & & \sigma) \end{array}$$

There are a great many facts about the analysis of English phonology that are raised but left unaddressed here. For one thing, the relevant pairings among 'long' and 'short' vowels in English have been obscured by the Great Vowel Shift and related diachronic phenomena; whether they should be characterized synchronically in terms of length or 'tenseness' (e.g. Chomsky and Halle 1968; Halle 1977) is not germane here. For another, there is some disagreement about exactly how (or even whether) to characterize the contexts of the rules in metrical terms. There are also many exceptions to these rules, both systematic and not; furthermore, there are other vowel neutralizations that compromise contrast (reduction of unstressed vowels, tensing of final vowels, etc.). These facts and others are tackled in

13. See §5.6 for discussion of the representations manipulated by these rules.

the combined efforts of the works that I cite in this section — and in the references therein — and the interested reader is urged to consult those works.[14]

3.3.1 Constraining underlying representations

To reiterate the point already made in §3.2, the underlying contrast between long and short vowels that is necessary in this case disqualifies two of the five analytical options presented in §3.1 for UCD. The prior underlying specification analysis in (3.1) would require that all vowels be underlyingly short and the relevant subset of them to be lengthened by Lengthening; the underspecification + feature-filling rule application analysis in (3.2), on the other hand, would require that all vowels be underlyingly unspecified for length, with two rules akin to Shortening and Lengthening filling in the relevant values. This leaves us with the remaining three analytical options, all three of which involve two feature-changing rules and which can thus accommodate an underlying contrast. Let's consider them in turn.

3.3.2 Complementary contexts of application

We can quickly dispense with the complementary contexts of application analysis. One problem with this analysis of this case of BCD is the same problem with the corresponding analysis of UCD discussed in §3.1.4: the complementarity of the effects of the rules is — by assumption, of course — simply recapitulated by stipulating that complementarity in their contexts of application.

But there is a further problem in this case that was not present in the case of UCD. In that case, the unbounded nature of the complementary distribution between voiced stops and spirants meant that the context of the otherwise more specific Spirantization rule, V—V, could simply be negated to create the complementary context of the otherwise more general Fortition rule, $\neg(V\text{—}V)$. Whatever independent issues are raised by allowing the statement of negative contexts of this sort, an equally straightforward solution is not available in the case of BCD. Simply negating the context of the otherwise more specific Lengthening rule does not render a context appropriate to the statement of the otherwise more general Shortening rule, because vowels in English are not short in *all* contexts except those where Lengthening applies: long and short vowels generally contrast outside the heads of branching main stress feet, so the scope of negation must somehow be limited to that context — requiring yet another descriptively powerful addition to the rule notation arsenal.

If there were independent motivation to state a suite of rules with the combined effect of Shortening, each of which carved out a chunk of the complementary context without the use of otherwise unnecessary notational devices, then of course this solution would be worthy of attention. This is not the case here, but it is in the example of Spanish rhotics to be discussed in §3.4.

14. There is a further condition on Lengthening that I am also putting aside here: the head vowel must be in an open syllable due to the independent rule of closed syllable shortening. Proposals to somehow unify closed syllable shortening with shortening of branching main stress foot heads include Luick (1898), Kiparsky (1968a, 1981a), Stampe (1979), Halle and Mohanan (1985), Myers (1985, 1987), Yip (1987), Prince (1991), and Rubach (1996); cf. Lahiri and Fikkert (1999).

3.3.3 Prior rule specification

Chomsky and Halle (1968: 181, 240ff) analyze the interaction between Lengthening and Shortening in prior rule specification terms.[15] Underlying forms such as */remĕdi+al/* and */jōvial/* are footed to become |*re('mĕdi)al*| and |*('jōvi)al*|, after which Shortening applies to produce |*re('mĕdi)al*| (vacuously) and |*('jŏvi)al*| (nonvacuously). Lengthening then simply undoes the effects of Shortening in these cases, rendering the correct surface forms [*re('mēdi)al*] and [*('jōvi)al*]. This is illustrated by the (abbreviated) derivations in (3.13).

(3.13) Prior rule specification: Shortening precedes Lengthening

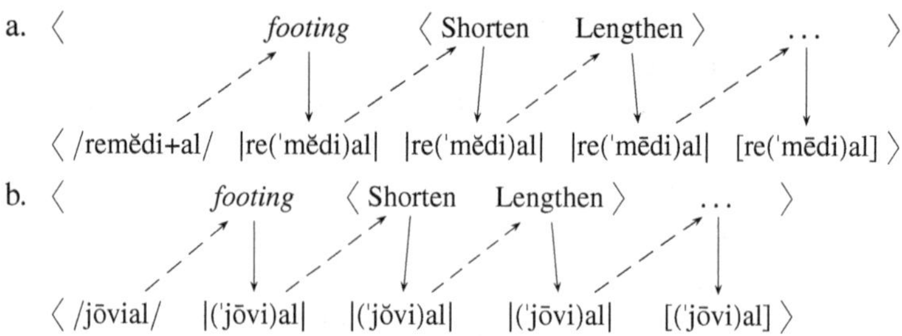

Chomsky and Halle impose this conjunctive order extrinsically, but arguments made by Kiparsky (1982: 154, 157) suggest that it follows intrinsically from each rule's behavior with respect to the lexical-phonological cycle: Shortening is cyclic (because it is blocked in nonderived environments) while Lengthening is postcyclic (because it isn't). Whether extrinsic or intrinsic, the order is conjunctive.

3.3.4 Disjunctive application

Kenstowicz (1994b: 218) and Halle (1995) claim that these rules apply disjunctively, mediated by the EC. The structural changes of the rules are incompatible: Lengthening lengthens vowels, while Shortening shortens them. Moreover, the structural description of Lengthening is properly included in that of Shortening: both apply to the heads of branching feet, but Lengthening applies more specifically to a [–high] head of a foot the nonhead of which is an *i* immediately followed by another vowel. Lengthening thus blocks Shortening, applying alone to |*re('mĕdi)al*| (⟶ [*re('mēdi)al*]) and |*('jōvi)al*| (⟶ [*('jōvi)al*]).[16]

(3.14) Disjunctive application of Lengthening and Shortening

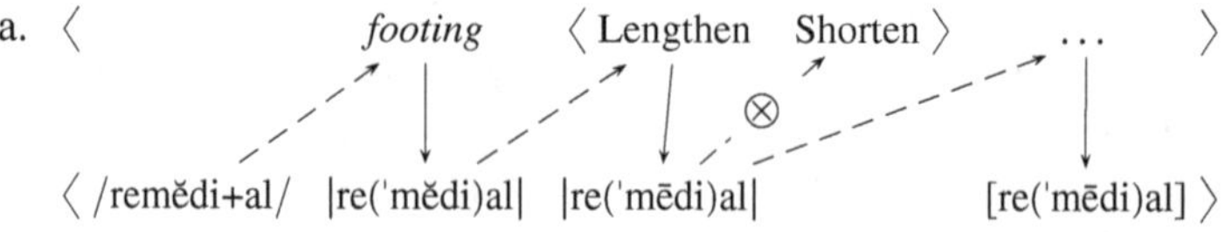

15. There are largely superficial differences between Chomsky and Halle's representational assumptions and those underlying the rule formulations in (3.12); these are beside the point here.

16. Note that Lengthening applies vacuously to |*('jōvi)al*|. If 'application' of Lengthening is what blocks Shortening, then vacuous application must count as application. See §5.6 for discussion.

b. ⟨ *footing* ⟨ Lengthen Shorten ⟩ ... ⟩

⟨ /jōvial/ |(ˈjōvi)al| |(ˈjōvi)al| ⊗ [(ˈjōvi)al] ⟩

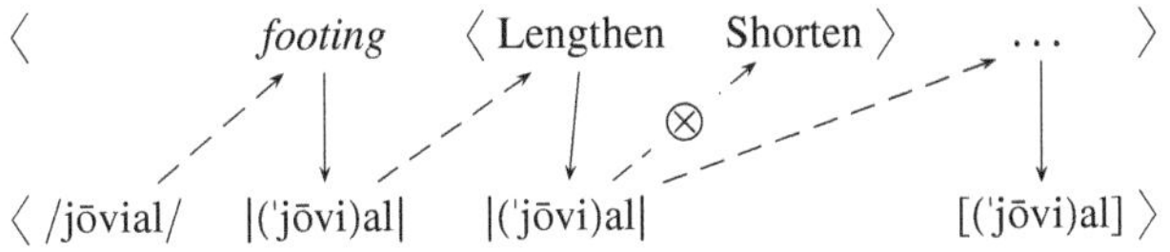

3.3.5 Conjunction or disjunction?

As made clear in (3.13) and (3.14), application of Lengthening and Shortening to forms that meet both structural descriptions results in the right surface representations whether the rules apply conjunctively or disjunctively. This pair of rules thus differs from the rule sets from Latin, Indonesian, Middle English, and Diola Fogny discussed in §2.4: recall that in those cases, a conjunctive alternative to disjunctive application required some serious (and detrimental) modification of the rules. By contrast, disjunctive application is only *possible* in the case under discussion here; it is not strictly necessary.

Given the availability of a working conjunctive alternative — using the very same rules, no less — insistence on a disjunctive analysis of the interaction between Lengthening and Shortening (and other cases like it) is thus quite curious. This is especially so considering the privileged status of counterfeeding in the literature. Recall from §3.1.3 that the prior rule specification analysis is a species of counterfeeding, which constitutes a significant subset of the class of opaque generalizations. Opacity is the most-invoked phenomenon in arguments for *SPE*'s conjunctive conception of rule application; Bromberger and Halle (1989) single out an example of counterfeeding in their argument for why extrinsic rule ordering is an irreducible element of phonological theory.

One would thus think that the conjunctive analysis of the English example in (3.13) would be celebrated as further evidence for the essential correctness of the overall *SPE* approach. One would be wrong, however, as evidenced by the fact that this example serves as the demonstrative piece of evidence for disjunctive application in Kenstowicz's (1994b) influential phonology textbook as well as in Halle's (1995) piece dedicated to the reassertion of the primal significance of the EC. So why would advocates of the conjunctive enterprise carve out a particular class of cases that can be analyzed perfectly well in terms of conjunctive counterfeeding and assert that they be analyzed disjunctively instead?

Prince (1997a) also wonders about the reasons for this argument.

> [This] example does not in fact provide much evidence for adjoining an Elsewhere Condition to extrinsic-ordering models of the SPE type: the relationship between the two rules is already obtained by the theory of serial ordering. Special lengthening is ordered *after* General shortening, and simply undoes the general shortening in its own narrow environment. This kind of effect, by which 'special' imposes itself on 'general' through ordinary rule-application, is predicted by ordering theories like SPE: there is no obvious need to re-predict it. (Prince 1997a: 2)

Indeed, the need for the EC in cases like this one is at the very least not obvious. Nevertheless, a couple of theoretically motivated arguments have been offered in the literature; these are reviewed in the remainder of this subsection.

'Psychological reality'

In his original proposal of the EC, Kiparsky (1973b: 98–100) argues that the conjunctive, fed-counterfeeding-on-focus alternative to disjunctive application predicts the existence of an intermediate representation that Kiparsky claims is not psychologically real. The argument crucially depends on a particular analysis and set of assumptions about the accessibility of derivational levels of representation for the purposes of metrical scansion put forth by Kiparsky (1972).

The facts, according to Kiparsky, can be summarized as follows. In Vedic Sanskrit, glides and high vowels were complementarily distributed according to Sievers' Law: glides after light syllables, high vowels elsewhere. However, "because of various other phenomena underlying glides had to be kept distinct from underlying high vowels" (Kiparsky 1973b: 99). The relevance of the EC here has to do with the analysis of Sievers' Law: neutralization in complementary contexts of the claimed underlying contrast between glides and high vowels requires the following two rules (adapted from Kiparsky 1973b: 99).

(3.15) Sievers' Law in Vedic Sanskrit

a. Glide Formation

$$\begin{bmatrix}\text{+high}\\\text{–cons}\end{bmatrix} \longrightarrow [\text{–syll}]\ /\ \breve{\sigma}\ \_$$

b. Vocalization

$$\begin{bmatrix}\text{+high}\\\text{–cons}\end{bmatrix} \longrightarrow [\text{+syll}]$$

Just like the English Lengthening and Shortening rules in (3.12), these two rules of Vedic Sanskrit can apply either conjunctively or disjunctively to produce the correct results. Conjunctively, Vocalization applies first to make all high vocoids syllabic (feeding Glide Formation), and then Glide Formation applies to make only those high vocoids after light syllables nonsyllabic (counterfeeding Vocalization). In a disjunctive analysis, Glide Formation applies to high vocoids after light syllables and blocks Vocalization from applying to those vocoids; Vocalization thus applies only to the remaining high vocoids elsewhere.

Kiparsky's main empirical concern is with the scansion of high vocoids in the hymns of the *Rigveda*: some high vocoids are only scanned as nonsyllabic glides, others are only scanned as syllabic vowels, and still others can be scanned either way. Kiparsky proposes that those high vocoids that must be scanned as glides are, derivationally speaking, glides through and through: they are underlyingly glides and occur only after light syllables, thus being subject to Glide Formation alone. Those high vocoids that must be scanned as vowels, on the other hand, are vowels all the way: they are underlyingly high vowels and do not occur after light syllables, thus being subject only to Vocalization.

Those high vocoids that can be scanned either way are what remains: underlying high vowels occurring after light syllables, or underlying glides occurring elsewhere. Both scansions are possible, Kiparsky argues, because metrical constraints may access either representations prior to or representations following the application of the rules comprising Sievers' Law in (3.15).

Kiparsky further hypothesizes that the set of derivational levels of representation to which metrical constraints have access — the "metrical range" — "cannot be discontinuous" (Kiparsky 1972: 194; see also Kiparsky 1973b: 99). This conjecture rules out conjunctive application of the rules in (3.15) because underlying glides after light syllables are required in a conjunctive analysis to undergo Vocalization before being re-formed by Glide Formation. But as noted above, underlying glides after light syllables are only scanned as nonsyllabic glides, never as syllabic vowels, meaning that their fleeting status as vowels must not be visible within the metrical range. Disjunctive application of the rules in (3.15) doesn't predict this intermediate representation; therefore, the conjecture is safe.

But it could of course be the case that Kiparsky's metrical range continuity restriction itself is simply wrong, as "plausible [a] restriction on the psychological availability of intermediate stages in a derivation" as it may intuitively seem (Kiparsky 1973b: 99). The relevant facts of the *Rigveda* are compatible with an alternative restriction on metrical accessibility; namely, that only the underlying and surface representations are metrically accessible (Howard 1975: 116).[17]

'No superfluous steps'

Recall from §3.1.3 that Pullum (1976) specifically discusses derivations of the type illustrated in (3.13b), which I called 'fed counterfeeding on focus' following Kavitskaya and Staroverov's (2010) terminology. In choosing a name for this type of derivation, Pullum invokes a traditional English rhyme depicting "incompetent and self-defeating activity" on the part of a fictitious 'Duke of York'.[18]

> Derivations that in some relevant respect have the form A → B → A I shall call *Duke of York derivations*, and the strategy of postulating such a derivation in order to achieve a description of some piece of linguistic data I shall call *the Duke of York gambit*. (Pullum 1976: 83)

Far from sharing in the "prejudice among linguists" against the Duke of York gambit that he documents in the paper, Pullum's own conclusions are as follows.

> [A] thorough investigation of the descriptive problems in which proposed Duke of York analyses are embedded does not reveal any basis for a general constraint that would prohibit the Duke of York gambit. This means that [those who have expressed a prejudice against such analyses] are in the strictest sense mistaken on a methodological matter. The guiding principle they implicitly appeal to in casting suspicion on Duke of York analysis cannot and does not exist; ... there are points both for it and against it but it cannot be trusted to select correct analyses over inadequate ones. [T]he strategy of avoiding (or of adopting) the Duke of York gambit will be reasonable precisely when the result is a reasonable analysis, and unreasonable precisely when it is not. (Pullum 1976: 100)

---

17. This alternative restriction is incompatible with Kiparsky's (1968b) claims (referenced by Kiparsky 1972: 175–176) concerning the analysis of the Finnish epic *Kalevala*, where it is proposed that the metrical range crucially includes only (continuous) *intermediate* levels of representation. That analysis would need to be reviewed on its own merits, a task that would take us too far afield here.
18. The version of the rhyme cited by Pullum is as follows: *The Grand Old Duke of York / He had ten thousand men / He marched them up a great high hill / And he marched them down again.*

Pullum's entertaining catalog of unfounded prejudices against the Duke of York gambit has somehow overshadowed this equally punchy concluding passage, because these prejudices have persisted. In a specific defense of the disjunctive analysis in (3.14b) as opposed to the conjunctive, Duke of York derivation in (3.13b), Halle and Idsardi (1998) present a dubious argument from authority by citing Chomsky on the supposed undesirability of such derivations.

> Chomsky (1995: p. 220) has noted "a linguistic expression L cannot be defined just as a pair (π, λ) formed by a convergent derivation. Rather, its derivation must be optimal, satisfying certain natural economy conditions: locality of movement, *no 'superfluous steps' in derivations*, and so on" (emphasis added). (Halle and Idsardi 1998: 1)

Neither Chomsky nor Halle and Idsardi offer any argument for the claim that derivations with 'superfluous steps' are not 'optimal'. Halle and Idsardi simply claim further that Duke of York derivations "such as [(3.13b)] . . . have justly been singled out as unacceptable because of the superfluous steps in them", but they cite no sources as agents of this passive clause. A parallel and equally unsubstantiated claim is made in earlier work by the same authors.[19]

> [O]bjections to [the Duke of York gambit] have been raised on the grounds that [it] subverts the essential difference between rules, which reflect idiosyncratic facts of a language, and repairs, which are consequences of general structural principles obeyed by the language. (Halle and Idsardi 1997: 344)

The general notion that derivation length should be minimized — in phonology, at least — can be found as early as Chomsky (1967) and Chomsky and Halle (1968). Chomsky (1967: 124–125) proposes a specific principle favoring disjunctive application, followed by a few speculative remarks about it, followed by a footnote clarifying just how speculative those remarks are.

> Principle 5: The underlying representing schema is selected in such a way as to maximize disjunctive ordering.
>
> . . . Princ. 5 is rather plausible. By maximizing disjunctive ordering we minimize the length of derivations, the amount of processing involved in production or perception of speech. It is not unreasonable to suppose that this should be a subsidiary consideration in the selection of a grammar.*
>
> *More precisely, this consideration bears on the interpretation of a grammar, since the sequence of rules constituting the grammar is not affected by the procedure for determining the value of the grammar and the assignment of disjunctive ordering. . . . In considering Princ. 5, one must bear in mind that the question of how a grammar is used in production or perception is, of course, quite open. Nevertheless, it is not unreasonable to assume, as a first approximation, that the process will increase in complexity as the number of applicable grammatical rules increases.

Chomsky and Halle (1968) are even more frankly speculative about how the competence grammar might be implemented in performance.

19. McCarthy (1999a: 6) notes that Halle and Idsardi (1997) nowhere clarify their assumptions regarding "the essential difference between rules . . . and repairs" referenced in this quotation; see Norton (2003: 125–126) for a valiant attempt to make sense of what Halle and Idsardi might mean here.

> The question of how an internalized grammar is used in performance ... is of course quite open. Nevertheless, it seems reasonable to suppose that the grammar should be selected in such a way as to minimize the amount of "computation" that is necessary, and that "length of derivation" is one factor in determining "complexity of computation." Naturally, this principle must be regarded as quite tentative. We will adhere to it where a choice arises, but we have very little evidence for or against it. (Chomsky and Halle 1968: 63)

Interestingly, much of Chomsky's work expresses strong views to the contrary on the more general matter of implementing competence in performance.[20]

> To avoid what has been a continuing misunderstanding, it is perhaps worth while to reiterate that a generative grammar is not a model for a speaker or a hearer. ... When we say that a sentence has a certain derivation with respect to a particular generative grammar, we say nothing about how the speaker or hearer might proceed, in some practical or efficient way, to construct such a derivation. (Chomsky 1965: 9)

> [A]lthough we may describe the grammar *G* as a system of processes and rules that apply in a certain order to relate sound and meaning, we are not entitled to take this as a description of the successive acts of a performance model... — in fact, it would be quite absurd to do so. (Chomsky 1968: 117)

> Recall that the ordering of operations is abstract, expressing postulated properties of the language faculty of the brain, with no temporal interpretation implied. (Chomsky 1995: 380)

There is a clear tension among these works, between the ideological desire to sharply distinguish competence from performance on the one hand and the natural urge to let premature intuitions about performance guide the construction of competence grammars on the other.[21] The problem with all of the claims quoted thus far in this subsection is that no empirical evidence is provided one way or the other. McCarthy (1999b, 2003c) and Norton (2003) are the only works known to me in which the consequences of Duke of York derivations are put to some sort of empirical test. Both authors conclude that the prejudice against the Duke of York gambit in the literature reviewed here and in Pullum (1976) is not unfounded.

McCarthy (1999b: 375ff; 2003c: 32ff) argues that there are no real examples of *feeding Duke of York derivations*, in which there are three rules where the first crucially feeds the second and the third rule crucially undoes the effect of the first.[22] For example, imagine a conjunctive order of the English rules in (3.12), with Lengthening preceding Shortening and with a Raising rule crucially sandwiched between them that raises all and only long foot heads. Raising would

20. These passages are quoted, in a slightly different context, by McCarthy (2002: 9–10). Note that the last of these passages comes from the same source as the somewhat contradictory passage quoted by Halle and Idsardi (1998), but then again the two passages are separated by 160 pages.
21. Much of Halle's own work simply abandons the ideology and is less hesitant about the natural urge; see the papers reprinted in Halle (2002), aptly titled *From Memory to Speech and Back.*
22. Duke of York derivations where there is no crucial rule sandwiched in the middle — like the derivation of /*jōvial*/ in (3.13b) — are what McCarthy calls *vacuous Duke of York derivations*. McCarthy (2003c: 30–31) demonstrates that *bleeding Duke of York derivations*, in which one rule bleeds a second and a third undoes the first, are analytically reducible to the vacuous type.

affect all vowels that are lengthened by Lengthening, and it would affect only some vowels elsewhere (those that are arbitrarily specified as long underlyingly, by hypothesis). Shortening will then come along and render all foot heads short, but the intermediate stage of derivation between Lengthening and Raising makes itself felt in the surface distinction between raised and nonraised vowels.

This hypothetical situation is illustrated in (3.16) with variations on two English forms, each with two possible underlying representations: one with an underlying short vowel in what will be the foot head position (|(*ˈrădi*)*al*|, |(*ˈrădi*)*cal*|) and the other with an underlying long vowel (|(*ˈrādi*)*al*|, |(*ˈrādi*)*cal*|). In the interests of space, the derivations here begin after footing has taken place.

(3.16) Lengthening precedes Raising precedes Shortening (hypothetical)

a.	|(ˈrădi)al|	$\xrightarrow[\text{Lengthen}]{}$	|(ˈrādi)al|	$\xrightarrow[\text{Raise}]{}$	|(ˈrēdi)al|	$\xrightarrow[\text{Shorten}]{}$	[(ˈrĕdi)al]
b.	|(ˈrādi)al|	$\xrightarrow[\text{Lengthen}]{}$	|(ˈrādi)al|	$\xrightarrow[\text{Raise}]{}$	|(ˈrēdi)al|	$\xrightarrow[\text{Shorten}]{}$	[(ˈrĕdi)al]
c.	|(ˈrădi)cal|	$\xrightarrow[\text{Lengthen}]{}$	⊙	$\xrightarrow[\text{Raise}]{}$	⊙	$\xrightarrow[\text{Shorten}]{}$	[(ˈrădi)cal]
d.	|(ˈrādi)cal|	$\xrightarrow[\text{Lengthen}]{}$	⊙	$\xrightarrow[\text{Raise}]{}$	|(ˈrēdi)cal|	$\xrightarrow[\text{Shorten}]{}$	[(ˈrĕdi)cal]

In real English, the two possible inputs in each case would converge on the same output. Both |(*ˈrădi*)*al*| and |(*ˈrādi*)*al*| are expected to surface as [(*ˈrādi*)*al*], with a long vowel guaranteed by the application of Lengthening; this is either because Shortening applies first in the conjunctive order (3.13) or because Lengthening disjunctively blocks Shortening (3.14). In similar fashion, both |(*ˈrădi*)*cal*| and |(*ˈrādi*)*cal*| are expected to surface as [(*ˈrădi*)*cal*], with a short vowel, because only Shortening is applicable in the derivations of these forms.

In the hypothetical situation depicted in (3.16), on the other hand, a three-way surface contrast is predicted to arise from these four underlying representations due to the conjunctive possibility of allowing Lengthening to precede and not block Shortening. Both |(*ˈrădi*)*al*| (3.16a) and |(*ˈrādi*)*al*| (3.16b) are subject to Lengthening, which leads to Raising and then Shortening, resulting in [(*ˈrĕdi*)*al*] in both cases. Contrariwise, neither |(*ˈrădi*)*cal*| (3.16c) nor |(*ˈrādi*)*cal*| (3.16d) are subject to Lengthening, but the latter form has a long vowel to begin with. This vowel is thus subject to Raising, leading to a surface contrast between [(*ˈrădi*)*cal*] (3.16c), without Raising, and [(*ˈrĕdi*)*cal*](3.16d), with Raising.

The unattestedness of feeding Duke of York derivations like (3.16) is unexpected in a theory that allows Duke of York derivations in general, thus offering some empirical support for the view that Duke of York derivations should be excluded. But note that feeding Duke of York derivations like (3.16) technically involve no *superfluous* steps: the first step is necessary to feed the second and the third is necessary to undo the first. Thus, proposing to disallow Duke of York derivations based exclusively on their superfluity, as Halle and Idsardi (1998) hastily propose to follow Chomsky (1995) in doing, would incorrectly *allow* the one type of Duke of York derivation that is most probably unattested.

For his part, Norton (2003: 129ff) observes that there are no attested cases in which some set of vowels is deleted in some context only to be replaced by an epenthetic vowel in the same context. This type of derivation should be attested if Duke of York derivations are possible, and yet what one finds instead is deletion and epenthesis in *complementary* contexts. For example, unstressed *i* in Palestinian Arabic deletes before a CV sequence, and the same vowel is inserted between two consonants followed by a consonant or word boundary (Brame 1974); these contexts are obviously complementary. Another example is Yokuts (Kuroda 1967; Kisseberth 1970a), where all short vowels delete in the doubly open syllable context VC — CV, and a short high vowel is epenthesized in the same context as in Palestinian Arabic — again, the contexts are complementary.

In cases where there is the opportunity for both deletion and epenthesis to apply in the same context, what one finds instead is that neither rule applies. For example, the nominative in Lardil is marked by deletion of the final stem vowel (Hale 1973; Wilkinson 1988), and unsuffixed monomoraic stems are augmented by word-final epenthesis of [a]: /*yiliyili*/ ⟶ [*yiliyil*] 'oyster species', /*yak*/ ⟶ [*yaka*] 'fish'. Both rules have the opportunity to apply to a CVCV stem: deletion would reduce the stem to monomoraic status, and epenthesis would augment it back to minimal bimoraicity. All CVCV stems might thus be expected to surface as CVC*a* in the nominative, but this is not the case in Lardil: /*mela*/ ⟶ [*mela*] 'sea', but /*wiṭe*/ ⟶ [*wiṭe*] 'inside' — neither deletion nor epenthesis applies.

Norton (2003: 133ff) discusses two subspecies of Duke of York derivation that may be attested: (i) cases in which constituent structure is built but subsequently destroyed, and (ii) cases in which the conflicting rules have different domains (levels/strata) of application. Still, Norton (2003: 135) concludes "that a disjunctive interaction between contrary processes is a universal property of language — the opposite of Pullum's conclusion", and offers a "Universal Interaction of Mutually Contrary Operations" as a universal principle: "Mutually contrary operations on segmental structure apply in distinct contexts." In other words, rules that could undo each other's effects never both apply to the same element.

Summary

There are examples of rule interactions for which the same rules can be ordered conjunctively or disjunctively to correctly map underlying representations to surface representations. Some researchers have argued that the disjunctive analysis is to be preferred in these cases on the grounds that derivation length is thereby minimized or that 'superfluous steps' are thereby avoided. The assumption behind this argument is that derivational step reduction is somehow desirable, but no solid evidence for the putative desirability of shorter derivations is provided; this assumption is thus unsupported by any kind of empirical evidence and is only weakly supported by unsubstantiated claims about the implementation of competence grammar in performance, claims that in fact conflict with generative grammar's ideological goal of separating competence from performance. But more recent work has shown that the availability of conjunctive analyses like these makes typological predictions that appear to be unattested in human languages, pointing to the conclusion that the disjunctive analysis may be the correct one after all.

3.4 Spanish rhotics

Spanish is somewhat unusual among the languages of the world in contrasting two rhotics, a tap *ɾ* and a trill *ɾ̄*.[23] These rhotics contrast only in (word-internal) intervocalic position: *toˈɾeɾo* 'bullfighter' vs. *toˈɾ̄eɾo* 'lighthouse keeper'; *ˈkaɾo* 'expensive' vs. *ˈkaɾ̄o* 'car'. Otherwise, they are in complementary distribution. First, only the trill occurs word-initially: *ˈɾ̄osa* 'rose', *ɾ̄aˈton* 'mouse'. Second, only the trill occurs syllable-initially after a consonant (effectively, after *n*, *l*, *s*): *ˈon.ɾ̄a* 'honor', *al.ˈɾ̄o.ta* 'flax residue', *is*^{z}*.ɾ̄a.ˈel* 'Israel'. Only the tap occurs elsewhere: as the second member of a complex onset (*ˈtɾen* 'train', *ˈo.βɾa* 'deed') and syllable-finally (*ˈpaɾ.te* 'part', *ˈmaɾ* 'sea').[24] These complementary contexts of occurrence of trills and taps are summarized for ease of future reference in (3.17).

(3.17) Complementary distribution of Spanish rhotics

a.	i.	# —	trills
	ii.	C $_{\sigma}[$ —	
b.	i.	$_{\sigma}[$C —	taps
	ii.	— $]_{\sigma}$	

Rehearsing the argument from §3.2 once again, the contrast between the tap and trill in intervocalic position makes it difficult to describe their complementary distribution in other contexts with either the prior underlying specification analysis or the underspecification + feature-filling rule application analysis. In this particular case, however, there are no alternations between positions of contrast and positions of complementary distribution; that is, there are no morphemes in Spanish that begin or end in one rhotic when it ends up in the contrastive intervocalic position but in the other rhotic when it ends up in another, noncontrastive position. This means that it is in principle possible to implement one of these two analyses. To do so, one would have to assume that taps and trills are underlyingly contrastive *only* in intervocalic position, and that in all other positions they are either all taps, all trills, or all underspecified rhotics.

And indeed, this is the approach pursued — explicitly or implicitly — in most if not all *SPE*-style analyses of Spanish rhotic distribution; for example, Harris (1969, 1983) specifies the rhotic as an underlying tap while Harris (2001, 2002) leaves it underspecified; in both cases, the contrast is assumed to exist only in intervocalic position in underlying representations. The difficulty lies in explaining why underlying representations are asymmetrically restricted: it's one thing to constrain underlying representations such that a contrast is not found in *any*

23. I follow Whitley (2003) and Hualde (2004, 2005) in using the IPA *ɾ* for the tap but adding the macron diacritic to better distinguish the trill *ɾ̄* (Harris 1983 also uses the macron; others sometimes use a tilde). I also set aside here the fact that there is significant phonetic variation in the production of both rhotics across the Spanish-speaking world, as well as the fact that there are emphatic and 'more careful speech' trills that occur optionally for many speakers in certain contexts.

24. This syllable-final context must be established at the word level, before resyllabification across word boundaries: |*ˈmaɾ.* # *a.ˈsul*| ⟶ [*ˈma.ɾa.ˈsul*] 'blue sea'.

position — this is the standard analysis of allophonic complementary distribution — but it's quite another to constrain underlying representations such that a contrast is only found in *some* positions.[25] Why those positions?

Bradley (2001a, b) argues that the explanation is on the surface, grounded in facts about articulation and perception. Briefly, Bradley's argument is that the rapid ballistic gesture required for the articulation of a tap is best implemented intervocalically, where its momentariness is also best perceived; this makes the intervocalic position the best position for any language to maintain a durational contrast between a tap and a trill (and the only position, if there is to be only one). Colina (2010) proposes a more diachronically motivated alternative account, but likewise aims to provide an account in which the grammar generates "the correct output regardless of the form of the underlying representation" (Colina 2010: 75).

To summarize: while it may be technically possible to analyze the distribution of Spanish rhotics assuming prior underlying specification (3.1) or underspecification + feature-filling rule application (3.2) in positions where there is no contrast, both types of analysis require underlying representations to be restricted in asymmetrical ways that can be better explained as restrictions on surface representations. Thus we are again left with the other three analytical options.

Even putting aside the problems with Duke of York derivations predicted by the prior rule specification analysis (as discussed in §3.3.5), it turns out to be difficult if not impossible to craft a 'more general' rule — the rule that establishes prior specification — in the case at hand. The same problem applies to the more general rule that must be blocked by the more specific rule(s) in a disjunctive application analysis; these two analyses are thus dispensed with together here.

The fact that the tap~trill contrast surfaces intact intervocalically means, of course, that there can be no rule in the analysis that affects intervocalic rhotics. What remains is the heterogeneous complement of this context; specifically, the positions where only trills are found — word-initially (3.17a.i) and syllable-initially after a consonant (3.17a.ii) — and the positions where only taps are found — as the second member of a complex onset (3.17b.i) and syllable-finally (3.17b.ii). These contexts can of course each be handled by separate rules in a complementary contexts of application analysis, as shown in (3.18). (I assume the *ad hoc* features [+rhotic], [+trill], and [+tap] for the sake of argument here.)

(3.18) Rules with complementary contexts accounting for (3.17)

a. i. $[+\text{rhotic}] \longrightarrow [+\text{trill}] \;/\; \# \_\_$

ii. $[+\text{rhotic}] \longrightarrow [+\text{trill}] \;/\; \text{C}\,{}_{\sigma}[\,\_\_$

b. i. $[+\text{rhotic}] \longrightarrow [+\text{tap}] \;/\; {}_{\sigma}[\,\text{C}\,\_\_$

ii. $[+\text{rhotic}] \longrightarrow [+\text{tap}] \;/\; \_\_\,]_{\sigma}$

25. In Harris's work, the underlying contrast is analyzed as being between a singleton and a geminate rhotic. This allows the postulation of a single underlying rhotic segmental melody, but shifting the burden of contrast from segmental melodies to melodic sequences (or doubly linked structures, or however the singleton-geminate distinction is represented) does not circumvent the argument in the text. In any event, see Lipski (1990), Bonet and Mascaró (1997), Bradley (2001b, 2006), Hualde (2004), Baković (2009a), and Colina (2010) for arguments against this analysis.

In order to establish the necessary elsewhere effect that is required for either the prior rule specification analysis or the disjunctive application analysis to function, the structural descriptions of either the pair of rules in (3.18a) or the pair in (3.18b) must be generalized to include the structural descriptions of the other pair of rules — but the intervocalic context must be excluded from this generalized structural description in order to allow the tap~trill contrast to surface there.

The only way to accomplish this appears to be to allow the use of negation, as in the complementary contexts of application analysis of UCD in (3.8): either the rules in (3.18a) or those in (3.18b) can be collapsed and generalized so that the structural description is ¬(V—V); the other, now more specific rules either apply after this generalized rule (assuming a prior rule specification analysis) or block it (assuming a disjunctive application analysis). But the use of a negative environment like this is suspect, just as it was in the case of (3.8) — although, somewhat paradoxically, for something like the opposite reason. In that case, its only justification was the need to stipulate complementarity in perverse pursuit of the complementary contexts of application analysis of a case of UCD; in this case, its only justification is the attempt to *avoid* the utterly unremarkable complementary contexts of application analysis in (3.18) of a case of BCD.

The key difference is that in this case of BCD, the specific context of contrast (between vowels) must be carved out from the set of all possible contexts defined by the otherwise all-inclusive structural description of any elsewhere rule. The English BCD case in §3.3 does not suffer from this issue because in that case it is the context of complementary distribution that is specific (heads of branching main stress feet); the structural description of the elsewhere rule (Shortening) can thus be all-inclusive up to that contextual point without infringing on the domain of contrast or resorting to the use of a negative environment. And in the case of UCD there is simply no context of contrast to carve out: allophonic complementary distribution is total, and its totality is what typically makes it difficult *not* to have an all-inclusive elsewhere rule (or prior underlying specification) — again, without resorting to the use of a negative environment.

This highlights a significant difference between UCD and the English vowel length case of BCD on the one hand and the Spanish rhotics case of BCD on the other: the former two are amenable to a straightforward disjunctive application analysis while the latter is not. To distinguish the two cases of BCD from each other, I will henceforth refer to cases of the English type as 'disjunctive BCD' and to cases of the Spanish type as 'complementary-contexts BCD'.

3.5 Summary

To summarize, we've observed in this chapter that there are five different ways to analyze complementary distribution under standard *SPE* assumptions.

Two of these analytical options were shown to be tailor-made for UCD, as typified by allophonic complementary distribution. The prior underlying specification analysis appears to require the least complicated machinery: one underlyingly specified phoneme representing the basic allophone, and one rule for each derived allophone. This is the type of analysis found in introductory textbooks and in otherwise relatively simplified descriptive statements, and is probably the most familiar to all linguists. The underspecification + feature-filling rule application analysis adds a couple layers of complexity: the crucial distinction between specified and unspecified features, and an additional context-free rule specifying the basic allophone that must be crucially bled whenever a context-specific rule for a derived allophone adds its own conflicting feature specification. This type of analysis is also very familiar to working phonologists, allowing for some minor variation in actual examples (more often than not simply because not all aspects of the analysis are spelled out at the level of detail considered here).

Given the contrast that exists in some contexts in cases of BCD, neither the prior underlying specification analysis nor the underspecification + feature-filling rule application analysis can be made to work for BCD. Instead, two other analytical options were shown to be more appropriate for cases of BCD. The complementary contexts of application analysis works best for cases of complementary-contexts BCD, where the contexts of contrast are more uniform than the contexts of complementary distribution (like the distribution of taps and trills in Spanish). The disjunctive application analysis works best for cases of disjunctive BCD, where the contexts of complementary distribution are more uniform than the contexts of contrast (like the distribution of long and short vowels in English). Another analytical option for disjunctive BCD, prior rule specification, introduces issues that are resolved by recasting it as a disjunctive application analysis: instead of the more general rule both feeding and being counterfed by the more specific rule, the more specific rule blocks the more general rule.

The complementary contexts of application analysis is inappropriate for prototypical cases of UCD, where the basic allophone has a nonuniform distribution, but mismatched analyses like these can be found in the literature. By contrast, the only disadvantage to the disjunctive application analysis of UCD appears to be the availability of the prior underlying specification and underspecification + feature-filling rule application alternatives that are consistent with the basic assumption of conjunctive application. It is thus notable that there are no disjunctive application analyses of UCD proposed in the literature: there is a basic sameness between UCD and disjunctive BCD that is apparently denied by practitioners of *SPE* by not unifying them under the banner of disjunctive application.

This basic sameness can be appreciated by considering that the Lengthening and Shortening rules in (3.12) stand in the same logical relationship to each other as do the Spirantization and Fortition rules in (3.9), respectively. First, the rules within each pair make contradictory and thus incompatible structural changes: the output of Lengthening is a long vowel while the output of Shortening is a short one; the output of Spirantization is [+cont] while the output of Fortition is [–cont]. Second, the rules in each pair share a necessary condition: Lengthening and Shortening both apply to the heads of branching main stress feet; Spirantization and Fortition both apply to voiced obstruents. Third, this necessary condition is sufficient for the more general rule of each pair (Shortening, Fortition) while it is not sufficient for the other, more specific rule (Lengthening, Spirantization).

These are of course the very prerequisites that are enshrined in the EC, to be met by all rules that apply disjunctively. Given the ubiquity of allophonic complementary distribution and the theoretical significance of disjunctive application and the EC — not to mention the common use of the same 'elsewhere' language to describe both types of cases — one would think that this basic sameness would have at least been explicitly noted early on, if not taken seriously as a challenge to analyze all cases of UCD in terms of disjunctive application. As discussed in the next chapter, this is the starting point of the analysis of 'elsewhere' in OT: both UCD and disjunctive BCD are analyzed in terms of the blocking (= forced violation) of more general constraints by higher-ranked, more specific constraints.

Chapter 4

Elsewhere in OT

IN THE PREVIOUS CHAPTER I explained how there are two basic types of complementary distribution, unbounded and bounded. Unbounded complementary distribution (UCD) is typified by allophony, where there is no contrast anywhere between the elements in complementary distribution. Bounded complementary distribution (BCD) does involve contrast in some contexts, and comes in two varieties: disjunctive BCD, where the contexts of complementary distribution are more uniform than the contexts of contrast, and complementary-contexts BCD, where the contexts of contrast are more uniform than the contexts of complementary distribution. In this chapter I provide OT analyses of UCD (§4.2) and disjunctive BCD (§4.3) of these types of complementary distribution, demonstrating that the correct, disjunctive application of the opposing processes involved in each case is an automatic consequence of the analysis. Moreover, each analysis parallels the other in fundamental respects that reflects the essential sameness of these phenomena in a way that their differing analyses in *SPE* never have.

I begin this chapter where we left off in Chapter 2, with a discussion of the OT analysis of each of the types of blocking discussed in that chapter: bleeding, counterfeeding, nonderived environment blocking, do-something-except-when blocking, and (of course) disjunctive application. This discussion highlights both the advantages and limitations of OT in accounting for each type of blocking, and paves the way for the more involved, ground-level demonstration that the basic tools of OT are both necessary and sufficient for an adequate account of UCD and disjunctive BCD as cases of disjunctive application. I leave the higher-level task of proving that disjunctive application follows inevitably from OT's most basic assumptions, constraint ranking and candidate comparison, to Chapter 6.

4.1 Blocking in OT

Our first task is to translate an *SPE* analysis into OT terms; to make the comparison between the two theories most effective, the translation will be as direct as possible. Schematically, a rule of the familiar *SPE* form $A \longrightarrow B \,/\, C \,\_\, D$ can be minimally described in OT by the ranking of a MARKEDNESS constraint penalizing the rule's structural description above a FAITHFULNESS constraint penalizing the *A* ⟶ *B* change dictated by the rule: ⟦𝕄:**CAD* ≫ 𝔽:**A*↦*B*⟧.

The figure in (4.1) spells out the details of this translation. The markedness constraint 𝕄:**CAD* derives from the structural description *CAD*, itself obtained from the FOCUS *A* in the EXTERNAL CONTEXT *C* — *D*. The faithfulness constraint 𝔽:**A*↦*B* derives from the FOCAL CHANGE *A* ⟶ *B*. Finally, the result of the ranking ⟦𝕄:**CAD* ≫ 𝔽:**A*↦*B*⟧ is the structural change *CBD* from *CAD*.

(4.1) Correspondences between rule-parts and ranked constraints

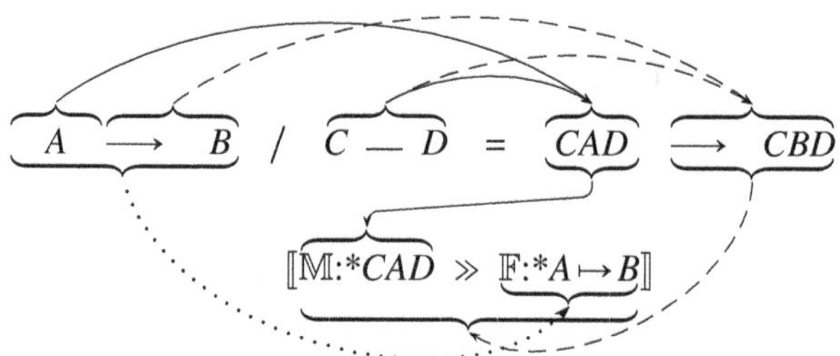

𝕄:**CAD* forces violation of 𝔽:**A*↦*B* in just those cases where 𝕄:**CAD* would otherwise be violated. This is most obviously the case when the input to the candidate comparison itself meets the structural description of the rule:

(4.2) Application of a rule in OT

/*CAD*/	𝕄:**CAD*	𝔽:**A*↦*B*
☞ *CBD*		*
CAD	* !	

The translation between an *SPE* rule and an ⟦𝕄 ≫ 𝔽⟧ ranking in OT requires three further comments. First, an actual *SPE* rule can be stated such that in some cases it applies *vacuously*.[1] This fact is somewhat disguised by the schematic example under discussion, where a nonvacuous distinction between the focus *A* and the result of changing it to *B* are presupposed. This makes the structural description *CAD* of the rule necessarily distinct from its structural change *CBD*, and this distinctness is by necessity reflected in the corresponding constraints in the OT translation: 𝕄:**CAD* must be assumed to be violated by *CAD* and not by *CBD*, while 𝔽:**A*↦*B* must be assumed to be violated by changing *CAD* to *CBD*.

Second, the ⟦𝕄:**CAD* ≫ 𝔽:**A*↦*B*⟧ ranking is assumed to be embedded within a constraint hierarchy that potentially includes other constraints that are violated by *CBD* candidates — 𝕄:**B*, for example, among others. Like 𝔽:**A*↦*B*, all of these other constraints must be ranked lower than 𝕄:**CAD* in order for *CBD* to emerge victorious over *CAD* from the input /*CAD*/.

1. Indeed, rules are typically stated vacuously whenever possible to make them 'simpler', assuming some simplicity metric (Chomsky and Halle 1968). The difference between vacuous and non-vacuous statements of rules has relevant formal consequences to be discussed in §5.3 and §5.6.

Third, the candidate set for the input /*CAD*/ is assumed to include candidates other than just *CAD* and *CBD*, some of which may satisfy $\mathbb{M}{:}{*}CAD$ without violating $\mathbb{F}{:}{*}A{\mapsto}B$, $\mathbb{M}{:}{*}B$, and other constraints violated by the desired change to *CBD*. At least one constraint violated by each of these other candidates must also be ranked above all constraints violated by *CBD*. One such possible candidate is *CAE*, which violates (among other possible constraints) $\mathbb{F}{:}{*}D{\mapsto}E$.

(4.3) Ensuring application of a rule in OT

/*CAD*/	$\mathbb{M}{:}{*}CAD$	$\mathbb{F}{:}{*}D{\mapsto}E$	$\mathbb{F}{:}{*}A{\mapsto}B$	$\mathbb{M}{:}{*}B$
☞ *CBD*			*	*
CAD	* !			
CAE		* !		

As illustrated in the subsections to follow, different types of blocking are described in OT by pitting a ranking of the form in (4.3) against other constraints that effectively prevent *CBD* from emerging victorious in specific circumstances.[2] Before proceeding, however, an important further remark is in order. The depth of an *SPE* derivation is limited only by the number of rules and the precise nature of their cumulative interactions on the form being derived. The result of a single rule's application — or indeed, of a pairwise rule interaction — may thus crucially differ from the ultimate output of the derivation, at least in principle. We must thus proceed here under the convenient fiction that *SPE* derivations are sufficiently shallow to allow meaningful comparison with OT.

4.1.1 Bleeding

The analysis of bleeding interactions in *SPE* takes advantage of the fact that some instances of ϕ meeting a bled rule's structural description (say, *CADX*) may be crucially changed by an earlier rule to a ϕ' that does not meet the bled rule's structural description but that is also inconsistent with the bled rule's structural change (say, $CA\underline{E}X$ instead of $C\underline{B}DX$). Because OT involves no serial derivation, bleeding must obviously be handled by other means. Assume (4.2) as the $[\![\mathbb{M} \gg \mathbb{F}]\!]$ ranking corresponding to the rule to be bled. The rule that bleeds (4.2) is of course also defined by a $[\![\mathbb{M} \gg \mathbb{F}]\!]$ ranking; following the schematic example suggested above, we have $[\![\mathbb{M}{:}{*}DX \gg \mathbb{F}{:}{*}D{\mapsto}E]\!]$.

(4.4) Nonvacuous application of another rule in OT

/*DX*/	$\mathbb{M}{:}{*}DX$	$\mathbb{F}{:}{*}D{\mapsto}E$
☞ *EX*		*
DX	* !	

2. The somewhat redundant $\mathbb{M}{:}{*}B$ is put aside in these illustrations, but will resurface in the discussions of UCD (§4.2) and disjunctive BCD (§4.3) further below.

Since either one of the faithfulness constraints now introduced can in principle be violated in order to satisfy 𝕄:**CAD*, these constraints must be ranked with respect to each other in order to ensure the same result as in (4.2). As illustrated in (4.3), the ranking ⟦𝔽:**D*↦*E* ≫ 𝔽:**A*↦*B*⟧ accomplishes this.[3]

One additional ranking among these constraints is necessary to account for a bleeding interaction between these two rules: ⟦𝕄:**CAD* ≫ 𝔽:**D*↦*E*⟧. Even though 𝕄:**CAD* cannot of its own accord justify violation of the higher-ranked of the two faithfulness constraints, the independent introduction of the need to satisfy 𝕄:**DX* means that the otherwise proscribed *D* ⟶ *E* change becomes the best way to satisfy both markedness constraints. This is illustrated in (4.5).

(4.5) Bleeding of a rule in OT

/*CADX*/	𝕄:**DX*	𝕄:**CAD*	𝔽:**D*↦*E*	𝔽:**A*↦*B*
☞ *CAEX*			*	
CBDX	* !			*
CADX		* !		

Let us add some substance to this schematic analysis by reconsidering the bleeding interaction between Lowering and Palatalization in Lamba discussed in §2.1.1. The rules are repeated here, with suitable ⟦𝕄 ≫ 𝔽⟧ ranking translations. From here on out I make an effort to use standard OT constraint(-family) names where relatively transparently applicable and *ad hoc*, more descriptive (though cumbersome) markedness constraint names that more directly recapitulate the structural descriptions of the relevant rules where otherwise deemed necessary.

(4.6) Lowering and Palatalization in Lamba, repeated from (2.4)

a. Lowering

[–back] ⟶ [–high] / [–high] C_0 —

≈ ⟦𝕄:AGREE(high) ≫ 𝔽:IDENT(high)⟧

b. Palatalization

k, s ⟶ ʧ, ʃ / — $\begin{bmatrix}\text{+high}\\ \text{–back}\end{bmatrix}$

≈ ⟦𝕄:NO-{k,s}i ≫ 𝔽:IDENT(pal)⟧

Given Lowering as the bleeding rule and Palatalization as the bled rule, the constraints in (4.6) can be plugged into the relevant slots of the schema in (4.5) to describe the bleeding interaction found in e.g. /*kos+ik+a*/ ⟶ *koseka*.

3. Note that this ranking has no effect on (4.4), since 𝔽:**A*↦*B* cannot possibly be sacrificed in order to satisfy 𝕄:**DX*. In general, a (nonmutual) bleeding interaction requires that the bled rule be in principle satisfiable by either of the two faithfulness constraints involved while the bleeding rule is satisfiable by only one of them. For more discussion, see Baković (in preparation).

(4.7) Lowering bleeds Palatalization in Lamba

/kos+ik+a/	$\mathbb{M}$:AGR(hi)	$\mathbb{M}$:NO-{k,s}i	$\mathbb{F}$:ID(hi)	$\mathbb{F}$:ID(pal)
☞ koseka			*	
koʃika	* !			*
kosika		* !		

Like the *SPE* analysis of bleeding, this OT analysis involves an interaction between two rules (≈ two ⟦$\mathbb{M} \gg \mathbb{F}$⟧ rankings) but achieves the result without serial derivation. This is possible because, given a substring that meets the structural descriptions of both rules, the structural change of either rule results in a substring that no longer meets the structural description of the bled rule. Effecting the structural change of the bleeding rule alone thus satisfies the markedness constraints that correspond to the structural descriptions of both rules simultaneously, without the need to also effect the structural change of the bled rule; indeed, effecting the structural change of the bled rule as well, as in a counterbleeding interaction, would be a gratuitous violation of faithfulness (McCarthy 1999b).

4.1.2 Bleeding vs. other types of blocking

Bleeding differs crucially from the four other types of blocking discussed in the brief history of blocking surveyed in Chapter 2: counterfeeding, nonderived environment blocking, do-something-except-when blocking, and disjunctive application. In the case of bleeding, the structural description of a bled rule is not met by the result of the bleeding interaction; it is instead bypassed by the structural change of the bleeding rule. In the case of other types of blocking, the structural description of a blocked rule *is* met by the result of the blocking interaction. Kiparsky (1971, 1973a) infamously classified rules the structural descriptions of which are met by some surface forms as *opaque* (or, more specifically, *non-surface-true*; McCarthy 1999b).[4] As I discuss at greater length in Baković (2011), this means that all of these types of blocking (that is, those other than bleeding) are examples of non-surface-true opacity by Kiparsky's definition.

The apparent problem for OT, then, is that opacity is generally believed to be difficult if not impossible to account for. The reason for the supposed difficulty is not far to seek in the cases at hand: because the structural description of a rule blocked by means other than bleeding is met by the result of the blocking interaction, then the markedness constraint corresponding to that structural description must be violated by the winning candidate in the corresponding OT analysis. Whether an OT analysis of each of these types of blocking is possible, then, depends entirely on whether the necessary markedness constraint violation can be justified by the need to satisfy some higher-ranked conflicting constraint(s).

In the following subsections I discuss how OT approaches each of these other four types of blocking. First, in §4.1.3, I discuss the difficulties OT encounters in

4. Rules the structural changes of which appear to have been unmotivated in some surface forms are also defined as opaque; McCarthy (1999b) refers to these as *non-surface-apparent*. These include counterbleeding interactions and others; see Baković (2007, 2011) for discussion.

accounting for counterfeeding and nonderived environment blocking, where the necessary markedness constraint violation is relatively difficult to justify. Then I discuss how do-something-except-when blocking (§4.1.4) and disjunctive application (§4.1.5) involve markedness constraint violations that are straightforwardly justified by higher-ranked conflicting constraints. I conclude in §4.1.6 with some discussion of other attested types of blocking that are possible to describe in OT.

4.1.3 Counterfeeding and nonderived environment blocking

Recall from §2.1.2 that counterfeeding interactions are ones in which a later-ordered rule *fails to feed* an earlier-ordered rule; this results in the earlier-ordered (= counterfed) rule's structural description being met by the surface representation.[5] Because the two rules are in a potential feeding relationship, making both focal changes would satisfy both structural descriptions.[6] Thus, no interaction between the two ⟦𝕄 ≫ 𝔽⟧ rankings corresponding to the two rules can produce anything other than feeding. To appreciate this, let's reconsider the counterfeeding interaction between Gliding and Deletion in Lomongo from §2.1.2.

(4.8) Gliding and Deletion in Lomongo, repeated from (2.7)

a. Gliding

$[-\text{low}] \longrightarrow [-\text{syll}] \;/\; \_\_\, \text{V}$ $\quad\approx$ ⟦𝕄:ONSET ≫ 𝔽:IDENT(syll)⟧

b. Deletion

$\begin{bmatrix}+\text{voi}\\-\text{son}\end{bmatrix} \longrightarrow \varnothing \;/\; \text{V}\,\_\_$ $\quad\approx$ ⟦𝕄:NO-V$\begin{bmatrix}+\text{voi}\\-\text{son}\end{bmatrix}$ ≫ 𝔽:MAX-C⟧

Given Deletion as the counterfeeding rule and Gliding as the counterfed rule, the constraints in (4.8) cannot be ranked in any way to describe the counterfeeding interaction found in e.g. /*o+bina*/ ⟶ [*oina*]. This is best illustrated with a comparative tableau (Prince 2002), where constraint cells explicitly indicate whether that constraint prefers the presumed loser in that row ('L'), the desired winner in the top row ('W'), or neither (empty); numbers indicate constraint violations.

(4.9) Deletion can't counterfeed Gliding in Lomongo

/o+bina/	𝕄:NO-V$\begin{bmatrix}+\text{voi}\\-\text{son}\end{bmatrix}$	𝔽:MAX-C	𝕄:ONSET	𝔽:ID(syll)
☞ oina		1	1	
~ obina	1 W	0 L	0 L	
~ wina		1	0 L	1 W

The key advantage of the comparative tableau format is that it makes clear the rankings that must hold in order for the desired winner to actually win: every

5. Modulo the intervention of other rules, as pointed out in fn. 5, p. 12 — but recall that we are assuming here that derivations are appropriately shallow for the purposes of theory comparison.

6. The exceptions to this are fed counterfeeding on focus relationships, some of which are amenable to disjunctive analysis (recall §3.1.3 and §3.3). We return to this point in §4.1.5.

constraint preferring a presumed loser must be dominated by at least one constraint preferring the desired winner — in other words, every L must be preceded by at least one W in every losing candidate row. This clearly does not hold in (4.9), where the presumed loser *wina* is preferred by ONSET and dispreferred by IDENT(syll) — and the ranking of these two constraints can't be reversed, since this is the ranking that guarantees the operation of Gliding in the first place.

Now recall from §2.5.1 that nonderived environment blocking interactions are in a way the opposite of counterfeeding interactions: in cases of counterfeeding, earlier-derived strings undergo a rule that later-derived strings do not; in cases of nonderived environment blocking, later-derived strings undergo a rule that earlier-derived strings do not. The problem encountered by an OT analysis of nonderived environment blocking is for this very reason the opposite of the problem encountered by the OT analysis of counterfeeding. To appreciate this, let's reconsider the interaction between Assibilation and Raising in Finnish.

(4.10) Raising and Assibilation in Finnish, repeated from (2.40)

a. Assibilation
t ⟶ s / — i ≈ ⟦𝕄:NO-ti ≫ 𝔽:IDENT(cont)⟧

b. Raising
e ⟶ i / — # ≈ ⟦𝕄:NO-e# ≫ 𝔽:IDENT(high)⟧

The comparative tableau of /*vete*/ ⟶ [*vesi*] in (4.11) below demonstrates that the only additional ranking of the constraints in (4.10) that must be posited to guarantee the correct outcome is ⟦𝕄:NO-e# ≫ 𝔽:IDENT(cont)⟧.

(4.11) Raising can feed Assibilation in Finnish

/vete/	𝕄:NO-e#	𝔽:ID(high)	𝕄:NO-ti	𝔽:ID(cont)
☞ vesi		1		1
~ vete	1 W	0 L		0 L
~ veti		1	1 W	0 L

The problem is that application of Assibilation must be blocked when Raising *hasn't* (nonvacuously) applied; e.g., in the case of /*äiti*/ ⟶ [*äiti*].

(4.12) Assibilation can't be blocked in Finnish

/äiti/	𝕄:NO-ti	𝔽:IDENT(cont)
☞ äiti	1	
~ äisi	0 L	1 W

Numerous proposals have been made in order to accommodate counterfeeding interactions, nonderived environment blocking, and other intransigent examples of opacity within OT; see McCarthy (2007b: 24ff) and Burzio (2011) for references and discussion. All of these accommodating proposals require something other than a ranking of the constraints that would otherwise be hypothesized to be responsible for the rules involved: selective reference to inputs or losing candidates, novel constraints of various types, or some degree of serial computation.

4.1.4 Do-something-except-when blocking

Recall from §2.5.2 that cases of do-something-except-when blocking are ones in which a rule is specifically blocked from creating certain structures that are typically absent from the language. Suppose, for example, that *A* becomes *B* in the context *C* — *D* except when followed by *X*: /*CADX*/ remains $C\underline{A}DX$ rather than becoming $C\underline{B}DX$, even though /*CAD*/ becomes $C\underline{B}D$ when not followed by *X*. This kind of blocking can be described in OT by ranking a markedness constraint like 𝕄:**BDX* above (4.2): ⟦𝕄:**BDX* ≫ 𝕄:**CAD* ≫ 𝔽:**A*↦*B*⟧.

(4.13) Do-something-except-when blocking of a rule in OT

/*CADX*/	𝕄:**BDX*	𝕄:**CAD*	𝔽:**A*↦*B*
☞ *CADX*		*	
CBDX	* !		*

In order to ensure do-something-except-when blocking rather than bleeding, any other constraint that could in principle be violated in order to satisfy 𝕄:**CAD* must also be ranked above 𝕄:**CAD*. This is illustrated in (4.14), using 𝔽:**D*↦*E* as an example of a representative faithfulness constraint.

(4.14) Ensuring do-something-except-when blocking of a rule in OT

/*CADX*/	𝕄:**BDX*	𝔽:**D*↦*E*	𝕄:**CAD*	𝔽:**A*↦*B*
☞ *CADX*			*	
CBDX	* !			*
CAEX		* !		

The blocking constraint represented here as 𝕄:**BDX* may be an output condition that unifies a conspiracy (Casali 1996; Casali 1997; Pater 1999). Recall the Yawelmani Yokuts case described in §2.5.2, for example: word-final monosyllabic suffix vowels are deleted *except when* such deletion would result in a tautosyllabic consonant cluster. The ranking ⟦𝕄:FINAL-C ≫ 𝔽:MAX-V⟧ corresponds to the deletion rule, and 𝕄:NOCOMPLEX is the blocking constraint. The faithfulness constraint 𝔽:DEP-C plays the role of ensuring blocking by preventing another way to avoid violation of 𝕄:FINAL-C, via consonant epenthesis.

(4.15) Blocking of vowel deletion in Yokuts: [xatmi] 'having eaten'

/xat+mi/	𝕄:NO-CMPLX	𝔽:DEP-C	𝕄:FINAL-C	𝔽:MAX-V
☞ xatmi			*	
xatm	* !			*
xatmit		* !		

Or, the blocking constraint may be a segment inventory condition (McCarthy and Prince 1995, 1999; Pulleyblank et al. 1995; Pulleyblank 1996). Take the case of Akan: [ATR] harmony (due to ⟦𝕄:AGREE(ATR) ≫ 𝔽:IDENT(ATR)⟧) applies to all vowels except the low, [–ATR] vowel *a*, which lacks a [+ATR] counterpart in the inventory (due to the blocking constraint 𝕄:ATR/LOW). 𝔽:IDENT(ATR)$_{\text{Root}}$ ensures blocking by preventing root vowels from harmonizing with the suffix *a*.

(4.16) Blocking of [ATR] harmony in Akan: [kurowa] 'town' (diminutive)

/kuro+wa/	𝕄:ATR/LO	𝔽:ID(ATR)$_{\text{Rt}}$	𝕄:AGR(ATR)	𝔽:ID(ATR)
☞ kurowa			*	
kurowɐ	* !			*
kʊrɔwa		** !		*

4.1.5 Disjunctive application

The analysis of disjunctive application in OT is nothing more than a special case of do-something-except-when blocking. The main thing that must be further specified is that the blocking constraint is violated only by a proper subset of the set of structures ALLOWED by the ⟦𝕄 ≫ 𝔽⟧ ranking corresponding to the blocked rule. This will be more formally defined and explained in §6.2.3, but for now we can say that a structure Σ is allowed by ⟦𝕄 ≫ 𝔽⟧ iff Σ satisfies 𝕄 by virtue of its performance on 𝔽 — that is, any minimally different structure Σ′ that performs differently than Σ on 𝔽 violates 𝕄. Some structures allowed by ⟦𝕄 ≫ 𝔽⟧ will (vacuously) satisfy the blocking constraint but some subset of them will violate it; furthermore, no structures disallowed by ⟦𝕄 ≫ 𝔽⟧ will violate the blocking constraint. Again taking ⟦𝕄:**CAD* ≫ 𝔽:**A*↦*B*⟧ as the ranking representing the blocked rule, a blocking constraint meeting these criteria is 𝕄:**CBDX*.[7]

(4.17) Disjunctive application in OT

/*CADX*/	𝕄:**CBDX*	𝔽:**D*↦*E*	𝕄:**CAD*	𝔽:**A*↦*B*
☞ *CADX*			*	
CBDX	* !			*
CAEX		* !		

7. Note that the more general constraint 𝕄:**BDX* does not meet the criteria because it is violated by structures that are not allowed by ⟦𝕄:**CAD* ≫ 𝔽:**A*↦*B*⟧ — such as *YBDX*, where $Y \neq C$.

I postpone further discussion of how this analytical schema applies to the OT analyses of UCD and disjunctive BCD until the end of this chapter in §4.4.

4.1.6 Even more types of blocking

Constraint ranking in OT has also been shown to make sense of otherwise stipulated blocking interactions between components of nonlinear analyses. Recall, for example, the metrical analysis of Latin stress sketched in §2.4.3.[8] The essential components of this analysis are that the main stress foot (a) is bimoraic (= two light syllables or a single heavy syllable), (b) is a trochee (= left-headed), and (c) stands at the right edge of the word, not including the final syllable.

The exclusion of the final syllable from condition (c) is commonly analyzed as being due to some interaction between extrametricality (on which see e.g. Hayes 1980, 1982, 1995; Harris 1983, 1992) and rightmost placement of the main stress foot, and there are essentially two ways to account for this interaction. One way is with ordering: extrametricality first removes the word-final syllable from metrical consideration, and the main stress foot is then placed at the right edge of what remains. The other way is with blocking: the demands of extrametricality block rightmost main stress foot placement, so the foot is placed as close to the right edge of the word as possible without including the word-final syllable.

This differs from other cases of blocking discussed thus far in that main stress foot placement isn't strictly 'blocked'; rather, a preference for rightmost stress placement is overruled and the next best option is taken instead: one syllable from the right edge of the word (or, as far to the right as possible given word-final syllable extrametricality). Prince and Smolensky (1993) make sense of this by placing the main stress foot with an alignment constraint (McCarthy and Prince 1993a, b) which is violated once for every syllable that separates the main stress foot from the end of the word.[9] When ranked below a constraint demanding non-final main stress foot placement (i.e., extrametricality), the result is the pattern found in Latin: ⟦𝕄:NONFINALITY ≫ 𝕄:EDGEMOST⟧.

(4.18) Extrametricality blocks rightmost foot placement

/patricia/	𝕄:NONFINALITY	𝕄:EDGEMOST
☞ pa('tri.ci)⟨a⟩		*
pa.tri('ci.a)	* !	
('pa.tri)ci⟨a⟩		** !

A tangible benefit of this blocking analysis over the alternative ordering analysis sketched further above is the fact that although extrametricality displaces rightmost stress, extrametricality itself is trumped when there would otherwise be nowhere to place the main stress foot. Monosyllabic content words such as

8. These remarks are based on the discussion in Prince and Smolensky (1993: 44–71).

9. The reliance on 'gradient' alignment constraints of this kind is attributed to a personal communication from Robert Kirchner. See McCarthy (2003b) for an extended argument against gradient constraints. (Notably, however, McCarthy does not include a reanalysis of the Latin case.)

(ˈrē) are stressed and so must be footed, meaning that extrametricality must be blocked from applying to them.[10] In the ordering analysis, this must be stipulated as a condition specifically blocking extrametricality "if it would render the entire domain of stress rules extrametrical" (Hayes 1995: 58). In the constraint ranking analysis, 𝕄:NONFINALITY is forced to be violated by a higher-ranked constraint demanding prosodification of lexical items: ⟦𝕄:LX≈PR ≫ 𝕄:NONFINALITY⟧.

(4.19) Prosodification of lexical items blocks extrametricality

/rē/	𝕄:LX≈PR	𝕄:NONFINALITY
☞ (ˈrē)		*
⟨rē⟩	* !	

This example highlights an important general characteristic of the analysis of blocking in OT. If the set of structures that violate a given blocking constraint ℂ is *generally absent* in the language, as Kisseberth (1970a) originally conjectured, then ℂ must obviously be undominated. But ℂ could in principle be crucially outranked by some constraints, meaning that the set of structures that violate ℂ are *not* generally absent in the language — and even that (again, in principle) only a subset of eligible rules is blocked by ℂ. In other words, a blocking constraint may define structures that are blocked from being created by only some of the rules that would otherwise be expected to create those structures.[11] Schematically (and putting aside the low-ranking role of faithfulness), if the blocked subset of rules is motivated by a set of markedness constraints $\mathbb{M}_x$ and the remainder of the set of eligible rules is motivated by a complement set of markedness constraints $\mathbb{M}_{x'}$, then ⟦$\mathbb{M}_{x'}$ ≫ ℂ ≫ $\mathbb{M}_x$⟧ describes this type of case. This schema and some broader consequences of process-specificity are discussed by McCarthy (1997: 237ff), in the context of an analysis of [RTR] harmony in southern Palestinian Arabic (cf. Davis 1995): leftward harmony is unblocked while rightward harmony is blocked by high front vowels, leading McCarthy to conclude that the ranking is ⟦$\mathbb{M}_{x'}$:RTR-LEFT ≫ ℂ:RTR/HI&FR ≫ $\mathbb{M}_x$:RTR-RIGHT⟧.

The overall approach to blocking in OT is thus very versatile. While problems are encountered with counterfeeding and nonderived environment blocking

10. Further evidence for footing of monosyllables is that they must be bimoraic, which follows from two assumptions: (i) that a word minimally consists of a foot (consistent with either strict (Selkirk 1984) or weak (Ito and Mester 2003b) layering of the prosodic hierarchy) and (ii) that feet in Latin are minimally bimoraic trochees (≈ condition (a) in the text). This entails that bisyllables such as (ˈ*aqua*) and (ˈ*putā*) also do not have an extrametrical final syllable, because the alternative parses (ˈ*a*)⟨*qua*⟩ and (ˈ*pu*)⟨*tā*⟩ would require a subminimal monomoraic foot on the initial syllable. Examples of light-heavy words like (ˈ*putā*) are optionally scanned as light-light in early Latin poetic texts by what is known as *Brevis Brevians* or iambic shortening (see Mester 1994: 11ff), suggesting enforcement of bimoraic *maximality* as well.
11. In Tunica (Haas 1940; Kisseberth 1970b, 1972), syncope *across* words is blocked from creating stress clashes, while syncope *within* words may create them — but only temporarily, as stress clashes are inadmissible on the surface in Tunica and are repaired by stress shift and destressing rules. This suggests that the anti-clash constraint holds only at the phrase level; the avoidance and repair of clash at this level is thus predicted and its creation at the word level is not a surprise.

(*qua* examples of opacity), bleeding is successfully handled without serial derivation — and do-something-except-when blocking, disjunctive application, and still other types of blocking are natural consequences of the approach.

4.2 Unbounded complementary distribution

The analytical basics of allophonic complementary distribution in terms of the interaction of markedness and faithfulness constraints in OT has been presented and discussed at length in the literature.[12] This analysis requires no constraints on underlying representations, distinguishing it from *SPE*'s prior underlying specification (§3.1.1) and underspecification + feature-filling rule application (§3.1.2) analyses. This conforms to the RICHNESS OF THE BASE hypothesis of OT, that there are no language-particular restrictions on input forms, itself a corollary of the hypothesis that the only difference between grammars is the ranking of a universal set of constraints.[13] Because there is no serial derivation in OT, there can be no Duke of York derivation as in the prior rule specification analysis (§3.1.3). The OT analysis comes closest to being like the disjunctive rule application analysis (§3.1.5), but without the need to stipulate disjunctive application or even to attempt to derive it from some *ad hoc* principle like the EC.

We assumed in §3.1 that Spirantization is the context-specific case ('between vowels') and that Fortition is the context-free case ('elsewhere') — in other words, that the voiced stops are the basic allophones of their respective phonemes. This assumption is formally expressed in an OT analysis by a ranking between relevant markedness constraints.[14]

(4.20) Markedness ranking: voiced continuants vs. voiced stops

a. 𝕄:NO-β
No voiced continuants.

b. 𝕄:NO-b
No voiced stops.

c. ⟦𝕄:NO-β ≫ 𝕄:NO-b⟧

By ranking the conflicting faithfulness constraint 𝔽:IDENT(cont) below the markedness constraint 𝕄:NO-β, as in (4.21b), we describe an inventory with voiced stops only due to the absolute dominance of 𝕄:NO-β. More precisely, this ranking defines a context-free fortition mapping: all underlying continuants are rendered stops in optimal candidates, violating the other markedness constraint 𝕄:NO-b and 𝔽:IDENT(cont) but sparing violation of 𝕄:NO-β.

12. The most prominent starting point is the set of contributions to Beckman et al. (1995); see in particular McCarthy and Prince (1995: 278ff) (or/also McCarthy and Prince 1999: 244ff).

13. See McCarthy (2002: 76–82) for discussion and references.

14. It is often also assumed that such rankings are universally fixed, to account for e.g. the observation that the presence of voiced continuants in a language's inventory typically entails the presence of voiced stops but not vice versa. This result can also be achieved by positing that the lower-ranked 𝕄:NO-b simply does not exist (Gouskova 2003). See also Prince (1997b, c, 2000, 2001) and de Lacy (2002, 2006) for a different take on the content and structure of universal markedness constraint hierarchies. It is unnecessary to take a position on the matter in the present context.

(4.21) Context-free fortition

a. 𝔽:IDENT(cont)

Corresponding segments agree in their value for [±cont].

b. ⟦𝕄:NO-β ≫ {𝔽:IDENT(cont), 𝕄:NO-b}⟧

To define the complementary distribution pattern of interest, with intervocalic spirantization and fortition elsewhere, what is left is the addition of the context-sensitive spirantization constraint 𝕄:NO-VbV to the top of the context-free fortition ranking in (4.21b). Since the output of spirantization violates NO-β, it must be that 𝕄:NO-VbV dominates 𝕄:NO-β. Since it also violates 𝔽:IDENT(cont) when the surface continuant is underlyingly a stop, 𝕄:NO-VbV must also be ranked above 𝔽:IDENT(cont), which it necessarily does by transitivity through 𝕄:NO-β.

(4.22) Intervocalic spirantization and fortition elsewhere

a. 𝕄:NO-VbV

No intervocalic voiced stops.

b. ⟦𝕄:NO-VbV ≫ 𝕄:NO-β ≫ {𝔽:IDENT(cont) , 𝕄:NO-b}⟧

There are other imaginable mappings that satisfy 𝕄:NO-VbV without spirantizing an underlying stop and thereby violating 𝕄:NO-β and 𝔽:IDENT(cont). Deletion of one of the flanking vowels, for instance, or deletion of the stop itself for that matter, would serve to satisfy all three of these constraints. Each of these output candidates, and other possible ones, must thus violate constraints that are ranked higher than 𝕄:NO-β, the highest-ranked constraint violated by the optimal spirantized candidate. I use 𝔽:MAX-V as a stand-in for these necessarily higher-ranked constraints, and I include one candidate that violates 𝔽:MAX-V, by deletion of the vowel to the left of the voiced obstruent, in the relevant tableaux. The complete complementary distribution hierarchy is thus as in (4.23).

(4.23) Complete complementary distribution hierarchy

⟦{𝕄:NO-VbV, 𝔽:MAX-V} ≫ 𝕄:NO-β ≫ {𝔽:IDENT(cont), 𝕄:NO-b}⟧

The tableaux in (4.24) and (4.25) illustrate the mappings that this hierarchy predicts for all four of the relevant conceivable types of inputs: intervocalic voiced stops /VbV/, intervocalic voiced continuants /VβV/, nonintervocalic voiced stops /Nb/, and nonintervocalic voiced continuants /Nβ/.

(4.24) Intervocalic spirantization: {/VbV/, /VβV/} ⟼ [VβV]

/VbV/	𝕄:NO-VbV	𝔽:MAX-V	𝕄:NO-β	𝔽:ID(ct)	𝕄:NO-b
VbV	*!				*
☞ VβV			*	*	
∅bV		*!			

/VβV/	M:NO-VbV	F:MAX-V	M:NO-β	F:ID(ct)	M:NO-b
VbV	* !			*	*
☞ VβV			*		
∅bV		* !		*	

(4.25) Fortition elsewhere: {/Nb/, /Nβ/} ⟼ [Nb]

/Nb/	M:NO-VbV	F:MAX-V	M:NO-β	F:ID(ct)	M:NO-b
☞ Nb					*
Nβ			* !	*	

/Nβ/	M:NO-VbV	F:MAX-V	M:NO-β	F:ID(ct)	M:NO-b
☞ Nb				*	*
Nβ			* !		

Note from the tableaux in (4.25) that fortition emerges elsewhere due to the irrelevance of the more specific, context-sensitive constraint M:NO-VbV in non-intervocalic contexts. Potential violation of F:MAX-V needn't be considered, as it must be in the tableaux in (4.24), and the more general, context-free constraint M:NO-β is free to decide in favor of the voiced stop candidate.

We are now in a position to examine the consequences of this analysis of unbounded complementary distribution as compared to the *SPE* analyses discussed in §3.1. Unlike the prior underlying specification analysis in (3.1) and the underspecification + feature-filling rule application analysis in (3.2), underlying representations are not constrained in any way in this OT analysis; complementarity is guaranteed by the higher rank of the more specific M:NO-VbV constraint. This is similar to the later ordering of the more specific Spirantization rule in the prior rule specification analysis in (3.7), but a key difference is that reranking of the constraints M:NO-VbV and M:NO-β, unlike the reordering of Spirantization and Fortition, completely obscures the potential effects of the more specific M:NO-VbV constraint because the more general M:NO-β consistently overrides it. As the tableaux in (4.26) show, no candidate with a voiced continuant can win under this ranking of the constraints. (The proof of this is provided in Chapter 6.)

(4.26) Context-free fortition:
{/VbV/, /VβV/} ⟼ [VbV]; {/Nb/, /Nβ/} ⟼ [Nb]

/VbV/	M:NO-β	F:MAX-V	M:NO-VbV	F:ID(ct)	M:NO-b
☞ VbV			*		*
VβV	* !			*	
∅bV		* !			

/VβV/	𝕄:No-β	𝔽:Max-V	𝕄:No-VbV	𝔽:Id(ct)	𝕄:No-b
☞ VbV			*	*	*
VβV	* !				
∅bV		* !		*	

/Nb/	𝕄:No-β	𝔽:Max-V	𝕄:No-VbV	𝔽:Id(ct)	𝕄:No-b
☞ Nb					*
Nβ	* !			*	

/Nβ/	𝕄:No-β	𝔽:Max-V	𝕄:No-VbV	𝔽:Id(ct)	𝕄:No-b
☞ Nb				*	*
Nβ	* !				

There are more constraints in the analysis than just 𝕄:No-VbV and 𝕄:No-β, however, so other possible constraint rerankings must be taken into consideration. As noted earlier, ranking 𝕄:No-b above 𝕄:No-β would simply undermine the assumption that voiced stops are the basic allophones of their respective phonemes, an assumption that is also made in the *SPE* analyses. Therefore, the ranking of 𝕄:No-β above 𝕄:No-b must be held fixed for any real comparison to be made. Similarly, alternative rankings of 𝔽:Ident(cont) and 𝔽:Max-V would define different input-output mappings for one or both cases, rendering them distinct from the structural changes made by the rules in the *SPE* analyses. The position of these constraints in the hierarchy must thus also be held fixed to make the right comparison between the two theories.

In sum, the OT analysis of unbounded complementary distribution achieves the complementarity of the mappings involved with nothing other than its most basic assumptions: a particular ranking of markedness and faithfulness constraints. There is no need for any artificial restrictions on underlying representations, and because there is no serial derivation, there is no need for any special condition ensuring disjunctive application. I now turn to the analysis of bounded complementary distribution, which has these same advantages.

4.3 Bounded complementary distribution

Consider now an OT analysis of the English lengthening and shortening facts discussed in §3.3. Assuming that there are markedness constraints against both long and short vowels and a conflicting faithfulness constraint 𝔽:Ident(long), ranking the faithfulness constraint on top as in (4.27d) describes an inventory with both short and long vowels — like the inventory of English.[15]

15. For space reasons, 𝕄:No-LongV and 𝕄:No-ShortV will sometimes be abbreviated below as 𝕄:No-V̄ and 𝕄:No-V̆, respectively.

(4.27) Contrastive long and short vowels

a. 𝕄:NO-LONGV
No long vowels.

b. 𝕄:NO-SHORTV
No short vowels.

c. 𝔽:IDENT(long)
Corresponding segments agree in length.

d. ⟦𝔽:IDENT(long) ≫ {𝕄:NO-LONGV, 𝕄:NO-SHORTV}⟧

I should note that I don't mean to suggest with 𝔽:IDENT(long) that there is a feature [±long] distinguishing long and short vowels, nor even that there is only one faithfulness constraint regulating both lengthening and shortening. 𝔽:IDENT(long) could be replaced by two separate constraints like 𝔽:MAX-μ and 𝔽:DEP-μ (see §5.6); this would only have some trivial consequences for the exact ranking of all the constraints in the analysis to follow.[16]

In order to complete the analysis of English, there must be at least two other context-sensitive markedness constraints that are responsible for the lengthening and shortening processes, both ranked above the entire hierarchy in (4.27d). These constraints, given in (4.28), are simply stated to be violated by the same strings that the Lengthening and Shortening rules in the *SPE* analysis nonvacuously apply to; ranking both constraints above 𝔽:IDENT(long) expresses the preference for the nonvacuous structural changes that those rules make.

(4.28) Context-sensitive markedness constraints

a. 𝕄:CIV
No short vowel in the head of a branching foot iff
  i. the head vowel is [–high], and
  ii. the nonhead vowel is /*i*/ followed by a vowel in hiatus.

b. 𝕄:TROCH
No long vowel in the head of a branching foot.

I state these constraints in terms that most straightforwardly line up with the statements of the corresponding *SPE* rules in (3.12) in order to facilitate theoretical comparison, though it should be obvious that neither constraint is really much of a candidate for universality. The constraint 𝕄:CIV in (4.28a), responsible for lengthening, is particularly complex and should probably be broken down into an interaction among several constraints (cf. van de Vijver 2003). For example, the condition that the nonhead vowel be /*i*/ in hiatus might be due to the anti-hiatal constraint 𝕄:ONSET, which would have to be ranked in such a way that it can force gliding of the /*i*/, the optimal result thus being e.g. (ˈ*rā*)⟨*djal*⟩ rather than (ˈ*rādi*)⟨*al*⟩. This analysis entails that the glided vowel is not the nonhead of a branching foot, and that there is instead a monosyllabic foot with lengthening of its head vowel being a response to a foot minimality requirement; i.e.,

16. The same considerations would apply if e.g. 𝔽:MAX(cont) and 𝔽:DEP(cont) had been employed instead of 𝔽:IDENT(cont) in the analysis of spirantization and fortition in §4.2 above.

Prince and Smolensky's (1993) 𝕄:FTBIN.[17] The constraint 𝕄:TROCH in (4.28b), responsible for shortening, is a bit more reasonable, corresponding loosely to constraints penalizing heavy-light feet; examples from the OT literature include 𝕄:RHHRM (Prince and Smolensky 1993), 𝕄:NO-(HL) (Cohn and McCarthy 1998), 𝕄:FTHARM (Baković 1996), and 𝕄:GRPHARM (McCarthy 2003c).[18]

Note that these two constraints stand in the same logical relationship to each other as 𝕄:NO-VbV and 𝕄:NO-β do. The more general constraint 𝕄:TROCH penalizes long vowels in the heads of branching feet, while the more specific constraint 𝕄:CIV penalizes short vowels in the heads of branching feet that meet some additional conditions. Through their mutual rank above 𝔽:IDENT(long), these constraints make conflicting demands on the subset of branching feet that meet the additional conditions of the more specific 𝕄:CIV. For this constraint to emerge victorious, it must also dominate the more general 𝕄:TROCH.[19]

(4.29) Complete complementary distribution hierarchy

⟦𝕄:CIV ≫ 𝕄:TROCH ≫ 𝔽:IDENT(long) ≫ {𝕄:NO-V̄, NO-V̌}⟧

I demonstrate the necessity of the ranking in (4.29) in the tableaux further below. The minimally contrasting pair of words (*ˈrădi*)⟨*cal*⟩ and (*ˈrādi*)⟨*al*⟩ are again used to illustrate the analysis. Each pair of tableaux shows how the correct choice is made between the two relevant output candidates for each word: the first with a long vowel in the head of the branching foot, (*ˈrādi*), and the second with a short vowel in that position, (*ˈrădi*).[20] The tableaux come in pairs because the underlying form of each of these words could have a long vowel or a short vowel; which is correct cannot be determined on the basis of these examples alone.

Consider shortening first, in (4.30). The choice between the candidates in the first tableau is the crucial one: if (*ˈrădi*)⟨*cal*⟩ has a long vowel underlyingly, then 𝕄:TROCH must be ranked above 𝔽:IDENT(long), forcing the latter's violation in the optimal form (*ˈrădi*)⟨*cal*⟩. The alternation in pairs like (*ˈtȳpe*) ~ (*ˈty̆pi*)⟨*cal*⟩ is thus accounted for by this ranking; the vowel is known to be underlyingly long in this case. And what if the vowel in (*ˈrădi*)⟨*cal*⟩ is underlyingly short, as in the second tableau? This case is shown by the simple choice between the candidates in that tableau: all of the constraints, save for the low-ranked 𝕄:NO-SHORTV, favor the correct form (*ˈrădi*)⟨*cal*⟩. The lack of alternation in pairs like (*ˈmy̆th*) ~ (*ˈmy̆thi*)⟨*cal*⟩ is thus also accounted for by this ranking.

17. Why the head of the foot must be [–high] (e.g., (*ˈtrĭvi*)⟨*al*⟩, *(*ˈtrī*)⟨*vjal*⟩) and why the (would-be) nonhead of the foot cannot be /*u*/ (e.g., (*ˈmănu*)⟨*al*⟩, *(*ˈmā*)⟨*nwal*⟩) are further questions that would need to be addressed in a full analysis along these lines; I leave these questions open here.
18. See also Prince (1991), Burzio (1994), Kenstowicz (1994a), Mester (1994), and Green (1996).
19. Burzio (1996) also discusses this particular ranking argument.
20. Constraints ranked higher than those considered here are assumed to narrow the candidate set down to these appropriately footed ones; this is equivalent in all relevant respects to the assumption that Lengthening and Shortening must follow footing in the *SPE* analysis. Inputs are correspondingly shown here with feet, just as the underlying representations were in the *SPE* analysis.

(4.30) Shortening: {/('rādi)⟨cal⟩/, /('rădi)⟨cal⟩/} ⟼ ('rădi)⟨cal⟩

/('rādi)⟨cal⟩/	𝕄:CIV	𝕄:TROCH	𝔽:ID(long)	𝕄:NO-V̄	𝕄:NO-V̆
('rādi)⟨cal⟩		* !		*	
☞ ('rădi)⟨cal⟩			*		*

/('rădi)⟨cal⟩/	𝕄:CIV	𝕄:TROCH	𝔽:ID(long)	𝕄:NO-V̄	𝕄:NO-V̆
('rādi)⟨cal⟩		* !	*	*	
☞ ('rădi)⟨cal⟩					*

Now consider those cases where the more specific and undominated markedness constraint 𝕄:CIV is relevant to the selection of the optimal candidate, occasioning lengthening. Regardless of the length of the head vowel in the input, 𝕄:CIV must be ranked above 𝕄:TROCH in order to force the violation of the latter in the optimal form (*'rādi*)⟨*al*⟩ in both tableaux. In the second tableau, where the head vowel is assumed to be underlyingly short, 𝔽:IDENT(long) — which must be ranked below 𝕄:CIV by transitivity through 𝕄:TROCH — is also necessarily (and predictably) violated. This accounts for the alternation in related word pairs like (*'remĕ*)⟨*dy*⟩ ~ *re*(*'mēdi*)⟨*al*⟩, where the vowel must be underlyingly short.

(4.31) Lengthening: {/('rādi)⟨al⟩/, /('rădi)⟨al⟩/} ⟼ ('rādi)⟨al⟩

/('rādi)⟨al⟩/	𝕄:CIV	𝕄:TROCH	𝔽:ID(long)	𝕄:NO-V̄	𝕄:NO-V̆
☞ ('rādi)⟨al⟩		*		*	
('rădi)⟨al⟩	* !		*		*

/('rădi)⟨al⟩/	𝕄:CIV	𝕄:TROCH	𝔽:ID(long)	𝕄:NO-V̄	𝕄:NO-V̆
☞ ('rādi)⟨al⟩		*	*	*	
('rădi)⟨al⟩	* !				*

The ranking arguments are not quite complete, however. Any other constraints that could be violated in order to satisfy the demands of the markedness constraints 𝕄:CIV and 𝕄:TROCH must also dominate 𝔽:IDENT(long), otherwise the preference for changing vowel length in both cases would not be guaranteed. One thing that these markedness constraints have in common is the 'head of a branching foot' specification, so some of these other constraints must be those responsible for footing, and these footing constraints must be assumed to be higher-ranked in any case (see fn. 20 above). Indeed, given the relatively simple statement of 𝕄:TROCH, footing constraints are the only constraints aside from 𝔽:IDENT(long) that can reasonably be violated in order to satisfy 𝕄:TROCH. The only other conflicting constraints left once these footing constraints are factored out, then, are ones that can be violated to satisfy 𝕄:CIV but not 𝕄:TROCH. Given the relatively complex statement of 𝕄:CIV, there are more than a few changes that can be performed to satisfy it. One of the conditions on 𝕄:CIV is that the head vowel be [–high]; faithfulness to this feature could be sacrificed. The other condition is that the nonhead vowel is /*i*/ followed by a vowel in hiatus; this is really a complex of conditions that can be mooted by changing the nonhead vowel to something other than /*i*/ or by somehow breaking the hiatus. Since the output of lengthening violates 𝕄:TROCH and 𝔽:IDENT(long), constraints violated by these other changes must be higher-ranked.

The opposite ranking of the constraints 𝕄:CIV and 𝕄:TROCH has no effect on the outcome of (*'rădi*)⟨*cal*⟩, but the outcome of (*'rādi*)⟨*al*⟩ is different: the more general and now higher-ranked constraint 𝕄:TROCH decides in favor of (*'rădi*)⟨*al*⟩, with a short vowel. Indeed, a candidate satisfying the more specific constraint 𝕄:CIV can never win under this ranking, because 𝕄:TROCH eliminates all of the relevant candidates before 𝕄:CIV even gets a chance at the pickings. This means that no ranking argument can be made between 𝕄:CIV and 𝔽:IDENT(long), and it is equivalent to saying in the *SPE* analysis that Lengthening doesn't exist in the grammar. This is shown in the following tableaux.

(4.32) Only shortening: {/('rādi)⟨(c)al⟩/, /('rădi)⟨(c)al⟩/} ⟼ ('rădi)⟨(c)al⟩

/('rādi)⟨cal⟩/	𝕄:TROCH	𝕄:CIV	𝔽:ID(long)	𝕄:NO-V̄	𝕄:NO-V̆
('rādi)⟨cal⟩	*!			*	
☞ ('rădi)⟨cal⟩			*		*

/('rădi)⟨cal⟩/	𝕄:TROCH	𝕄:CIV	𝔽:ID(long)	𝕄:NO-V̄	𝕄:NO-V̆
('rādi)⟨cal⟩	*!		*	*	
☞ ('rădi)⟨cal⟩					*

/('rādi)⟨al⟩/	𝕄:TROCH	𝕄:CIV	𝔽:ID(long)	𝕄:NO-V̄	𝕄:NO-V̆
('rādi)⟨al⟩	*!			*	
☞ ('rădi)⟨al⟩		*	*		*

/('rădi)⟨al⟩/	𝕄:TROCH	𝕄:CIV	𝔽:ID(long)	𝕄:NO-V̄	𝕄:NO-V̆
('rādi)⟨al⟩	*!		*	*	
☞ ('rădi)⟨al⟩		*			*

Once again, the OT analysis accounts for disjunctive application without constraints on underlying representation and with no need to take special steps in order to avoid a Duke of York derivation. The priority of lengthening over shortening is due to the only possible ranking between the more general 𝕄:TROCH and the more specific 𝕄:CIV that allows them to both be active in the grammar; this is because specific only partially eclipses general when specific is ranked higher but general totally eclipses specific when specific is ranked lower.

4.4 Summary

The primary difference between unbounded and bounded complementary distribution is the basic contrastive status of the elements (featural, prosodic, etc.) that are incompatibly affected by the mappings in question. In unbounded cases, the elements are noncontrastive everywhere, and in bounded cases they are contrastive outside of the proper subset of contexts where there is complementarity. In the foregoing OT analyses, this was reflected in the difference between the basic rankings in (4.21c) vs. (4.27d), repeated together in (4.33).

(4.33) Basic (non)contrastiveness rankings

a. UCD: voiced obstruent continuancy is basically noncontrastive
⟦𝕄:No-β ≫ {𝔽:Ident(cont), 𝕄:No-b}⟧

b. Disjunctive BCD: vowel length is basically contrastive
⟦𝔽:Ident(long) ≫ {𝕄:No-LongV, 𝕄:No-ShortV}⟧

Because the markedness constraint 𝕄:No-β is dominant in the unbounded case (4.33a), all that is necessary to ensure complementarity of values of the noncontrastive [±cont] feature is a more specific markedness constraint that conflicts with and dominates 𝕄:No-β; that constraint is 𝕄:No-VbV. In the bounded case (4.33b), the faithfulness constraint 𝔽:Ident(long) must be dominant in order to ensure the basic contrastiveness of vowel length, and so the complementarity of vowel length in the relevant subset of contexts must be due to the interaction between two conflicting markedness constraints other than 𝕄:No-LongV and 𝕄:No-ShortV, one more specific and higher ranked than the other; these constraints are 𝕄:CiV and 𝕄:Troch, respectively. Focusing attention on just the faithfulness constraints and constraints above them, then, we have the following crucial rankings that characterize both types of complementary distribution.

(4.34) Complementary distribution rankings

a. UCD: intervocalic voiced continuants, else voiced stops
⟦𝕄:No-VbV ≫ 𝕄:No-β ≫ 𝔽:Ident(cont)⟧

b. Disjunctive BCD: long vowels in *CiV* context, else short
⟦𝕄:CiV ≫ 𝕄:Troch ≫ 𝔽:Ident(long)⟧

Note the correspondence between these rankings and the schematic ranking for disjunctive application in (4.17): ⟦𝕄:**CBDX* ≫ 𝕄:**CAD* ≫ 𝔽:**A*↦*B*⟧.[21] Just as in the schematic ranking, the top-ranked blocking constraint in both the UCD and disjunctive BCD rankings is violated only by a proper subset of the set of structures allowed by the lower ⟦𝕄 ≫ 𝔽⟧ ranking: *VbV* represents the set of structures that violate 𝕄:No-VbV which is a proper subset of the structures that are allowed by ⟦𝕄:No-β ≫ 𝔽:Ident(cont)⟧, and (ˈ*rădi*)⟨*al*⟩ represents the set of

21. To focus the discussion on the constraints of immediate interest, I have left out the other undominated constraints from all three cases: 𝔽:**D*↦*E* from the schematic ranking, 𝔽:Max-V from the UCD ranking, and constraints responsible for footing from the disjunctive BCD ranking.

structures that violate 𝕄:CIV which is a proper subset of the structures that are allowed by ⟦𝕄:TROCH ≫ 𝔽:IDENT(long)⟧. This is how the essential sameness of the two types of complementary distribution is captured in OT. In both cases, the more specific constraint is dominant, forcing violation of the more general constraint in just those contexts where both constraints are relevant. As shown in (4.26) for UCD and (4.32) for disjunctive BCD, the opposite ranking of these two markedness constraints simply renders the more specific one completely ineffectual, as if it did not even exist in the grammar (as will be proven in Chapter 6). The defining characteristics of OT, constraint ranking and candidate comparison, are thus perfectly suited to account for both types of complementary distribution.

Chapter 5

The Elsewhere Condition

> The ideal result would be the discovery of some sufficient and necessary condition K which would have to hold for rules to be disjunctively ordered.
>
> *Kiparsky (1973b: 94)*

MOST PHONOLOGISTS, it is safe to say, are familiar with the rudiments of the Elsewhere Condition (henceforth the EC), if not also with some of the motivation for its statement or some specific formulation of it. A phonologist's familiarity with the literature on the EC usually goes at least as far back as its extensive discussion in the lexical phonology and morphology literature (Kiparsky 1982 *et seq.*), if not further back to Kiparsky's (1973b) seminal article. Kiparsky's (1973b) original statement of the EC is repeated in (5.1) below.

(5.1) The Elsewhere Condition, repeated from (2.19)

Two adjacent rules of the form

$A \longrightarrow B \,/\, P \,\_\, Q$
$C \longrightarrow D \,/\, R \,\_\, S$

are disjunctively ordered if and only if:

a. the set of strings that fit *PAQ* is a subset of the set of strings that fit *RCS*, and

b. the structural changes of the two rules are either identical or incompatible.

Kiparsky (1973b: 94) briefly notes Anderson's (1969) earlier statement of the same basic principle (see also Anderson 1974), discussed in §2.3.[1] But whether Anderson or Kiparsky should be credited with the introduction of the principle is

1. Kiparsky's acknowledgement of Anderson (1969) is somewhat backhandedly accompanied by a footnote stating that "Pat Wolfe has pointed out to me that there are some problems with the Middle English example which Anderson cites" (Kiparsky 1973b: 94, fn. 4). These "problems" may have to do with the coupling of lengthening and lowering; recall the discussions in §2.2.3 and §2.4.2.

complicated by the fact that "Paul Kiparsky was a primary source of ideas during the initial stages of [Anderson's] work" (Anderson 1969: xi).[2]

Kiparsky (1973b) also notes that "[a] version of [the EC] is consistently employed in Pāṇini's Aṣṭādhyāyī", and that this version

> is explicitly formulated in the Mahābhāṣya (for example, ad P. 6.1.89 *etyed-hatyūṭhsu*; see Kielhorn (1960, vol. 3, p. 69) and constitutes Paribhāṣā LVII of the Paribhāṣenduśekhara: *yena nāprāpte yo vidhir ārabhyate sa tasya bāḍhako bhavati* ("a rule which is given [in reference to a particular case or particular cases to which, or to all of which] another [rule] cannot but apply [or in other words, which all already fall under some other rule], supersedes the latter"—Kielhorn's translation). (Kiparsky 1973b: 94, fn. 3)

Anderson (1969, 1974) also explicitly acknowledges "the corresponding principle which governs much of Pāṇini's grammar" (Anderson 1974: 107):

> [T]his extended principle of disjunctive order is quite similar to that employed by Panini ... which also does not require formal identity of operation, but only that the cases to which the one rule applies be a subset of the class of cases to which the other applies. ... Thus, the principle of disjunctive ordering is essentially Panini's principle of the precedence of the more specific rule. (Anderson 1969: 142–143)

With this question of the EC's lineage out of the way, we can focus on what it is meant to do: to enforce disjunctive application between two rules that meet the core conditions in (5.1a, b). The EC identifies rule pairs that apply disjunctively through ostensibly simple comparisons between the structural descriptions and structural changes of rules. The condition on structural descriptions (5.1a) is met by any pair of rules that share a necessary condition that is sufficient for application of one rule but that is not sufficient for application of the other. The rules discussed in §3.1 and §3.3 meet this requirement. A voiced obstruent is a necessary condition for both Spirantization and Fortition, but it is a sufficient condition only for Fortition; Spirantization also requires that the voiced obstruent occur between vowels. Likewise, the head of a branching main stress foot is a necessary condition for both Lengthening and Shortening, but is a sufficient condition only for Shortening; Lengthening also requires that the head of the foot be [–high] and that the nonhead be an /*i*/ in hiatus. The condition on structural changes (5.1b) also holds of these pairs of rules, since the rules in each case make opposite, and hence incompatible, demands on some representational property (obstruent continuancy in one case, vowel length in the other).

Whether there are other types of situations in which two rules apply disjunctively is for all practical purposes irrelevant to the EC, except perhaps to the extent

2. Kiparsky (1973b: 94) also notes that a "similar principle is referred to in" a 1971 prepublication version of Koutsoudas et al. (1974); this is the Proper Inclusion Precedence Principle discussed in §3.1.2. Neither Koutsoudas et al. (1974) nor the closely related article by Sanders (1974) references Kiparsky (1973b) or Anderson (1969). See also Hastings (1974) and Iverson (1976) for related ideas from around the same time period, and see Janda and Sandoval (1984: 2ff) for what is perhaps the most detailed and comprehensive chronicle of all these interrelated principles.

that such situations can also be predicted by some generalized version of the EC. Let's assume for the sake of argument that the spirit of the formulation of the EC in (5.1) correctly identifies all rule pairs that apply disjunctively. Even granted this empirical correctness, careful examination of the EC reveals that there is far more *ad hoc* stipulation than explanation involved in its statement. The two core conditions and other details specified in the statement of the EC are all implicated in this charge, in Kiparsky's (1973b) original version as well as in subsequent modifications of the EC. These modifications may have been made in response to deficiencies in the EC (both perceived and demonstrated), but the fact has remained that the theoretical foundation of the EC is no more secure than it ever was: each and every aspect of the EC could easily be defined otherwise, with the consequences of such redefinitions being strictly and directly empirical.

In the remaining sections of this chapter I substantiate the claims just made with detailed discussion of several different claims and assumptions made in the statements of the two most familiar versions of the EC, the one in Kiparsky (1973b) and the one in Kiparsky (1982). I begin in §5.1 with Kiparsky's (1973b) claim that the more specific and more general rules must already be adjacent in the ordering. In §5.2, I discuss Kiparsky's (1982) claim that the more specific rule not only blocks but also precedes the more general rule in the ordering. I then scrutinize the core conditions of the EC: proper inclusion of structural descriptions (§5.3) and identity/incompatibility of structural changes (§5.4). This is followed by discussion of two critically ambiguous assumptions about how blocking works. The first is that blocking is local, not global (§5.5), meaning that application of the more general rule can be blocked only in local contexts of conflict with the more specific rule, not also in other contexts in the form under evaluation. The second is that blocking is circumstantial, not applicational (§5.6), meaning that application of the more general rule can be blocked not only by actual, nonvacuous application of the more specific rule but also by the circumstantial emergence of the more specific rule's structural change.

In each of these sections I demonstrate how the claim or assumption under discussion has been, can be, or should be differently conceived, and how the consequences of these different conceptions are strictly empirical. Toward the end of each section I also briefly remark on how the empirically correct conception of the claim or assumption follows automatically from the basic assumptions of OT.

5.1 The adjacency requirement

In both Kiparsky's (1973b) and Anderson's (1974) statements of the EC, two rules apply disjunctively only if they are *already adjacent* in the ordering. Kiparsky (1973b: 104) acknowledges that this requirement may be unnecessary, speculating that the EC "might be applicable not just to rules which are adjacent in the ordering, but also to rules which are separated by other rules." The adjacency requirement appears to be an otherwise unmotivated hold-over from disjunctive application via the parenthesis notation (recall §2.2.1); as Prince (1997a: 3, n. 4) notes, adjacency is "obviously necessary for reduction via parentheses". But the assumptions behind the parenthesis notation appear to be more complicated than this; for example, it is generally assumed that reduction via parentheses cannot be side-stepped by otherwise arbitrary nonadjacent ordering (cf. fn. 4 below).

But the result of sufficiently complex expansions involving parentheses and other notations can *introduce* nonadjacency, prompting Chomsky and Halle (1968: 36) to specifically note that "rules may be disjunctively ordered with respect to one another even if they are not adjacent in the ordering". The example under discussion in this passage is the rule in (5.2a), "an abbreviation for the [ordered] sequence of rules" in (5.2b) (adapted from Chomsky and Halle 1968: 35).

(5.2) Disjunctive application between nonadjacent expansions

a. $\mathrm{V} \longrightarrow [\text{+stress}] \mathbin{/} X\text{—}\, \mathrm{C}_0(\check{\mathrm{V}}\mathrm{C}_0^1) \mathbin{/} \text{—} \left(\begin{Bmatrix} \text{+affix} \\ {}^{\prime}\sigma \end{Bmatrix} \right)]$

b. i. $\mathrm{V} \longrightarrow [\text{+stress}] \mathbin{/} X\text{—}\, \mathrm{C}_0\check{\mathrm{V}}\mathrm{C}_0^1\text{+affix}]$

ii. $\mathrm{V} \longrightarrow [\text{+stress}] \mathbin{/} X\text{—}\, \mathrm{C}_0\text{+affix}]$

iii. $\mathrm{V} \longrightarrow [\text{+stress}] \mathbin{/} X\text{—}\, \mathrm{C}_0\check{\mathrm{V}}\mathrm{C}_0^1{}^{\prime}\sigma]$

iv. $\mathrm{V} \longrightarrow [\text{+stress}] \mathbin{/} X\text{—}\, \mathrm{C}_0{}^{\prime}\sigma]$

v. $\mathrm{V} \longrightarrow [\text{+stress}] \mathbin{/} X\text{—}\, \mathrm{C}_0\check{\mathrm{V}}\mathrm{C}_0^1]$

vi. $\mathrm{V} \longrightarrow [\text{+stress}] \mathbin{/} X\text{—}\, \mathrm{C}_0]$

The order in (5.2b) is guaranteed to be unique by the expansion conventions of Chomsky and Halle (1968: 394), but some disjunctively ordered pairs in this order are nonadjacent: "in [(5.2b)], rule [(i)] is disjunctively ordered with respect to rule [(vi)], but not with respect to rule [(iii)]" (Chomsky and Halle 1968: 36).[3]

Harris (1974) also offers a specific argument against the adjacency requirement. The two disjunctively ordered rules in question are Harmony and Lowering in Brazilian Portuguese, reproduced in (5.3) from Harris (1974: 69, 74).

(5.3) Harmony and Lowering in Brazilian Portuguese

a. Harmony

$$\begin{bmatrix} \mathrm{V} \\ \alpha\,\text{round} \\ \alpha\,\text{back} \end{bmatrix} \longrightarrow \begin{bmatrix} -\text{low} \\ \langle\text{+high}\rangle \end{bmatrix} \mathbin{/} \text{—}\, \mathrm{C}_0 \left[\begin{bmatrix} \mathrm{V} \\ -\text{low} \\ \langle\text{+high}\rangle \end{bmatrix} \right]_{\text{Stem}} \mathrm{V}\ldots \Big]_{\text{Verb}}$$

b. Lowering

$$\begin{bmatrix} \mathrm{V} \\ \text{+stress} \\ \begin{Bmatrix} -\text{high} \\ \text{+E} \end{Bmatrix} \end{bmatrix} \longrightarrow [\text{+low}] \mathbin{/} \text{—}\, \mathrm{C}_0 \Big]_{\text{Root}} \ldots \Big]_{\text{Verb}}$$

There is more to be said about how the rules in (5.3) come to be disjunctively ordered by the EC (see §5.3 below for some discussion), but the relevant point

3. This is Chomsky and Halle's preliminary version of the Main Stress Rule in their 'sketch of English phonology' (Chapter 2), but the same considerations apply to the sequence of expansions of the prefinal (1968: 99) and final (1968: 109–110) statements of the rule in their Chapter 3.

here is Harris's argument that Harmony is crucially separated from Lowering by the Truncation and Stress rules reproduced in (5.4) from Harris (1974: 65).

(5.4) Truncation and Stress in Brazilian Portuguese

a. Truncation

$[[\mathrm{X}\ \underset{\substack{\downarrow\\ \varnothing}}{\mathrm{V}}]_{\mathrm{St}}\ \mathrm{V}\ \mathrm{Y}]_{\mathrm{Vb}}$

b. Stress

$\mathrm{V} \longrightarrow [\text{+stress}]\ /\ \text{—}\ \mathrm{C_0VC_0}]_{\mathrm{Verb}}$

Briefly, the ordering arguments proceed as follows. First, Harmony (5.3a) must be ordered before Truncation (5.4a), because truncated theme vowels nevertheless trigger raising of root vowels (Harris 1974: 69); Truncation in turn must be ordered before Stress (5.4b), because surface penultimate vowels are stressed and theme vowels are penultimate before they are truncated (Harris 1974: 65).

(5.5) Harmony (5.3a) precedes Truncation (5.4a) precedes Stress (5.4b)

/serv+i+o/ $\underset{\text{Harmony}}{\longrightarrow}$ |sirvio| $\underset{\text{Truncation}}{\longrightarrow}$ |sirvo| $\underset{\text{Stress}}{\longrightarrow}$ [ˈsirvo] 'I serve'

Stress must in turn independently (and, Harris claims, intrinsically) be ordered before Lowering (5.3b), because the focus of Lowering mentions [±stress]. The total order is thus ⟨Harmony > Truncation > Stress > Lowering⟩. Even though Harmony and Lowering are not adjacent in the ordering, Harmony still blocks Lowering. This is illustrated by the derivation of ˈ*movo* 'I move' in (5.6), adapted from Harris (1974: 78). This is thus a case in which the adjacency requirement of Kiparsky's (1973b) EC would make the wrong empirical prediction.

(5.6) Harmony nonadjacently blocks Lowering

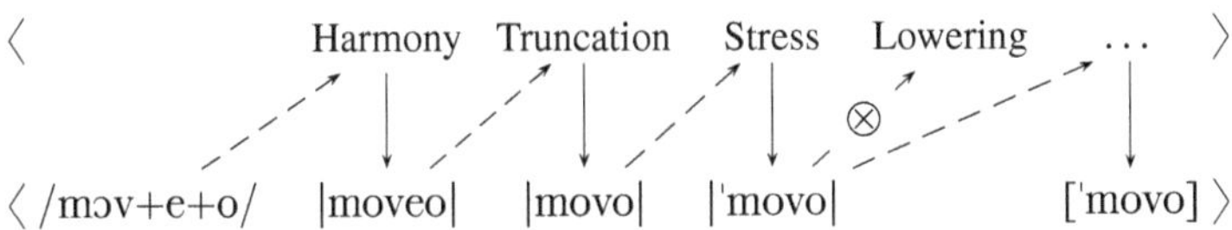

Kiparsky (1982) drops the adjacency requirement without comment and less strictly requires that the rules be "in the same [lexical-phonological] component" instead. Kiparsky's (1982) revised version of the EC is reproduced in (5.7).

(5.7) The Elsewhere Condition (Kiparsky 1982: 136–137)

Rules A, B in the same component apply disjunctively to a form ϕ if and only if

(i) The structural description of A (the special rule) properly includes the structural description of B (the general rule)

(ii) The result of applying A to ϕ is distinct from the result of applying B to ϕ

In that case, A is applied first, and if it takes effect, then B is not applied.

The problem with the adjacency requirement is thus not that it is *wrong*, but that it is *arbitrary*. Whether the EC should require that the two rules be adjacent (or even in the same component) cannot be justified outside of its empirical consequences. The requirement can be relaxed, strengthened, or completely changed depending on what the facts to be accounted for turn out to be.[4]

Because there are no ordered rules in OT, there can be no directly comparable requirement. But there are ranked constraints in OT, so one might imagine an adjacency requirement on constraint conflict or its adjudication. But conflict between two constraints holds regardless of their positions in a constraint hierarchy, and conflict between nonadjacent constraints is adjudicated in the same way as conflict between adjacent constraints: the higher-ranked of two conflicting constraints is satisfied at the expense of the lower-ranked of the two. Blocking of a more general constraint by a more specific constraint depends only on their ranking relative to one another: specific must outrank general, because the opposite ranking renders the more specific constraint inert under the thumb of the more general constraint. This follows from how constraint interaction works in OT; it is not somehow peculiar to specific-general pairs of constraints.

On the other hand, how the potential conflict between constraints in different *components* is resolved in the derivation of a form depends in part on the architecture of lexical-phonological grammars in OT. If components are defined by output-output faithfulness relations within a single constraint hierarchy (e.g. Burzio 1996; Benua 1997), then conflict between constraints will be resolved via the relative ranking of those constraints within that hierarchy. If components are instead independent, serially ordered constraint hierarchies as in Stratal OT (Kiparsky forthcoming; Bermúdez-Otero forthcoming), then the higher-ranked constraint in the later-ordered component will ultimately prevail; the derivation will proceed in all relevant respects like a prior rule specification analysis in which the later-ordered specific rule overwrites the earlier-ordered general rule.

5.2 Imposing precedence

Another arbitrary issue concerns whether the EC imposes one of the two possible linear orders between the specific and general rules that it yokes in disjunctivity, and if so, which order. On the one hand, the specific rule $\mathcal{S}$ might be made to precede — and if it applies, to block — the general rule $\mathcal{G}$. On the other hand, $\mathcal{G}$ might be made to precede $\mathcal{S}$, with $\mathcal{G}$ being blocked if the form in question also meets the structural description of $\mathcal{S}$ — which would then apply later in the derivation. Finally, there is also the possibility that neither order between $\mathcal{S}$ and $\mathcal{G}$ is imposed by the EC, only blocking of $\mathcal{G}$ by $\mathcal{S}$. The first and third of these positions have been explicitly suggested in the phonological literature on the EC; specific instances of these suggestions are discussed in turn below.

4. But note how easy it would be to defeat the EC if adjacency were indeed a prerequisite. Two rules that might otherwise be subject to the EC (and that would thus be expected to apply disjunctively) can be made to apply conjunctively instead by arbitrarily separating them in the ordering. This arbitrariness wouldn't be perverse, either: a situation in which disjunctive application is expected but not observed should be sufficient empirical motivation for otherwise arbitrary nonadjacent ordering, provided that there isn't any conflicting evidence for adjacency.

5.2.1 Specific before general is required

Kiparsky's (1973b) original version of the EC (5.1) does not explicitly address the question of ordering, but Kiparsky's (1982) version (5.7) directly stipulates the specific-before-general position: "A [= the more specific rule $\mathcal{S}$] *is applied first, and if it takes effect, then* B [= the more general rule $\mathcal{G}$] is not applied" (emphasis added). This appears to be the usual understanding of how disjunctive application is generally meant to work, whether or not the EC is involved in determining it. Consider, for example, Chomsky's definition (emphasis added):

> [T]wo rules R_1 [= $\mathcal{S}$] and R_2 [= $\mathcal{G}$], *linearly ordered so that R_1 precedes R_2*, are said to be DISJUNCTIVELY ORDERED if R_2 cannot apply to a given string at a certain stage of the cycle if R_1 has already applied to this string at this stage of the cycle. (Chomsky 1967: 120)

Consider also what Chomsky and Halle have to say (emphasis added):

> [T]he two subcases [$\mathcal{S}$] and [$\mathcal{G}$] *are ordered not only as shown* [i.e., as $\mathcal{S}$ before $\mathcal{G}$], but are "disjunctively ordered," in the sense that if [$\mathcal{S}$] applies, then [$\mathcal{G}$] is not permitted to apply. Thus a sequence of rules abbreviated in terms of the parenthesis notation constitutes a disjunctively ordered block; *as soon as* one of these rules is applied, the remaining rules are skipped within any one cycle of a derivation. (Chomsky and Halle 1968: 30)

Despite the apparent consistency of this assumption in the literature, no definitive argument for specific-before-general order over the two logical alternatives noted earlier (general-before-specific order, imposition of neither order) has ever been made in the literature, so far as I am aware (*pace* Halle and Vergnaud's [1982] unconvincing effort, to be discussed in §5.2.2 below). But there is clearly an intuitive appeal to the specific-before-general position despite the relative lack of reasoned support for it: if it is application of $\mathcal{S}$ that blocks application of $\mathcal{G}$, we must first attempt application of $\mathcal{S}$ in order to determine whether $\mathcal{G}$ can apply.

Bever (1967: 109ff) proposes an implementation of disjunctive application that formalizes this intuition. The essence of this proposal is the following: given two disjunctively ordered rules $\mathcal{S}$ and $\mathcal{G}$, application of $\mathcal{S}$ not only performs the structural change of $\mathcal{S}$ but also leaves behind a rule exception feature [$-\mathcal{G}$]. This diacritic is a condition on $\mathcal{G}$'s application: $\mathcal{G}$ cannot apply to segments marked [$-\mathcal{G}$]. This implementation of disjunctive application is exemplified in (5.8) below with the case of English Lengthening (3.12a = $\mathcal{S}$) and Shortening (3.12b = $\mathcal{G}$). Because the segment to which $\mathcal{G}$ is otherwise applicable is marked by $\mathcal{S}$ with the [$-\mathcal{G}$] diacritic, $\mathcal{G}$ is disjunctively blocked from actually applying to that segment.[5]

(5.8) Lengthening blocks Shortening via a rule exception feature

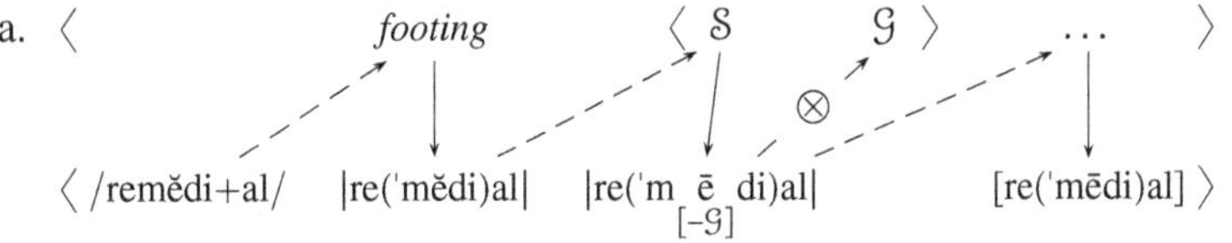

5. These illustrations only mark the focus of $\mathcal{S}$ as [$-\mathcal{G}$], but complementary insertion and deletion rules require that more of the surrounding context be so marked; see Bever (1967: 110) for discussion. Another situation in which this distinction makes a difference is noted in fn. 26, p. 107.

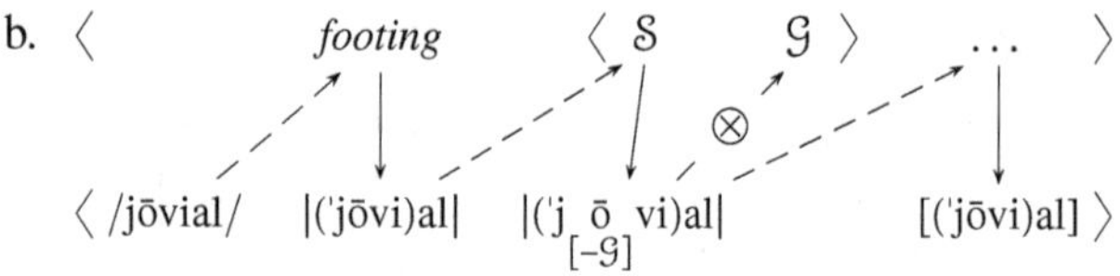

Naturally, the rule exception feature implementation of disjunctive application only works under the specific-before-general order: 𝒮 must apply first in order to mark the relevant segments so that 𝒢 can 'know' to be blocked from also applying to those segments. 𝒮 and 𝒢 must of course still be related to each other independently of their application; that is, 𝒢 needs to be recognized as more general (in the relevant sense) than 𝒮 so that 𝒮 is ordered before 𝒢 and leaves behind the rule exception feature [−𝒢] as a diacritic on the segment(s) to which it applies.

5.2.2 General before specific is possible

There is no explicit proposal in the literature to the effect that the EC imposes general-before-specific order, but there is at least one example where this order is argued to be independently necessary and therefore that it should at least be allowed.[6] The analysis of tone and accent in Tonga by Goldsmith (1981, 1984a, b) independently requires a general-before-specific order of rules, prompting him to propose that neither order between specific and general is imposed or required.

> [The EC] is not (and was not proposed as) a principle predicting relative rule ordering. In particular, the [EC] does *not* predict that the more specific of two rules in the appropriate relationship will apply first ... the more general rule should fail to apply not when the more specific rule *has* applied, but where the condition for the more specific rule is met. (Goldsmith 1984b: 36)[7]

The situation in Tonga involves Meeussen's Rule (5.9a), which is blocked by a more specific rule of Accent Shift (5.9b) even though the former bleeds — and thus must precede — the latter. These rule statements follow the formulations in Goldsmith (1984a: 246, 250; 1984b: 30, 35); despite superficial dissimilarities, they indeed meet the structural description inclusion requirement of the EC. Accent is marked here with a vertical tick mark rather than an asterisk over the vowel in order to distinguish it from an asterisk marking ungrammaticality.

(5.9) General (a) and specific (b) accent rules in Tonga

a. Meeussen's Rule

$\dot{V}\ C_0\ \dot{V} \longrightarrow \dot{V}\ C_0\ V$ (right-to-left iterative)

b. Accent Shift

-ȧ- $\dot{V}\ V \longrightarrow$ -ȧ- $V\ \dot{V}$ (strong recent past only)

The key cases are ones in which there is a substring of three accented vowels that meets the structural description of the more specific Accent Shift (5.9b), and

6. The discussion in this subsection builds on that of Prince (1997a: 3, n. 4).
7. Parallel discussion is also found in Goldsmith (1984a: 249).

each of the accents on the first two vowels of that substring is also subject to deletion by the more general Meeussen's Rule (5.9a). An example illustrating the interaction between these two rules is given in (5.10a); the examples in (5.10b, c) illustrate the independent application of each of the two rules.

(5.10) Interactions between Meeussen's Rule (MR) and Accent Shift (AS)

a. i. /bá-á-bá-lang-a/ ⟶ [bá-a-bá-lang-a] 'they looked at them'

ii. *[bá-a-ba-lang-a] MR

iii. *[bá-á-ba-láng-a] AS

b. /bá-á-bá-silik-a/ ⟶ [bá-a-ba-silik-a] MR 'they treated them'

c. /ndi-á-bá-lang-a/ ⟶ [ndi-á-ba-láng-a] AS 'I looked at them'

Given the underlying form in (5.10a) and left to its own devices, Meeussen's Rule (5.9a) would apply iteratively from right to left, deleting both the second and third accents as shown in (5.10a.ii) (cf. (5.10b), where only Meeussen's Rule applies to delete all accents after the first). Meeussen's Rule is instead blocked by the EC from deleting the third accent, because if the more specific Accent Shift (5.9b) were itself left to its own devices, it would shift that accent to the following unaccented vowel as shown in (5.10a.iii) (cf. (5.10c), where only Accent Shift applies). But Meeussen's Rule is not blocked from deleting the *second* accent: this it does in (5.10a.i), thus bleeding the actual application of Accent Shift.

This particular analysis also crucially depends on two other specific assumptions about the EC, proper appreciation of which requires a rather detailed deconstruction of the key case of /bá$_1$-á$_2$-bá$_3$-la$_4$ng-a$_5$/ in (5.10a). The specific substring Σ of this form that matches the structural description of the more specific Accent Shift rule (5.9b) is /-á$_2$-bá$_3$-la$_4$/, and the proper substring σ of Σ which first matches the structural description of the more general Meeussen's Rule (5.9a) in its right-to-left iterative sweep is /-á$_2$-bá$_3$/. The vowels of Σ that would be affected by Accent Shift are /á$_3$/, which would lose its accent, and /a$_4$/, which would gain it. The vowel of σ that would be affected by the first attempt to iteratively apply Meeussen's Rule from right to left is /á$_3$/, which would lose its accent.

Restricting attention to the proper substring σ that is included in both structural descriptions, then, the structural changes of both rules are technically identical: /á$_3$/ would be deaccented by application of either rule. So in order for the EC to block application of Meeussen's Rule to σ, rules that make identical changes must be eligible for specific-general pairing by the EC; cf. the discussion in §5.4 further below. But Goldsmith appears to assume otherwise, paraphrasing the EC thusly: "if the outputs of two adjacently ordered rules are mutually inconsistent, and if the set of forms to which one rule can apply properly includes the other, then the two are in a disjunctive relationship" (Goldsmith 1984a: 249). Goldsmith must assume that the additional change made by Accent Shift — the accenting of a previously unaccented vowel — makes it "mutually inconsistent" with the output of Meeussen's Rule, which says nothing at all about that vowel.[8]

8. Indeed, these two rules clearly serve closely related clash-avoidance functions; see Kisseberth (1970b: 11ff) for relevant discussion of a similar pair of rules in Tunica.

The other assumption underlying Goldsmith's analysis is that the EC does not block application of Meeussen's Rule *tout court*; Meeussen's Rule is only blocked from applying to the specific substring σ that matches its structural description and that is properly included in the longer substring Σ that also matches the structural description of Accent Shift (see §5.5). The full analysis requires that Meeussen's Rule continue its right-to-left iterative sweep after being blocked from applying to /ą́$_3$/ and to apply to the next substring /ą́$_1$-ą́$_2$/, deleting the accent on /ą́$_2$/. The result is [*bą́$_1$-ą$_2$-bą́$_3$-la$_4$ng-ą$_5$*], which no longer meets the structural description of Accent Shift — Meeussen's Rule thus bleeds Accent Shift.

This is thus a case where the more general rule is not blocked by the *actual* application of the more specific rule, but merely by the *potential* application of that rule later in the derivation. Halle and Vergnaud (1982) state that Goldsmith's analysis "is quite unprecedented in the literature" and continue as follows:

> [T]he disjunctivity required is not the traditional one [but rather one requiring] far-reaching modifications in the algorithm for rule application [that] are not to be welcomed since they render the rules extremely powerful, for now whether or not a given rule applies to a given string no longer depends purely on the form of the string, but may also depend on what other rules might apply to the input string. (Halle and Vergnaud 1982: 81)

Halle and Vergnaud do not specify how they understand the "traditional" type of disjunctivity to work, but we can assume for the sake of argument that it is something along the lines of the rule exception feature implementation outlined in §5.2.1 above. At the point in derivational time when a more general rule $\mathcal{G}$ is considered for application to a string, that string includes any [$-\mathcal{G}$] rule exception feature diacritics left behind by any more specific $\mathcal{S}$ rules that have applied previously. Thus the application of a rule "depends purely on the form of the string" under the rule exception feature implementation, which requires $\mathcal{S}$-before-$\mathcal{G}$ order.

Even under this "traditional" view, the EC must independently determine that two rules $\mathcal{S}$ and $\mathcal{G}$ are related to each other (i.e., in terms of structural description inclusion and structural change identity/incompatibility) so that it can add to $\mathcal{S}$ the proviso that it leave behind the [$-\mathcal{G}$] diacritic on the relevant segments. Given this, the resulting set of blocking requirements is arguably more complex than the set that appears to be entailed by Goldsmith's analysis. Instead of $\mathcal{S}$ adding a [$-\mathcal{G}$] diacritic and being ordered before $\mathcal{G}$ so that $\mathcal{G}$ can be blocked by the diacritic, Goldsmith's EC simply needs to add a blocking condition to $\mathcal{G}$ to the effect that *$\mathcal{G}$ is not applicable to strings matching the structural description or change of $\mathcal{S}$.* We must thus encode the structural description and change of $\mathcal{S}$ as conditions that block the application of $\mathcal{G}$.[9]. These differences are summarized in (5.11), using the Spirantization (= $\mathcal{S}$) and Fortition (= $\mathcal{G}$) rules from §3.1.5 as examples.

9. See Malouf (2005a, b) for an implementation of disjunctive application along these lines.

(5.11) Different sets of blocking requirements

	"Traditional" view	*Goldsmith (1981, 1984a, b)*
a.	$\mathcal{S}$ and $\mathcal{G}$ are related by the EC: $\mathcal{S}$ = VbV $\longrightarrow$ VβV $\mathcal{G}$ = β $\longrightarrow$ b	$\mathcal{S}$ and $\mathcal{G}$ are related by the EC: $\mathcal{S}$ = VbV $\longrightarrow$ VβV $\mathcal{G}$ = β $\longrightarrow$ b
b.	Application of $\mathcal{S}$ adds [$-\mathcal{G}$] : $\mathrm{VbV} \xrightarrow[\mathcal{S}]{} \mathrm{V} \underset{[-\mathcal{G}]}{\beta} \mathrm{V}$	(No diacritic is added.)
c.	$\mathcal{S}$ is ordered before $\mathcal{G}$.	(No order is imposed on $\mathcal{S}$ and $\mathcal{G}$.)
d.	$\underset{[-\mathcal{G}]}{\beta}$ blocks $\mathcal{G}$.	VbV or VβV blocks $\mathcal{G}$.

In both cases, the EC must relate $\mathcal{S}$ and $\mathcal{G}$, and based on this relation a blocking condition must be added to $\mathcal{G}$. In the "traditional" view, this blocking condition requires that $\mathcal{S}$ precede $\mathcal{G}$ in the ordering so that $\mathcal{G}$ may have access to the [$-\mathcal{G}$] mark left behind by the application of $\mathcal{S}$. In Goldsmith's analysis, on the other hand, the blocking condition is simply the structural change of $\mathcal{S}$, acquired directly from the relation that needs to be established between the two rules anyway.

In any event, whether Goldsmith's analysis can be considered "unprecedented in the literature" depends on how broadly we construe the literature and the analysis. It may be true that Goldsmith's suggestion was unprecedented in the literature *on the EC* (and on disjunctive application more generally) up to that point, but a wealth of work in the early 1970s (e.g. Kisseberth 1970a and Hill 1970, among many others) — Halle and Vergnaud's possible opinions of this work notwithstanding — had established a clear precedent for at least the *possibility* that rules might have access to information that is not strictly in their input strings. Moreover, as I document in §5.6 further below, Halle himself in later work argues for a modification of the EC the consequences of which are identical to those of Goldsmith (1981, 1984a, b) — with no acknowledgment of Goldsmith's proposal and with no disavowal of the misplaced critique thereof by Halle and Vergnaud.

The analysis of elsewhere interactions in OT does require a particular ordering relationship between the more specific and more general constraints; namely, that the more specific dominate the more general, in order for the more specific constraint to have any effect at all. This means that the OT analog of the rule order in Goldsmith's analysis, one in which the more specific constraint blocks the more general constraint even though the latter dominates the former, would not only be unprecedented — it would be impossible as a matter of definition. But this analog is not necessarily a homologue: an OT reanalysis of Goldsmith's analysis is beyond our current scope, but it need not involve a ranking paradox.[10]

5.3 The inclusion condition

It turns out that there are good reasons to question whether the core condition in (5.1a)/(5.7i), that the structural description of the more general rule be prop-

10. See Blumenfeld (2006) for an OT analysis of tone in Tonga, though the specific issues under consideration here are not directly addressed in that work.

erly included in the structural description of the more specific rule, is sufficiently justified as a prerequisite for disjunctive application. Suppose, for example, that Lengthening and Shortening in English (3.12) were stated so that both apply strictly nonvacuously; that is, Lengthening applies to short vowels only and Shortening applies to long vowels only. The structural description of Lengthening would then no longer properly include the structural description of Shortening! These rules would thus be predicted to apply conjunctively rather than disjunctively, even though they would have the same individual effects as corresponding rules that *do* meet the proper inclusion of structural descriptions requirement.[11]

One might think that Chomsky and Halle's (1968) simplicity metric could be invoked to disallow strictly nonvacuous rule statements like these, but one would be wrong: the simplicity metric only selects from among different grammars "which are all compatible with whatever data are available from a certain language" (Chomsky and Halle 1968: 330). Since two rules will apply disjunctively if and only if they meet the EC requirements and conjunctively otherwise, then a grammar with two rules that meet the EC requirements and a grammar with two minimally different rules that do not meet those requirements describe different sets of data and are thus not comparable by the metric. Chomsky and Halle's view on the matter is not at all unique: Halle (1978: 127) reiterates the same point ("Appeal to the simplicity metric is irrelevant where alternative descriptions either cover different sets of facts or where they employ different theoretical devices"), and Goldsmith and Laks (forthcoming: 7) offer the following historical perspective on the interpretation of the simplicity metric: "In case of multiple accounts of the same data ... formal simplicity was to be used to choose among the accounts".

Even if the simplicity metric could be brought to bear on the question of allowing strictly nonvacuous rule statements, there are some rules that *must* apply strictly nonvacuously — namely, insertion and deletion rules.[12] Consider Halle and Idsardi's (1997) analysis of Eastern Massachusetts English *r*, which is deleted syllable-finally and inserted prevocalically after nonhigh vowels. The relevant rules apply complementarily in word-final position in Halle and Idsardi's analysis: syllable-final *r* is inserted between a nonhigh vowel and a word-initial vowel; otherwise, syllable-final *r* is deleted.[13] The formulations of the relevant rules from Halle and Idsardi (1997: 343–344) are reproduced in (5.12).

11. Thanks to Roger Schwarzschild and Hubert Truckenbrodt for helping me to see this point, and to Alan Prince for discussion of it; see also Prince (1997a: 3, n. 5). Thanks also to John McCarthy for discussion of some of the broader implications, though he may not agree with my conclusions. Note that the same point holds even if only Shortening is stated in this strictly nonvacuous way.
12. Lengthening and Shortening may be instances of insertion and deletion themselves; see §5.6.
13. There are detectable contrasts between words with underlying *r* in the relevant contexts and those without, *pace* Pullum (1976: 90–91). There are also further empirical, analytical, and theoretical facts and issues that are not germane here; see e.g. Whorf (1943), Vennemann (1972), Kahn (1976), Broadbent (1991), McCarthy (1991, 1993, 1999a), Harris (1994), Blevins (1997), Halle and Idsardi (1997), Baković (1999b), Orgun (2001), Krämer (2005), Uffmann (2007), and references therein.

(5.12) Deletion and Insertion of *r* in Eastern Massachusetts English

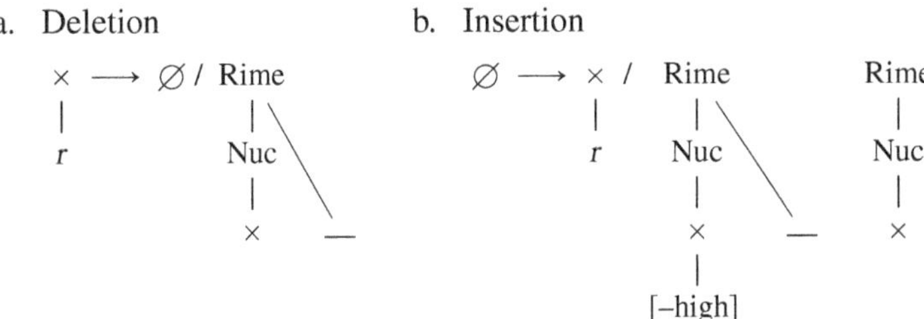

Halle and Idsardi (1997) leave the issue unaddressed (focusing instead on a related issue to be discussed in §5.6 below), but as McCarthy (1999a: 7) points out, Deletion requires that a syllable-final *r* be present in order to be deleted while Insertion requires that a syllable-final *r not* be present in order to insert one there. Deletion and insertion rules necessarily apply nonvacuously, and so there can be no proper inclusion between their structural descriptions.

One way to avoid the problem of strictly nonvacuous rules is to require that the structural *change* of one rule be properly included in the structural description of the other.[14] Whether Lengthening is applicable to all vowels or only short vowels, its structural change is a long vowel in the head of a branching foot meeting further conditions; this is properly included in the structural description of Shortening, again whether this latter rule is applicable to all vowels or only long vowels. Likewise, the structural change of Insertion is syllable-final *r* meeting further conditions; this is properly included in the structural description of Deletion, which is applicable to any syllable-final *r*.

Kiparsky (1973b: 104–105) suggests an alternative modification of the structural description inclusion requirement: "a subset relationship in the external context—namely, *P—Q, R—S* in [(5.1)]—rather than the whole structural analysis —*PAQ, RCS*—might suffice to establish disjunctivity." Adopting Kiparsky's terminology, I refer to this as the EXTERNAL CONTEXT INCLUSION requirement as opposed to the original WHOLE STRUCTURAL ANALYSIS INCLUSION requirement. The difference between these boils down to whether the *focus* of each rule — the element to the left of the arrow designated to undergo the change — is considered in the calculation of proper inclusion: external context inclusion does not consider foci while whole structural analysis inclusion does.

External context inclusion also avoids the problem of strictly nonvacuous rules. Ignoring the rules' foci effectively wipes out the distinction between strictly nonvacuous rules and their potentially vacuous counterparts, since the only difference between these is in the relative specification of their foci. But this was not Kiparsky's explicit intent in considering the possibility of external context inclusion; he was instead (somewhat speculatively) considering another type of case in which the focus of the otherwise more general rule might be more specified than the focus of the otherwise more specific rule. The example Kiparsky discusses involves two rules of Sanskrit, reproduced in (5.13).

14. I refer to this as the SC⊊SD requirement for convenience: 'SC' = structural change, 'SD' = structural description, and '⊊' = proper inclusion. The formal details of SC⊊SD and other SC/SD relations are discussed at length in Baković (in preparation).

(5.13) Sanskrit rules

a. Assimilation

$$[+\text{coronal}] \longrightarrow [\alpha\text{place}] \;/\; \_\_ \# \begin{bmatrix} \alpha\text{place} \\ +\text{coronal} \\ -\text{continuant} \end{bmatrix}$$

b. Aspiration

$$\begin{bmatrix} +\text{coronal} \\ +\text{continuant} \end{bmatrix} \longrightarrow \d{h} \;/\; \_\_ \#$$

Both rules apply word-finally, but Assimilation (5.13a) also requires a following word-initial coronal stop to assimilate to; thus, the external context of Assimilation properly includes that of Aspiration (5.13b). However, the focus of the 'more specific' Assimilation rule is a coronal while the focus of the 'more general' Aspiration rule is more specifically a coronal *fricative*, meaning that the whole structural analysis of Assimilation does *not* include that of Aspiration. Nevertheless, Kiparsky claims, these rules must apply disjunctively: in situations where the structural descriptions of both rules are met, Assimilation applies and blocks Aspiration: $s\#c \longrightarrow \acute{s}\#c$, $*\d{h}\#c$. Kiparsky notes that coronal fricatives also *optionally* assimilate to other coronal fricatives ($s\#\acute{s} \longrightarrow \acute{s}\#\acute{s} \sim \d{h}\#\acute{s}$) and to consonants at other places of articulation ($s\#p \longrightarrow \phi\#p \sim \d{h}\#p$); Aspiration must of course also be blocked when this assimilation rule opts to apply.[15]

It is important to note that this type of case is crucially different from the strictly nonvacuous rule cases discussed further above. Consider that the set of strings that meet the structural change of Assimilation, which includes assimilated word-final coronal stops, is not properly included in the set of strings that meet the structural description of Aspiration, which may not. The SC$\subsetneq$SD requirement accommodates strictly nonvacuous rules, but not the type of case under discussion here; external context inclusion accommodates both. In fact, external context inclusion is loose enough to accommodate cases in which the foci of the two rules have very little to do with each other. Recall, for example, the Harmony and Lowering rules in Brazilian Portuguese from §5.1; the rules are repeated here with their external contexts lined up (after Harris 1974: 77).

(5.14) Harmony and Lowering in Brazilian Portuguese, repeated from (5.3)

a. Harmony

$$\begin{bmatrix} \text{V} \\ \alpha\ \text{round} \\ \alpha\ \text{back} \end{bmatrix} \longrightarrow \begin{bmatrix} -\text{low} \\ \langle +\text{high} \rangle \end{bmatrix} \;/\; \_\_\, C_0 \left[\begin{bmatrix} \text{V} \\ -\text{low} \\ \langle +\text{high} \rangle \end{bmatrix} \right]_{\text{Stem}} \text{V}\ldots \Big]_{\text{Verb}}$$

b. Lowering

$$\begin{bmatrix} \text{V} \\ +\text{stress} \\ \left\{ \begin{matrix} -\text{high} \\ +\text{E} \end{matrix} \right\} \end{bmatrix} \longrightarrow [+\text{low}] \;/\; \_\_\, C_0 \Big]_{\text{Root}} \ldots \Big]_{\text{Verb}}$$

15. If Aspiration is a rule deleting unlicensed supralaryngeal place features (debuccalization), then its interaction with Assimilation can be recast in prosodic licensing terms (Ito 1986); see §5.4.2.

The external context of Lowering properly includes the external context of Harmony: both specify that the segment to be affected is followed by C_0 within a verb, but Harmony further specifies intervening vowels separated by a stem boundary.[16] But the whole structural analysis of Lowering does not include the whole structural analysis of Harmony, and in fact their foci only share the fact that they are vowels: the focus of Harmony is a vowel with the same values for [±round] and [±back], while the focus of Lowering is a stressed vowel that is either [–high] or a member of a "minority class of third conjugation roots with underlying high vowels that are unexpectedly lowered in certain forms" that is marked with the lexical diacritic feature '+E' (Harris 1974: 74).

There are two problematic issues that external context inclusion raises, one notational and the other more substantive. The first, notational issue is the fact that slash and dash ('/', '—') are "auxiliary expressions" (as opposed to "primitives") in the SPE formalism (Chomsky and Halle 1968: 390ff): a rule of the form $A \longrightarrow B \;/\; P \,\text{—}\, Q$ is automatically expanded by convention to a transformation of the form $PAQ \longrightarrow PBQ$. Crucial reference to the presence of dash ('—') in the external context of a rule grants more substance to this auxiliary expression than appears to have been intended by Chomsky and Halle (1968).

The second, more substantive issue concerns conditions on rule foci. A significant consequence of external context inclusion is that the only condition on foci comes from the clause requiring that structural changes be incompatible — or, as more practically stated by Kiparsky (1982) in (5.7), that the application of one of the two rules to a form ϕ be distinct from application of the other rule to ϕ. The problem is that in the case of complementary deletion and insertion rules, there is no form ϕ to which both rules are applicable: a form with the relevant element in the right context can only undergo deletion, and a form without the element in that context can only undergo insertion. Further formalization of incompatibility/distinctness is thus needed to accommodate such rules (see §5.4.2).

Even if it is possible to address these issues in a principled manner, the choice between one formulation of the inclusion requirement or another is, again, an entirely arbitrary one. The exigencies of description might require that one or another be adopted, with no substantive consequence for the *SPE* theory in which the EC is couched. There is something significant about the distinction between whole structural analysis inclusion and external context inclusion, however, that deserves closer scrutiny. To borrow a useful term in a related context from Prince (1997b, c, 2000, 2001), whole structural analysis inclusion is a more STRINGENT requirement than is external context inclusion. Given two structural descriptions A and B, if the whole structural analysis of A is included in that of B, then the external context of A is by definition also included in that of B — but not necessarily vice versa. Adopting the less stringent demands of external context inclusion is thus a move in the direction of the even less stringent demands of mere *overlap*

16. A minor complication not addressed by Harris (1974) is that the supposedly more general external context of Lowering specifies a root boundary that is not specified by the supposedly more specific external context of Harmony. It just so happens that there are no stems in Brazilian Portuguese that match the external context of Harmony that don't also match the external context of Lowering, meaning that the same root boundary could be (redundantly) specified in the Harmony rule.

between structural descriptions: if the external context of A is included in that of B, then A and B also overlap — but again, not necessarily vice versa.

So why even demand anything more stringent than overlap? Though nowhere explicitly discussed in the literature, there are very good reasons within *SPE* to distinguish the more stringent inclusion relationships from overlap for the purposes of establishing disjunctive application between rules. When two rules with incompatible structural changes merely overlap, we do not necessarily expect only one possible blocking interaction between them — and if we did, it is not obvious how one would establish which of the two rules blocks the other. For example, consider the following pair of rules in Nootka (Sapir and Swadesh 1978).

(5.15) Labialization and Delabialization in Nootka

a. Labialization

[+dorsal] ⟶ [+round] / [+round] —

b. Delabialization

[+dorsal] ⟶ [–round] / — $]_\sigma$

The structural descriptions of these two rules are not in any kind of inclusion relationship because Labialization but not Delabialization is applicable to *syllable-initial* dorsals preceded by round vowels (/*ħaju+qi*/ ⟶ *ħaju+q*^{w}*i* 'ten on top') and Delabialization but not Labialization is applicable to syllable-final dorsals *preceded by nonround vowels* (/*ɬa:k*^{w}*+ʃit͡ɬ*/ ⟶ *ɬa:k+ʃit͡ɬ* 'to take pity on'). But the structural descriptions do overlap, because they are both met by syllable-final dorsals preceded by round vowels; here, only the structural change of Delabialization is achieved: /*m'u:q*/ ⟶ *m'u:q*, **m'u:q*^{w} 'throwing off sparks'.

Now suppose that there could be no language just like Nootka except that Labialization prevails (/*m'u:q*/ ⟶ *m'u:q*^{w}, **m'u:q*). How could blocking of Labialization by Delabialization be *guaranteed in principle*? Neither rule can be identified as being in a unique relationship with respect to the other; unlike proper inclusion, overlap is mutual.[17] Cases like this one have thus been quietly handled with conjunctive ordering: Delabialization prevails because it applies after and overwrites the prior effect of Labialization, even though the result is a Duke of York derivation (Campbell 1973; Pullum 1976; McCarthy 1999b, 2003c, 2007a, b) — and the opposite order is of course also possible under this account.

Constraint conflict in OT, and the need to adjudicate it via ranking, always and only arises when constraints make incompatible demands on a string. The distinction between overlap and more stringent inclusion relationships is irrelevant: all cases of conflict result in violation (= blocking) of the lower-ranked constraint. When constraints conflict in overlapping contexts, either ranking is possible and both constraints are independently active where they don't conflict — just as with ordering of overlapping rules, except of course without the consequences of Duke of York derivations. When constraints conflict because the context of one is properly included in the context of the other, however, then either ranking is still possible but only one results in both constraints being independently active.

17. One might perhaps conjecture that, say, rules with syllabic contexts block overlapping rules with nonsyllabic contexts, but this is clearly grasping at straws.

5.4 The change condition

5.4.1 Identical or incompatible

Kiparsky's (1973b) EC requires that structural changes be "either identical or incompatible". As noted in §2.3, the "identical" case is intended to cover stress rules — the class of examples that originally motivated disjunctive application, and that was once accounted for with the parenthesis notation (recall §2.2.1).[18] Stress rules all assign stress to a vowel, and so the changes they make are on the face of it "identical": V $\longrightarrow$ [+stress]. This identity is, however, only skin deep: a rule's structural change is more than just the specification of the change effected by a rule on its focus. The standard *SPE* rule format $A \longrightarrow B \,/\, P \,\_\_\, Q$ expands by convention to $PAQ \longrightarrow PBQ$ (Chomsky and Halle 1968: 397); *PAQ* is the structural description (as Kiparsky (1973b) clearly assumes) and *PBQ* is the structural change (not *B* or $A \longrightarrow B$). The structural changes of two rules that assign stress to different vowels in a form can thus not be identical, strictly speaking, and so the question is how they can be understood to be incompatible in some way.

Kiparsky (1982: 137) drops the "identical or" portion of the change condition and restates the incompatibility condition this way: "[t]he result of applying [the more specific rule] is distinct from the result of applying [the more general rule]". The "result of applying" parts of this statement make clear that the relevant comparison is between the full structural changes of the rules, not just the changes effected by the rules on their foci. Most if not all work on the EC subsequent to Kiparsky (1982) appears to agree on the correctness of only requiring that structural changes be incompatible (now "distinct").[19]

But the question remains: how can the structural changes of stress rules be understood to be incompatible? Kiparsky offers the following explanation.

> The earlier version [i.e., (5.1)] had to apply also to cases where the structural changes are identical. But, as pointed out by Howard (1975), the case where the changes are identical was only necessary for stress rules. For example, the two rules collapsed in the schema V $\longrightarrow$ V́ / — C_0 (V C_0) # must apply disjunctively so that a stress is assigned to the final syllable only if there is no penult (i.e. in monosyllables). However, if we adopt metrical phonology, the two stress patterns (… $\overset{\text{F}}{\text{S W}}$# and … $\overset{\text{F}}{|}$#) are distinct if we construe distinctness for metrical structure in the obvious way as incompatibility of labeling or bracketing. And in any case, the metrical version of the rule simply assigns a maximally binary foot to the right edge of a word, and so does not properly constitute a schema abbreviating two rules. We therefore need only specify distinctness of outputs… (Kiparsky 1982: 173–174, n. 2)

18. Paradoxically, Johnson (1972: 113ff) proposes to dispense with the parenthesis notation precisely because it can be used to establish disjunctive application between rules *other than stress rules*.
19. This appears to be true even when Kiparsky's (1973b) formulation of the EC is explicitly adopted. For example, Halle (1995: 27) notes that "Kiparsky's stress examples … have a solution that requires no reliance on the Elsewhere constraint" but also reproduces the "identical or incompatible" requirement. This is likely an oversight, unless Halle is implicitly acknowledging the existence of other types of rules making identical changes that nevertheless must apply disjunctively.

In other words, there are two possible reinterpretations of the old disjunctive application analysis of stress rules given metrical stress theory. The first is that there is an inherent incompatibility between the structural changes of relevant metrical stress rules: penultimate stress and final stress are incompatible because the final syllable cannot be both the head of one foot and the nonhead of another. The second is that stress involves rules and principles of metrical structure assignment for which disjunctive application is irrelevant: if stress feet are preferably and maximally binary, left-headed, and built at the right edge, then polysyllabic forms will allow and thus require penultimate stress while monosyllables will disallow this and stress will be final, on the one and only syllable.[20]

What this discussion reveals is that the structural change requirement is entirely arbitrary. Why must the structural changes be incompatible — or distinct, or whatever term is on offer, so long as it is well defined (see §5.4.2) — other than to correctly delimit the set of cases in which disjunctive application is observed? The EC must stumble to state the empirically correct requirement because it does not follow from anything within the set of *SPE* assumptions in which the EC is couched. In OT, on the other hand, the restriction to incompatible changes needn't be stated because it follows from constraint ranking and candidate comparison. Incompatibility between the candidates preferred by distinct constraints is what makes those constraints conflict; one constraint is satisfied by violation of the other, and this is what requires them to be ranked with respect to each other.

5.4.2 Defining incompatibility

The terms "incompatible" and "distinct" (and "identical", for that matter) are not defined in Kiparsky (1973b, 1982). Howard (1975: 110, fn. 1) raises this point and concludes somewhat charitably that "[o]n the basis of the examples cited [by Kiparsky (1973b)], it seems reasonable to conclude that incompatible changes involve contrary specifications for the same feature, or assimilation and deletion."

The "contrary specifications" set includes the types of examples highlighted in Chapters 3 and 4. These are examples for which there is a workable (though problematic) conjunctive alternative with the more specific rule overwriting the result of the more general rule. (This analysis was referred to as *fed counterfeeding on focus* in §3.1.3; I use this term here to refer to this type of case regardless of the analysis.) The "assimilation and deletion" set includes the example of Diola Fogny; the relevant rules of which are repeated here for convenience.

(5.16) Diola Fogny rules, repeated from (2.21) and (2.31)

a. Assimilation

$$\begin{bmatrix} \text{C} \\ \text{+nasal} \end{bmatrix} \longrightarrow [\alpha\text{place}] \;/\; \text{—} \begin{bmatrix} \text{–cont} \\ \alpha\text{place} \end{bmatrix}$$

b. Deletion

$$\text{C} \longrightarrow \varnothing \;/\; \text{—}\,\text{C}$$

20. Alternatively, the Free Element Condition (Prince 1985; Halle and Kenstowicz 1991) might prevent final stress on polysyllables due to the prior presence of a penultimate stress foot.

Assimilation and Deletion are both applicable to nasals followed by noncontinuants, to which only more specific Assimilation is allowed to actually apply, blocking more general Deletion. Unlike the more familiar cases of fed counterfeeding on focus, recall from §2.4.1 that a conjunctive interaction between these two rules as stated is not possible: if Deletion were to precede Assimilation, then there would be no nasals left to assimilate (= Deletion bleeds Assimilation), and if Assimilation were to precede Deletion, then all assimilated nasals would later be deleted (= Deletion 'masks' Assimilation; cf. Guerssel 1978).[21]

So Assimilation must block Deletion, but how exactly is this enforced by the EC? The structural changes of Assimilation and Deletion — more generally, the structural changes of any deletion rule and any feature-changing rule that target the same focus — can be commonsensically described as *distinct from* each other, but they are not obviously *incompatible*. The key word here is 'obviously': with no formal definition of incompatibility, we must guess at the intended interpretation. Kiparsky's (1973b) intention appears to be that the structural changes of two rules are incompatible if (a) there is a conjunctive order between the rules that would enable both to apply nonvacuously in the derivations of some forms (Assimilation before Deletion for Diola Fogny; either order for fed counterfeeding on focus cases), and (b) application of one of the rules (Deletion in Diola Fogny; either rule in other cases) *nullifies* the effect of the application of the other rule (by masking in Diola Fogny; by reversal in other cases).[22,23]

Alternatively, however, one can appeal to the (now quite standard) *prosodic licensing* analysis of Diola Fogny (Ito 1986), which can be described as follows. Deletion is stray erasure (Steriade 1982), which only targets those consonants that have not been incorporated into syllable structure. The coda position of a syllable in Diola Fogny does not license place features, and so consonants cannot be syllabified as codas unless their place features are independently licensed by another consonant in onset position — this is indeed what motivates place features to spread from a noncontinuant in an onset to a would-be coda nasal.[24]

Neither Deletion nor Assimilation are stand-alone rules under this analysis, but to the extent that we can talk about them as if they were, Assimilation bleeds Deletion: spreading of place leads to successful syllabification of a coda nasal, thereby preventing it from being stray erased. There is thus no apparent need for

21. Note the difference between the potential conjunctive interactions between these two rules, which target the same foci, and the potential conjunctive interactions between similar rules that target different foci. In Indonesian and other Austronesian languages (Halle and Clements 1983: 125; see also Pater 1999, 2001; Blust 2004; and references therein), the focus of Assimilation is a preconsonantal nasal and the focus of Deletion is a post-nasal voiceless stop. Assimilation precedes Deletion in a counterbleeding interaction: a nasal assimilates to a following voiceless stop before the stop deletes. The opposite order between the rules would be a bleeding interaction, as expected.
22. 'Reversal' covers both the feature-change reversals apparent in the fed counterfeeding on focus cases discussed thus far and deletion/insertion reversals of the type discussed in §5.3 above.
23. Given that the structural change of Deletion results in strings that do not meet the structural descriptions of either Assimilation or Deletion, the interaction between these types of rules — as well as between their corresponding $[\![\mathbb{M} \gg \mathbb{F}]\!]$ rankings in an OT analysis — differs significantly from reversals. For discussion, see Baković (in preparation).
24. There must of course be independent reasons why onset continuants can't spread and nonnasals can't be spread to. Also, word-final consonants are allowed in Diola Fogny and so must be given special dispensation — perhaps, as Ito (1986) suggests, by adjoining them to the prosodic word.

disjunctive application in this kind of case, making it feasible to say that two structural changes are incompatible only if one of them is a reversal of the other.

5.5 Global blocking vs. local blocking

Suppose that a form ϕ contains some set F of two or more potential foci for $\mathcal{G}$, and that only a proper subset f of F are potential foci for $\mathcal{S}$. Assuming what I call LOCAL BLOCKING, $\mathcal{G}$ is blocked from applying only to the proper subset of foci f; assuming what I call GLOBAL BLOCKING, $\mathcal{G}$ is blocked from applying to the entire set of foci F.[25] Attested cases of blocking are local: $\mathcal{G}$ is only blocked from applying to the specific foci in the proper subset f to which $\mathcal{S}$ is also applicable, and is otherwise free to apply to the complement set f', the remainder of the potential foci of $\mathcal{G}$ in F. If blocking were global, then application of $\mathcal{S}$ to any one potential focus of $\mathcal{G}$ would block application of $\mathcal{G}$ to all potential foci of $\mathcal{G}$.

Global blocking entails that a contrast between elements that are otherwise distributed complementarily could potentially emerge in the set of f'-foci of $\mathcal{G}$. That is, forms with only f'-foci would undergo $\mathcal{G}$, as expected, but forms with both f-foci and f'-foci would undergo only $\mathcal{S}$. The intuitively bizarre result is that the specification of a given f'-focus is determined by $\mathcal{G}$ only if there is no f-focus in the same form; if there is one, then the specification of the f'-focus is either determined by some other rule or by its underlying specification.

Spanish provides a straightforward example of a local blocking interaction between a more specific Assimilation rule (5.17a) and a more general Neutralization rule (5.17b), both of which affect syllable-final nasals.

(5.17) Rules affecting nasal place in Spanish

a. Assimilation

$$[\text{+nasal}] \longrightarrow [\alpha\text{place}] \;/\; \text{—}\,]_\sigma\; [\alpha\text{place}]$$

b. Neutralization

$$[\text{+nasal}] \longrightarrow [\text{+coronal}] \;/\; \text{—}\,]_\sigma$$

I arbitrarily represent the syllable-final nasals affected by these rules as underspecified *N* in underlying forms, because whether they have one or another place of articulation underlyingly is irrelevant. Application of Assimilation and consequent blocking of Neutralization is illustrated in the derivation of *ˈbaŋko* 'bank' in (5.18a). Successful application of Neutralization due to the inapplicability of Assimilation to a nasal that is not followed by a consonant is illustrated in the derivation of *balˈkon* 'balcony' in (5.18b).

(5.18) Interaction between Assimilation and Neutralization

a. ⟨ . . . Assim . . . Neut ⊗ . . . ⟩

⟨ /baNko/ |baNko| |baŋko| |baŋko| [ˈbaŋko] ⟩

25. This section borrows liberally from Baković (2009b).

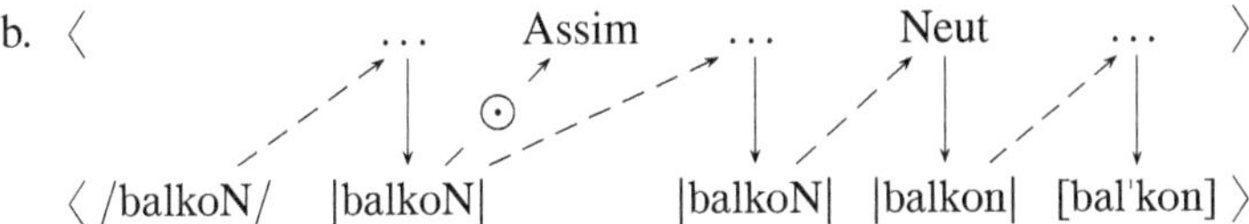

The locality of blocking can be appreciated by considering the derivation of *riŋ'kon* 'corner (of a room)' in (5.19). The first nasal meets the structural descriptions of both Assimilation and Neutralization; application of Assimilation blocks application of Neutralization to this first nasal, as illustrated in (5.19a). The second nasal only meets the structural description of Neutralization and so Neutralization applies to that nasal, as illustrated in (5.19b).

(5.19) Local blocking of Neutralization by Assimilation

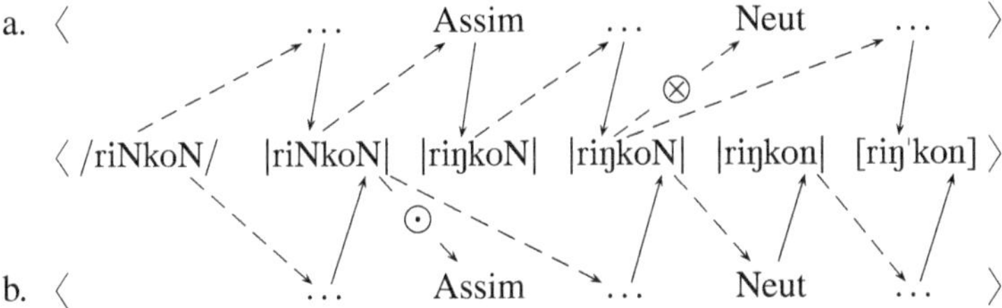

If blocking were global rather than local, Neutralization would be blocked from applying to the second nasal of (5.19) as well as to the first. We would thus expect a contrast among different nasals to be able to surface in just this type of context — that is, in nasals that only meet the more general structural description of Neutralization but where there happens to be another nasal somewhere else in the form that also meets the more specific structural description of Assimilation.[26]

26. To be clear, the distinction between local blocking and global blocking is not simply a matter of whether $\mathcal{G}$ and $\mathcal{S}$ are applicable to distinct foci within the same form. The sets of complementary stress rules that originally motivated disjunctive application are always applicable to distinct foci within the same form; blocking is necessarily achieved in such cases, but the bizarre result of global blocking is not produced. Metrical stress theory has obviated the relevance of disjunctive application in these cases in any event, as discussed in §5.4, but we nevertheless proceed with an illustration. Consider the English verb stress rule, adapted from Chomsky and Halle (1968: 77) via Kiparsky (1973b: 94): $V \longrightarrow [+\text{stress}]\ /\ \_\ C_0(\breve{V}C_0^1)\#$. The longer, more specific expansion of this rule, with the structural description $\_\ C_0\breve{V}C_0^1\#$, assigns stress to a penultimate syllable if the final vowel is short and followed by at most one consonant (*'edĭt, de'velŏp*). If there is no penultimate syllable (*'rŭn, 'hĭt*), or if the final vowel is long (*re'sīgn, e'rāse*) or in a syllable that is closed by more than one consonant (*e'lăpse, re'spĕct*), then the shorter, more general expansion of the rule, with the structural description $\_\ C_0\#$, assigns stress to the final syllable. In forms matching the structural descriptions of both expansions, the longer one is applicable to the penultimate syllable and the shorter one is applicable to the final syllable; only the longer one applies, blocking the shorter one. What's crucially different about this sort of case is that while the two expansions of the rule are necessarily applicable to different foci — a penultimate syllable or a final syllable — the focus of the shorter expansion is included in the broader structural description of the longer expansion, modulo the fact that the longer expansion imposes additional conditions on the final syllable. (This is thus a case in which the rule exception feature implementation of disjunctive application outlined in §5.2.1 would have to ensure that not just the focus but all segments in the substring matching the structural description of $\mathcal{S}$ are marked $[-\mathcal{G}]$; recall fn. 5, p. 93.) In the Spanish case illustrated in (5.19), the word-final focus of the more general Neutralization rule is not included anywhere in the structural description of Assimilation. It is this disjointness of domains of application that produces the bizarre global blocking result.

Surprisingly, the empirically correct local interpretation of blocking does not follow from the EC and thus must be separately stipulated.[27] Chomsky and Halle (1968) note this issue and acknowledge the need to stipulate the correct result.

> Clearly we must stipulate that if rules R_1 and R_2 are disjunctively ordered—R_1 preceding R_2—and if R_1 applies to the substring *Y* of a string *XYZ* but is independent of *X* and *Z*, then R_2 may apply to *X* and *Z* but not to *Y* in a stage of the cycle to which R_1 applies. (Chomsky and Halle 1968: 366)

The question comes down to how 'application of $\mathcal{S}$' (= R_1 in Chomsky and Halle's discussion) is encoded in the derivation so as to correctly block $\mathcal{G}$ (= R_2). It needs to be encoded locally, at the level of the individual focus ('$\mathcal{S}$ has applied to this focus$_k$, so $\mathcal{G}$ may not apply to it$_k$'),[28] and not globally, at the level of the entire form ('$\mathcal{S}$ has applied to this form$_i$, so $\mathcal{G}$ may not apply to it$_i$').

As discussed earlier (§5.2.1), one way to encode 'application of $\mathcal{S}$' in the derivation of a form is to assign a rule exception feature [$-\mathcal{G}$] to the foci affected by $\mathcal{S}$. This appears to correctly achieve local blocking, since the potential foci of $\mathcal{G}$ that are not themselves affected by $\mathcal{S}$ should not be marked [$-\mathcal{G}$]. The main obstacle to this conclusion is that rule exception features are generally assumed to be assigned to entire morphemes, not to individual segments (Chomsky and Halle 1968: 172ff), which would result in global blocking. Thus either the assignment (or percolation) of rule exception features to entire morphemes is wrong, or the rule exception feature implementation of disjunctive blocking is incorrect. In any event, whether blocking is local or global is treated entirely as an empirical matter, and the theme throughout this chapter is thus repeated here: the empirically correct form of blocking remains to be explained rather than stipulated.

Anderson (1974) also addresses this "interesting indeterminacy in the theory of disjunctive ordering", citing related discussions in Bever (1967), Howard (1972), and Johnson (1972) (cited by Anderson as Johnson 1970).

> While this theory specifies the conditions under which the application of one rule precludes the application of some other, it was only meant to cover cases in which the domains of the two rules *overlapped to some extent*. Cases have been illustrated . . . that demonstrate the fact that, when one part of a disjunctive schema applies to one part of a form, it does not preclude the application of the other part of the schema to some *completely unrelated* portion of the same form. . . . [W]e leave the issue unresolved at this point, except to note that disjunctive ordering is presumed not to obtain if the portion of the form analyzed by the SD [= structural description] of the longer (or more specific) rule is *totally disjoint* from the portion analyzed by the SD of the shorter (or less specific) rule. (Anderson 1974: 108–109, emphasis added)

Where to draw the line between substrings that "overlap to some extent" and those that are "completely unrelated" or "totally disjoint" turns out not to be a

---

27. Spanish-type cases are thus typically handled otherwise. Harris's (1984) analysis, for example, presupposes that the rules in (5.17) are strictly feature-filling: Assimilation and Neutralization only affect *placeless* nasals, previously made so by a nasal debuccalization rule. Assimilation precedes and thus bleeds Neutralization: just those nasals that have already undergone Assimilation cannot undergo Neutralization. For a critique of Harris's (1984) analysis, see Baković (2001).

28. Or at the level of the substring matching the structural description of $\mathcal{S}$; again, recall fn. 5, p. 93.

trivial question. For example, recall Goldsmith's analysis of Tonga discussed in §5.2. The rules and a key example of their interaction are repeated in (5.20).

(5.20) Tonga rules and their interaction, repeated from (5.9) and (5.10)

a. Meeussen's Rule

$\acute{V}\ C_0\ \acute{V} \longrightarrow \acute{V}\ C_0\ V$ (right-to-left iterative)

b. Accent Shift

-á- $\acute{V}\ V \longrightarrow$ -á- $V\ \acute{V}$ (strong recent past only)

c. /bá-á-bá-lang-a/ ⟶ [bá-a-bá-lang-a] 'they looked at them'

Two substrings match the structural description of Meeussen's Rule (5.20a) in its iterative right-to-left sweep through the form in (5.20c), /bá$_1$-á$_2$-bá$_3$-la$_4$ng-a$_5$/. The first is the substring /á$_2$-bá$_3$/. This opportunity to deaccent /á$_3$/ is blocked by the fact that the substring /-á$_2$-bá$_3$-la$_4$/ — which properly includes /á$_2$-bá$_3$/ — also matches the structural description of Accent Shift (5.20b), which aims to shift the accent from /á$_3$/ to /a$_4$/. This application of Accent Shift is crucially bled, however, by the second, successful attempt by Meeussen's Rule to apply to this form — this time to the substring /bá$_1$-á$_2$/, deaccenting /á$_2$/. But why is this second attempt not also blocked? After all, the substring /bá$_1$-á$_2$/ "overlaps to some extent" with the substring matching the structural description of Accent Shift, /-á$_2$-bá$_3$-la$_4$/. The key, of course, is that /bá$_1$-á$_2$/ is not *properly included* in /-á$_2$-bá$_3$-la$_4$/ and that the rules now have *different foci*: /á$_2$/ for Meeussen's Rule, /á$_3$/ and /a$_4$/ for Accent Shift. These represent two separate problems for the EC, which I address in turn.

First, proper inclusion. The EC is only concerned with the relationship between the structural descriptions of $\mathcal{S}$ and $\mathcal{G}$; it says nothing about *actual individual substrings* that match those structural descriptions in any given case. This is most explicit in the case of Kiparsky's (1982) definition in (5.7) ("[t]he structural description of A … properly includes the structural description of B"), and only slightly more indirectly in the case of Kiparsky's (1973b) definition in (5.1) ("the set of strings that fit *PAQ* is a subset of the set of strings that fit *RCS*").

This clause could of course be suitably redefined, requiring a proper inclusion relationship between the actual individual substrings matching the structural descriptions of both rules. This definition seems more natural anyway, as pointed out to me by Roger Schwarzschild (p.c.); after all, rules themselves pick out the actual individual substrings of a form that match their structural descriptions, whether they then apply simultaneously or iteratively to those substrings (see the extensive discussion in Kenstowicz and Kisseberth 1979: 318ff). The fact that this clause of the EC can be defined otherwise, however, is the point here; the fact that it *is* defined otherwise by Kiparsky (1973b, 1982) simply highlights it.

Second, different foci. Again, the relevant clause of the EC is only concerned with the relationship between the structural changes of $\mathcal{S}$ and $\mathcal{G}$; it says nothing about the *actual individual foci* that undergo those changes in any given case. This reference to the form of the structural change in the rule is crucial: since the whole point of the EC is for application of $\mathcal{G}$ to be blocked by the applicability of $\mathcal{S}$, the individual foci in fact never undergo $\mathcal{G}$'s structural change.[29] Relating $\mathcal{S}$ and $\mathcal{G}$ via the EC thus *requires* reference to the form of $\mathcal{G}$'s structural change, since it cannot involve reference to any actual change performed by $\mathcal{G}$.

Reference to rule form in this case may be inescapable, but the structural change clause could be supplemented with the stipulation that at least one focus targeted by each of the rules is the same segment in the substrings under consideration.[30] The point remains that whether Accent Shift should block the second attempt by Meeussen's Rule to apply to (5.20c) — more generally, whether blocking is local or global — depends on more than what is actually stated by the EC.

In OT, only local blocking of a more general constraint $\mathbb{G}$ by a more specific constraint $\mathbb{S}$ is possible. Suppose that a form has two foci f_1 and f_2 to which $\mathbb{G}$ is applicable, but that $\mathbb{S}$ is only applicable to f_1. If $[\![\mathbb{S} \gg \mathbb{G}]\!]$, then $\mathbb{G}$ will be forced to be violated by $\mathbb{S}$ only with respect to f_1, the focus to which both constraints are applicable; since $\mathbb{S}$ is irrelevant to the fate of f_2, $\mathbb{G}$ will be satisfied there. This is due to minimal violation, a fundamental property of OT governing all constraint conflict resolution (Prince 1993): no constraint is violated more than is necessary to ensure better satisfaction of higher-ranking constraints. Local blocking follows directly from minimal violation; there is no need to ensure it separately.

5.6 Applicational vs. circumstantial blocking

Halle (1995) and Halle and Idsardi (1997) advance another modification to the definition of the EC. Both statements of this modification are quoted here.

> [T]he less restrictive rule may not apply to a string that has the form of the more restrictive rule. [This definition] is somewhat more general than the one given in [Kiparsky (1973b)], where "disjunctivity" was limited to strings to which the more "restrictive" rule had applied. (Halle 1995: 27)

> Any two rules meeting the Elsewhere Condition prerequisites are subject to the following constraint: the less complex rule may not apply to a string that has the form of the output of the more complex rule. That is, the less complex rule is blocked if the current representation is compatible with the structural change of the more complex rule. (Halle and Idsardi 1997: 346)

Halle and Idsardi's statement is a little more explicit than Halle's, but here is some further explication. Suppose that the more specific (or "more restrictive", or "more complex") rule $\mathcal{S}$ has the form $A \longrightarrow B \,/\, C \_ D$. Given a form containing a substring *CAD* at the time of $\mathcal{S}$'s turn in the derivation, $\mathcal{S}$ will apply nonvacuously to produce *CBD*; application of any more general rule $\mathcal{G}$ will thus be blocked,

29. Reference to rule form is also crucial to Goldsmith's particular argument for the general-before-specific ordering of Meeussen's Rule before Accent Shift: since more specific Accent Shift also never applies to the form in (5.20c) due to bleeding by the second attempt to apply Meeussen's Rule, it must be the form of Accent Shift's structural change — the structural change it *would have made*, if left to its own devices — that blocks the first attempt to apply Meeussen's Rule.

30. I say "at least one focus" because Accent Shift has two foci: the vowel-to-be-deaccented and the vowel-to-be-accented. Only the former is the same segment as the focus of Meeussen's Rule in the case under discussion, which is why the structural changes of these rules must be taken to be identical for the purposes of being related by the EC (recall the discussion in §5.2.2).

as expected under Kiparsky's (1973b) original definition. The modification under discussion ensures that a form that, *for any reason*, happens to contain the substring *CBD* — that is, a substring matching the output of $\mathcal{S}$ — will also block application of $\mathcal{G}$. I refer to the original definition of blocking as APPLICATIONAL BLOCKING, and to this modified definition as CIRCUMSTANTIAL BLOCKING.

The idea behind this terminology is that circumstantial blocking requires that the form of $\mathcal{S}$'s output be *circumstantially present* in the form in order to block $\mathcal{G}$, while applicational blocking requires explicit, *nonvacuous application* of $\mathcal{S}$ to have produced that output. This distinction should be familiar from the discussion toward the end of §5.2.2 further above: circumstantial blocking corresponds directly to the definition of blocking proposed by Goldsmith (1981, 1984a, b) to allow $\mathcal{S}$ to block $\mathcal{G}$ even when $\mathcal{G}$ precedes $\mathcal{S}$, while applicational blocking corresponds directly to the "traditional" definition that Halle and Vergnaud (1982) appear to assume in their critique of Goldsmith's definition. We will consider the relevance of this point toward the end of the present section.

The empirical base of Halle (1995) is the interaction between Lengthening and Shortening in English. The rules are repeated in (5.21) for convenience. Recall that these are adapted from Kenstowicz (1994b: 218); Halle (1995) only offers informal prose statements (e.g., "Shorten the head vowel of a branching foot").[31]

(5.21) English Lengthening and Shortening rules, repeated from (3.12)

a. Lengthening

$$\begin{bmatrix} \text{V} \\ \text{-high} \end{bmatrix} \longrightarrow \bar{\text{V}} \;/\; \begin{array}{ccc} \_\_ & \text{C}\; i & \text{V} \\ | & & | \\ (\text{'}\sigma & & \sigma) \end{array}$$

b. Shortening

$$\text{V} \longrightarrow \breve{\text{V}} \;/\; \begin{array}{ccc} \_\_ & \text{C}_0 & \text{V} \\ | & & | \\ (\text{'}\sigma & & \sigma) \end{array}$$

As evidence for the empirical correctness of circumstantial blocking and the incorrectness of applicational blocking in this case, Halle (1995: 28) points to the fact that the underlyingly long branching foot heads in words like (*'jōvi*)⟨*al*⟩ and *Shake*(*'spēāri*)⟨*an*⟩ are not subject to Shortening "even though Lengthening is not responsible for the long vowel in their stems." Thus what Halle (1995) intends to achieve with circumstantial blocking is for Shortening to be blocked by the presence of any long vowel in the environment of Lengthening, regardless of whether that vowel is specifically long due to the application of Lengthening.

The legitimacy of this argument crucially depends on the representation of length and the consequent character of the rules that manipulate this dimension of contrast. Briefly summarizing the more explanatory discussion to follow, the issue is this: a featural representation of length only requires circumstantial blocking if vacuous rule application does not 'count' as application for the purposes of applicational blocking; a prosodic representation of length, on the other hand,

31. Halle (1995: 27) cites Myers (1987) in connection with this statement of Shortening even though Myers (1987: 495ff) argues that the effects of Shortening follow from a resyllabification rule that closes a stressed syllable followed by an unstressed, nonextrametrical syllable, which feeds closed syllable shortening (which is not itself foot- or even stress-sensitive). Myers (1987: 510ff) ultimately derives both closed syllable shortening and its ordering with respect to resyllabification from the interaction of the English syllable template with universal principles of syllabification.

makes it possible to state Lengthening and Shortening as complementary insertion and deletion rules, respectively, necessitating circumstantial blocking.

Suppose first that length is represented by a feature like [±long]. The standard assumption behind (feature-changing) rules specifying a value of a feature to the right of the arrow is that they target foci with *either value* of the feature and change that value if necessary. Lengthening and Shortening would thus both be stated to apply to vowels of any length, as illustrated in (5.22).

(5.22) feature-changing-Lengthening and feature-changing-Shortening

a. feature-changing-Lengthening

$$\begin{bmatrix} \text{V} \\ -\text{high} \end{bmatrix} \longrightarrow [+\text{long}] \ / \ \begin{array}{ccc} \underline{\quad} & \text{C} \ i & \text{V} \\ | & & | \\ ({}^{\prime}\sigma & & \sigma) \end{array}$$

b. feature-changing-Shortening

$$\text{V} \longrightarrow [-\text{long}] \ / \ \begin{array}{ccc} \underline{\quad} & \text{C}_0 & \text{V} \\ | & & | \\ ({}^{\prime}\sigma & & \sigma) \end{array}$$

Now take a case like (*'jōvi*)⟨*al*⟩. Feature-changing-Lengthening may not be "responsible" for the length of the branching foot head because it is long to begin with, but the rule technically does apply, albeit vacuously, to the vowel in question. If vacuous application 'counts' as application — and there appears to be no reason to assume otherwise — then applicational blocking is sufficient to block feature-changing-Shortening and circumstantial blocking is unnecessary.[32]

Now assume instead the standard view, that vowel length distinctions are represented prosodically via association of a single vocalic element in the segmental melody either to (a) one vs. two skeletal slots (McCarthy 1979, 1981; Clements and Keyser 1983) or (b) one vs. two moras (McCawley 1968; Hyman 1985; Hayes 1989) on a separate tier between syllables and the melody.[33] Under this representational regime, Lengthening adds a skeletal slot or mora and associates it with an erstwhile short vowel, while Shortening removes (the association to) a skeletal slot or mora from an erstwhile long vowel. Lengthening and Shortening are thus complementary insertion and deletion rules, respectively, as illustrated more formally in (5.23); the moraic representation of length is arbitrarily adopted here.

---

32. See Bever (1967: 122–123) on the importance of vacuous application counting for blocking purposes. But it should be noted that although the standard assumption is that the rules in (5.22) should be stated as generally as possible, with no specification of length to the left of the arrow, there is in fact nothing that specifically *prevents* these rules from being stated to apply only to vowels to which they apply nonvacuously. (See §5.3 for further discussion of this point.) Note also that Kenstowicz (1994b: 218) states the rules in (5.21) as if they apply to vowels of any length, suggesting [±long], but moraic representations are defended later in the text (e.g. Kenstowicz 1994b: 291ff).

33. See Broselow (1995) and Perlmutter (1995) for comprehensive reviews of the literature on skeletal slots, moras, and the multiple association representation of quantity.

(5.23) Lengthening-as-insertion and Shortening-as-deletion

a. Lengthening-as-insertion   b. Shortening-as-deletion

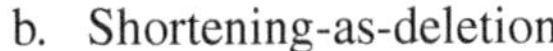

a. V C *i* V; [–high]; $\varnothing \longrightarrow \mu$ / μ — μ; ('σ σ)

b. V C_0 V; $\mu \longrightarrow \varnothing$ / μ — μ; ('σ σ)

Shortening-as-deletion is blocked from applying to forms like ('*jōvi*)⟨*al*⟩ because the long vowel in this case cannot have been made long by Lengthening-as-insertion, which specifically adds a mora only where there wasn't one before — it does not somehow vacuously rewrite one of two moras on an already long vowel.[34] But circumstantial blocking saves the day: the relevant substring *looks like* the output of a nonvacuous application of Lengthening-as-insertion.

Circumstantial blocking is in fact necessary for all complementary deletion and insertion rules. Recall from §5.3 the interaction between insertion and deletion of *r* in Eastern Massachusetts English as analyzed by Halle and Idsardi (1997); this case requires circumstantial blocking in order for insertion to correctly block deletion in the full range of cases. The rules are repeated in (5.24).

(5.24) Deletion and Insertion of *r* in E. Mass. English, repeated from (5.12)

a. Deletion   b. Insertion

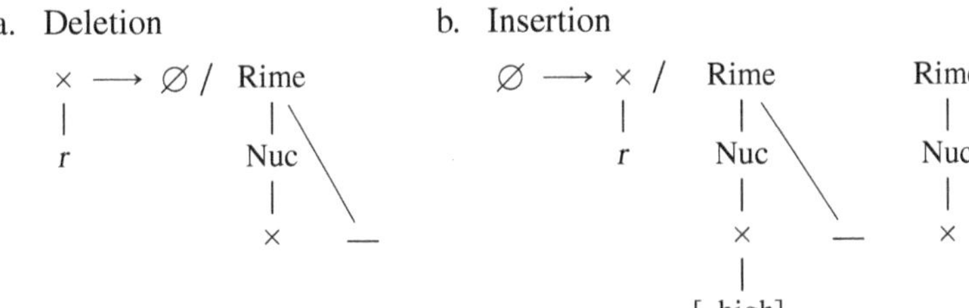

Halle and Idsardi (1997: 345) credit François Dell with noting that application of more general Deletion must be blocked not only if more specific Insertion has applied, but also if the output of Insertion just so happens to be present because it surfaces unchanged from the underlying representation (or, in principle, from any other potential source). The reason is that there are examples of word-final *r*s in the context of Insertion that are not deleted but that were certainly not inserted; i.e., the 'linking' (= underlying) *r* in e.g. *Homer arrived* as opposed to the 'intrusive' (= inserted) *r* in e.g. *Wandar arrived.* Since Insertion cannot possibly be stated so as to have applied, even vacuously, to forms with linking *r*, its application alone cannot suffice to block Deletion; the independent existence of

34. What if Lengthening-as-insertion were to try to add a *third* mora to an already long vowel? Such a move must be prevented either by something like the Linking Constraint of Hayes (1986: 331) — "[a]ssociation lines in structural descriptions are interpreted as exhaustive" — or by the imposition of a bimoraic maximum on syllables (see e.g. Prince 1980: 526). Given known implementational difficulties with the Linking Constraint and the independent utility of a bimoraic maximum in explaining closed syllable shortening in English and other languages, I assume the latter.

a form that *could have resulted* (but did not) from a nonvacuous application of Insertion must therefore also be able to block application of Deletion.

Circumstantial blocking thus appears to be absolutely necessary only in cases of complementary deletion and insertion rules, because such rules do not and cannot apply vacuously. One must ask whether things could be otherwise. If it just so happened that applicational rather than circumstantial blocking were correct, then we would expect complementary deletion and insertion rules to behave in a very different manner from other complementary rules. For example, intrusive *r* would exist but linking *r* would not: the *r* in *Homer arrived* would be deleted because it wasn't inserted, while the *r* in *Wandar arrived* would not be deleted because it couldn't be, having been inserted. This would contrast with e.g. the interaction between Harmony and Lowering in Brazilian Portuguese (see again below): since both are [±low]-affecting rules applying to vowels with either value of [±low], any substring matching the structural description of more specific Harmony will be blocked from undergoing more general Lowering even if the application of Harmony is vacuous. Empirically speaking, this is a perfectly plausible alternative state of affairs. The fact that complementary deletion and insertion rules behave just like other complementary rules in actuality is simply serendipitous, as well as a complete and very curious accident according to the EC.

The issue here is again the theme of this chapter: the choice between circumstantial and applicational blocking is theoretically arbitrary within *SPE*. Not so in OT, where the empirically correct consequences of circumstantial blocking unavoidably follow from how constraints evalutate candidates and how constraint conflicts are resolved. For example, both forms with underlying long vowels like (ˈ*jōvi*)⟨*al*⟩ and forms with lengthened vowels like *re*(ˈ*mēdi*)⟨*al*⟩ satisfy more specific CIV and violate more general TROCH equally; the ranking ⟦CIV ≫ TROCH⟧ thus ensures that both forms will surface with long vowels, 'blocking' the shortening effect of TROCH. More generally, satisfaction of any higher-ranked, more specific markedness constraint $\mathbb{S}$ takes priority over satisfaction of any lower-ranked, more general markedness constraint $\mathbb{G}$, causing the latter to be violated in all and only those cases where violation of the former is at stake.

Responding to a reviewer who asks whether circumstantial blocking "does not amount to a trans-derivational constraint", Halle and Idsardi (1997) are a little more explicit about what they assume circumstantial blocking requires.

> The reinterpretation of the Elsewhere Condition is not a trans-derivational constraint because no access to previous or subsequent representations in the derivation (or other derivations) is necessary. Rather, the application of a rule to the current representation is blocked in one particular circumstance—if the form is compatible with the structural description or change of a more specific rule. Thus, what is required is a limited access to the formal encodings of other rules... (Halle and Idsardi 1997: 346–347)

This "limited access to the formal encodings of other rules" is demonstrably insufficient for at least one class of examples, however — ones in which an additional rule crucially intervenes between $\mathcal{S}$ and $\mathcal{G}$; specifically, one that counterbleeds $\mathcal{S}$. Recall, for example, Harris's (1974) Brazilian Portuguese example discussed in §5.1. The rules and an illustrative derivation are repeated in (5.25) below. As illustrated in (5.25e), Harmony blocks Lowering even though Truncation intervenes, counterbleeding Harmony and thus making it such that the input to Lowering is *not*, in fact, "compatible with the structural description or change of" Harmony. Assuming for the sake of argument that this case is representative and that blocking does indeed obtain in situations like these, then circumstantial blocking will indeed require "access to previous or subsequent representations in the derivation" in order to block $\mathcal{G}$; for example, any representation prior to $\mathcal{G}$'s turn in the ordering that matches the structural description or change of $\mathcal{S}$.

(5.25) Brazilian Portuguese, repeated from (5.3), (5.4), and (5.6)

a. Harmony

$$\begin{bmatrix} \text{V} \\ \alpha\,\text{round} \\ \alpha\,\text{back} \end{bmatrix} \longrightarrow \begin{bmatrix} -\text{low} \\ \langle +\text{high} \rangle \end{bmatrix} / \,\text{—}\, C_0 \left[\begin{bmatrix} \text{V} \\ -\text{low} \\ \langle +\text{high} \rangle \end{bmatrix} \right]_{\text{Stem}} \text{V}\ldots \Big]_{\text{Verb}}$$

b. Lowering

$$\begin{bmatrix} \text{V} \\ +\text{stress} \\ \begin{Bmatrix} -\text{high} \\ +\text{E} \end{Bmatrix} \end{bmatrix} \longrightarrow [+\text{low}] / \,\text{—}\, C_0 \Big]_{\text{Root}} \ldots \Big]_{\text{Verb}}$$

c. Truncation

$$[[\text{X}\ \underset{\substack{\downarrow \\ \varnothing}}{\text{V}}]_{\text{St}}\ \text{V}\ \text{Y}]_{\text{Vb}}$$

d. Stress

$$\text{V} \longrightarrow [+\text{stress}] / \,\text{—}\, C_0 V C_0]_{\text{Verb}}$$

e. Truncation counterbleeds Harmony; Harmony still blocks Lowering

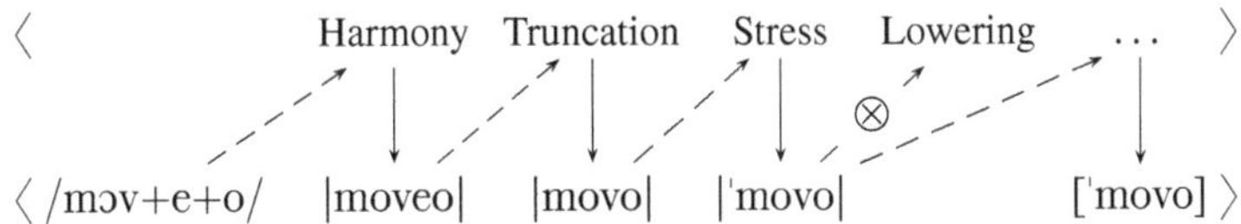

Even if this case is not representative, Halle and Idsardi (1997) seem to be splitting hairs pretty finely in the quotation above. The fact is that their characterization of circumstantial blocking is identical in all relevant respects to the definition of blocking that Goldsmith (1981, 1984a, b) requires for his analysis of Tonga, as discussed in §5.2.2: because $\mathcal{G}$ precedes $\mathcal{S}$ in Goldsmith's analysis, blocking of $\mathcal{G}$ must depend on whether "the form is compatible with the structural description or change of" $\mathcal{S}$ — that is, the exact same "limited access to the formal encodings of other rules" advocated now by Halle and Idsardi. But it was exactly this aspect of Goldsmith's definition of blocking that was denounced by Halle and Vergnaud (1982: 81) for entailing "far-reaching modifications in the algorithm for rule application" that "are not to be welcomed since they render the rules extremely powerful, for now whether or not a given rule applies to a given string no longer depends purely on the form of the string, but may also depend on what other rules might apply to that input string" — and these are precisely the sorts of properties of "trans-derivational constraints" that the reviewer in question is asking of Halle and Idsardi's crucial use of circumstantial blocking.

5.7 Concluding remarks

In this chapter I have identified several claims and assumptions of the EC that, in Prince and Smolensky's (1993: 119) words, "could very well be otherwise." This makes the EC something of a slippery principle, meaning that in at least some cases it might be easily circumvented via careful rule formulation. The EC needs to be more aggressive: pairs of rules that can be properly identified as being *potentially* related by the EC must be independently *made to be* related by the EC.

Perhaps something along the lines of the principle suggested by Chomsky (1967) and Chomsky and Halle (1968) is correct: that derivation length is minimized and disjunctive application is maximized. As noted in §3.3.5, there does indeed seem to be something to the idea that derivation length should be minimized, at least to the extent that (feeding) Duke of York derivations will thereby be avoided (McCarthy 1999b, 2003c) or, more generally, that rules that could undo each other's effects will thereby never apply to same element (Norton 2003). But as Norton (2003: 136–137) notes, the EC can at best only play a small role in this endeavor given that the EC's proper inclusion requirement leaves out all other cases of mutually undoing rules that apply in overlapping contexts (such as Nootka; recall §5.3). This point is also made by Pullum (1976), who writes:

> If it is to be required that no description contain an instance of the Duke of York gambit for any form generated, this will have to be accomplished by an *ad hoc* theoretical principle in the purely nonpejorative sense that the constraint will be set up for this special purpose. Independent constraints on the form of phonological descriptions will in some cases be in agreement with an anti-Duke of York principle and sometimes not. (Pullum 1976: 94)

The EC is clearly inadequate as an "anti-Duke of York principle". For one thing, the EC only lays claim to a fraction of the set of potential Duke of York derivations: those in which there is a proper inclusion relationship between structural descriptions. For another, the fact that the EC can be easily circumvented by careful rule formulation means that it does not even have a lock on that fraction.

OT, which eschews derivations, eschews Duke of York derivations *a fortiori*. Proper inclusion is not a prerequisite for constraint conflict in OT; only overlap is required. So one can reasonably ask whether the same issue alluded to above — that disjunctive application ($\approx$ constraint conflict) can be evaded via careful rule ($\approx$ constraint) formulation — also applies to OT, and the answer is that it does not. If conflicting constraints are formulated carefully enough to avoid overlap, then they will either not apply as intended in cases where they are independent of each other or they will simply apply in accidentally complementary contexts. Elsewhere interactions fall out directly from OT's basic architecture, following from it as a theorem. We finally turn our attention to this in the next chapter.

Chapter 6

The Elsewhere guarantee

(This is an oversimplified first cut at the true result; such claims must be stated carefully.)

Prince and Smolensky (1993: 88–89)

BECAUSE THE FOCUS OF THIS BOOK has been on disjunctive application, a phenomenon discussed mainly in the context of *SPE* assumptions, I have attempted to facilitate theory comparison by translating *SPE* rules into OT terms in a somewhat idealized way (recall §4.1): a rule corresponds relatively directly to an $[\![\mathbb{M} \gg \mathbb{F}]\!]$ ranking, where $\mathbb{M}$ corresponds to the structural description of the rule and $\mathbb{F}$ corresponds to the focal change effected by the rule. This idealization is maintained in this chapter through to the statement and proof of what I call the Elsewhere Theorem on Constraint-ranking. The ETC builds on Pāṇini's Theorem on Constraint-ranking (PTC; Prince and Smolensky 1993), and the proofs of both theorems underscore the fact that elsewhere interactions follow from the most basic assumptions of OT.

Another idealization that will be made here, following an idealization made implicitly in the literature on the EC, is that the specific and general mappings are only applicable to at most one focus per form. Prince and Smolensky (1993) also make this idealization explicit: citing "complexities surrounding the issue", the authors warn that they "will formally state and prove [PTC] only in the case of constraints which are Boolean at the whole-parse level: constraints which assign a single mark to an entire parse when they are violated, and no mark when they are satisfied" (Prince and Smolensky 1993: 89). I follow this lead, acknowledging the complexities and vowing to return to the issue in §6.4 below.

Because blocking is the norm in OT, PTC and the ETC do not somehow add disjunctive application to the descriptive possibilities of the theory in the way that the EC necessarily does for *SPE*, where the basic mode of rule interaction is conjunctive. So why bother to state and prove PTC and the ETC at all? A somewhat utilitarian answer is that "it allows the analyst to spot certain easy ranking arguments" (Prince and Smolensky 1993: 89). For the purposes of the overall argument of this book, the point is to demonstrate not only that it is possible to describe disjunctive application in OT — as we did in Chapter 4 — but also that the coexistence of a specific-general pair of incompatible mappings in a single grammar entails that the specific mapping blocks the general one when both are applicable. If such blocking does not obtain, it is because both mappings do not in fact coexist in the grammar. The intended effect of the EC is the same: it is meant to enforce disjunctive application between coexisting specific and general rules. The point of stating and proving PTC and the ETC is thus to show how this effect follows from the logic of OT without the need for any auxiliary statements.

6.1 Pāṇini's Theorem on Constraint-ranking

PTC describes a specific set of conditions under which a given constraint $\mathbb{S}$ is guaranteed to be INACTIVE with respect a particular class of candidate sets, purely as a function of a precise formal relationship between $\mathbb{S}$ and another constraint $\mathbb{G}$. Intuitively — and as already revealed in the place-holding names given to these hypothetical constraints — $\mathbb{S}$ must be more specific than (and must conflict with) $\mathbb{G}$. The details of this formal relationship and of the particular class of candidate sets for which inactivity of $\mathbb{S}$ is guaranteed are discussed in this section.

First we must define constraint activity. Informally, a constraint is active on an input if it crucially rules out some candidate output(s) competing for optimality. Prince and Smolensky (1993: 89, 119) offer this more formal definition.

(6.1) Dfn. **Active.**

> Let $\mathbb{C}$ be a constraint in a constraint hierarchy $\mathbb{CH}$ and let i be an input. $\mathbb{C}$ is active on i in $\mathbb{CH}$ if $\mathbb{C}$ separates the candidates in Gen(i) which are admitted by the portion of $\mathbb{CH}$ which dominates $\mathbb{C}$.

A few clarifications are in order here. First, 'Gen(i)' refers to the candidate set associated with (= generated from) the input i. Second, $\mathbb{C}$ *separates* a set of candidates if there are at least two candidates in the set that are distinguished by $\mathbb{C}$ (one satisfies $\mathbb{C}$ and the other violates it, or one violates $\mathbb{C}$ more than the other). Finally, a candidate is *admitted* by a (portion of a) constraint hierarchy if it performs no worse on that (portion of the) hierarchy than any competing candidates.[1]

For $\mathbb{C}$ to be *inactive* on a particular input i, then, $\mathbb{C}$ must not distinguish among candidates in the subset of Gen(i) that is not already filtered out by higher-ranked constraints. Or, as Prince and Smolensky themselves clarify,

> the portion of $\mathbb{CH}$ which dominates $\mathbb{C}$ filters the set of candidate parses of i to some degree, and then $\mathbb{C}$ filters it further. When $\mathbb{C}$ is not active for an input i in $\mathbb{CH}$, the result of parsing i is not at all affected by the presence of $\mathbb{C}$ in the hierarchy. (Prince and Smolensky 1993: 89)

With these preliminaries out of the way, we can proceed with discussion of the conditions described by PTC guaranteeing constraint inactivity.

1. Prince and Smolensky (1993: 89) actually define the term 'accepts' this way, but use 'admitted' in the same sense for the purposes of the definition of constraint activity reproduced in (6.1). And, as Vieri Samek-Lodovici (p.c.) points out, the set of candidates that are admitted/accepted by a portion $\mathbb{P}$ of a hierarchy is the set of candidates that are *optimal* according to $\mathbb{P}$.

6.1.1 Pāṇinian constraint relation

Prince and Smolensky (1993: 90, 119) offer the following formal definition of the relationship which must hold between $\mathbb{S}$ and $\mathbb{G}$ in order for inactivity of $\mathbb{S}$ to be guaranteed under the remaining conditions to be defined further below.

(6.2) Dfn. **Pāṇinian Constraint Relation**

> Let $\mathbb{S}$ and $\mathbb{G}$ be two constraints. $\mathbb{S}$ stands to $\mathbb{G}$ as special [= *specific*] to general in a Pāṇinian relation if, for any input *i* to which $\mathbb{S}$ applies non-vacuously, any parse of *i* which satisfies $\mathbb{S}$ fails [= *violates*] $\mathbb{G}$.

And again, a couple of clarifications are in order. First, this definition technically does not require that $\mathbb{S}$ *be more specific than* $\mathbb{G}$; it only requires that $\mathbb{S}$ *not be more general than* $\mathbb{G}$. Awareness of this technicality is useful in illustrating what is probably the most straightforward type of example that PTC has something to say about: conflict between two constraints that are diametrically opposed to each other (Prince 1997c, 1998, 2000). For example, suppose that $\mathbb{M}$:NO-CODA, demanding that syllables end in vowels, has an evil twin $\mathbb{M}$:YES-CODA demanding that syllables end in consonants. These constraints stand in a Pāṇinian relation regardless of which is considered $\mathbb{S}$ and which is considered $\mathbb{G}$, because nonvacuous satisfaction of either constraint (= $\mathbb{S}$) entails violation of the other (= $\mathbb{G}$).[2]

The other clarification concerns the notion 'nonvacuous application'. Prince and Smolensky define it like this: "$\mathbb{C}$ *applies non-vacuously* to an input *i* if it separates Gen(*i*)"; in other words, "if some of the parses of [*i*] violate [$\mathbb{C}$] while others satisfy it" (Prince and Smolensky 1993: 89 and 119, original emphasis). Note that nonvacuous application is a special case of activity.[3] The difference is that the activity of a constraint is assessed relative to a hierarchy in which the constraint is embedded, with some other constraints assumed to be ranked above it, while the nonvacuous application of a constraint is assessed independently of other constraints. A Pāṇinian relation is thus established between two constraints regardless of what other constraints may exist and regardless of what the ranking of the two constraints may be with respect to other constraints (or to each other). As I argue in §6.2 below, however, complete ignorance of the rest of the hierarchy is insufficient; we must consider a stricter and more accurate prerequisite than nonvacuous application of $\mathbb{S}$ for the purposes of establishing the right kind of relatedness between $\mathbb{S}$ and $\mathbb{G}$. In the meantime, we proceed with the understanding that the nonvacuous application prerequisite is sufficient for at least some types of constraints that might be considered in place of $\mathbb{S}$ in (6.2).

6.1.2 Proving the theorem

Armed with an understanding of the definitions of constraint activity and Pāṇinian relatedness, we are now in a position to tackle PTC itself. The statement of the theorem from Prince and Smolensky (1993: 90, 119, 241) is reproduced in (6.3).

2. See §6.2.2 for explanation of why it must be '*nonvacuous* satisfaction' here.
3. I thank Vieri Samek-Lodovici for discussion of this point.

(6.3) **Pāṇini's Theorem on Constraint-ranking** (PTC)

> Let $\mathbb{S}$ and $\mathbb{G}$ stand as specific to general in a Pāṇinian relation. Suppose these constraints are part of a constraint hierarchy $\mathbb{CH}$, and that $\mathbb{G}$ is active in $\mathbb{CH}$ on some input *i*. Then, if $\mathbb{G} \gg \mathbb{S}$, $\mathbb{S}$ is not active on *i*.

The following is a proof of PTC, more compactly paraphrasing the equivalent proof offered by Prince and Smolensky (1993: 241).

> For $\mathbb{G}$ to be active in $\mathbb{CH}$ on *i*, $\mathbb{G}$ must distinguish among the candidates that are still in the running for optimality after Gen(*i*) has already been filtered through the portion of $\mathbb{CH}$ ranked above $\mathbb{G}$. This means that some of these candidates satisfy $\mathbb{G}$ and others violate $\mathbb{G}$. Only those that satisfy $\mathbb{G}$ survive, and some or all of them make it to $\mathbb{S}$ (depending on the presence and content of constraints in between). Since all of these candidates satisfy $\mathbb{G}$, they must all violate $\mathbb{S}$ — for if any of them satisfied $\mathbb{S}$ they would violate $\mathbb{G}$, by the definition of Pāṇinian relatedness. $\mathbb{S}$ is thus not active on *i*, as stated by PTC. □

And yet again, a clarification is in order. The wording of the final clause of PTC — "$\mathbb{S}$ is not active on *i*" — is more parochial than the advertised result of the theorem, that $\mathbb{S}$ is not active on *any input*: "the more specific constraint must dominate the more general one in order for it to have *any visible effects in the grammar*" (Prince and Smolensky 1993: 88, emphasis added). The issue is with the key restrictor on the result of PTC: the proviso that "$\mathbb{G}$ is active in $\mathbb{CH}$ on *i*", which sets aside inputs on which $\mathbb{G}$ is itself inactive. $\mathbb{G}$ can be inactive for either of two reasons: (i) the candidates that survive filtering by the higher-ranked portion of $\mathbb{CH}$ all satisfy $\mathbb{G}$, or (ii) they all violate $\mathbb{G}$.

The first class of situations simply takes a shorter path to the same PTC conclusion. Since all of the relevant candidates satisfy $\mathbb{G}$, they must all violate $\mathbb{S}$ — for if any of them satisfied $\mathbb{S}$ they would violate $\mathbb{G}$, by the definition of Pāṇinian relatedness. $\mathbb{S}$ is thus also not active in this class of situations.

This leaves the second class of situations, in which the relevant candidates all violate $\mathbb{G}$. The definition of Pāṇinian relatedness does not say anything about $\mathbb{S}$ given violation of $\mathbb{G}$, and so $\mathbb{S}$ can in principle be active in this class of situations. In order to demonstrate inactivity of $\mathbb{S}$, either (a) there can be no situation in which the portion of $\mathbb{CH}$ above $\mathbb{G}$ passes down only candidates that violate $\mathbb{G}$, or (b) candidates that violate $\mathbb{G}$ cannot be distinguished by $\mathbb{S}$ for independent reasons. On the face of it, (a) is implausible: there's little that can be done to guarantee that all possible higher-ranked portions of $\mathbb{CH}$ will pass down at least one candidate that satisfies $\mathbb{G}$. So we proceed with consideration of (b).

What we are interested in knowing is if there are any situations in which a set of candidates that all violate $\mathbb{G}$ can be separated by $\mathbb{S}$. By the definition of Pāṇinian relatedness, it is possible for at least some of the candidates in this set to satisfy $\mathbb{S}$. The question thus boils down to whether any of the candidates in the set can violate $\mathbb{S}$ — and the only possible answer is that, in principle, yes. But it is unclear what the practical consequences of this fact are, especially in terms of the cases of disjunctive application that are of immediate interest in this book. The markedness constraints that we assume here to directly substitute for the structural descriptions of rules that can be related by the EC always conflict in such a way that violation of the markedness constraint corresponding to the structural description of the more general rule consistently entails satisfaction of the markedness constraint corresponding to the structural description of the more specific rule. Whatever relation we choose to establish between the markedness constraints corresponding to the structural descriptions of specific and general rules will thus have to reflect this fact. Since we have already independently determined that Pāṇinian relatedness is insufficient for our purposes, we turn now to an examination of that insufficiency and to the kind of relatedness that we need to define in order to talk about the cases of interest in this book.

6.2 Elsewhere relatedness

The definition of Pāṇinian relatedness in (6.2) is insufficient for our purposes in two specific ways. First, the prerequisite that $\mathbb{S}$ 'apply nonvacuously' does not take into account the standard OT assumption that candidate sets are INCLUSIVE — that is, that Gen(i) is "a large space of candidate analyses [obtained] by freely exercising the basic structural resources of the representational theory" (Prince and Smolensky 1993: 6). The problem here is that there are inputs to which $\mathbb{S}$ applies nonvacuously but whose inclusive candidate sets include candidates that are bound to satisfy both $\mathbb{S}$ and $\mathbb{G}$, precisely the state of affairs that is supposed to be impossible if $\mathbb{S}$ stands to $\mathbb{G}$ as specific to general in a Pāṇinian relation.

The second insufficiency is the one-sidedness of the definition: satisfaction of $\mathbb{S}$ entails violation of $\mathbb{G}$ (and conversely, satisfaction of $\mathbb{G}$ entails violation of $\mathbb{S}$) but nothing is entailed either by violation of $\mathbb{S}$ nor by violation of $\mathbb{G}$. In particular, the definition allows for $\mathbb{S}$ and $\mathbb{G}$ to both be violated by a given candidate, leaving open a narrow but real possibility that $\mathbb{S}$ can be active even when outranked by $\mathbb{G}$.

I address these two insufficiencies of the definition of Pāṇinian relatedness in this section, resulting in the definition of what I call the ELSEWHERE MAPPING RELATION which forms the basis of the proof of the ETC in §6.3.

6.2.1 Nonvacuous application

We begin with the observation that the "for any input i to which $\mathbb{S}$ applies nonvacuously" part of the definition of a Pāṇinian constraint relation in (6.2) means that for the purposes of establishing Pāṇinian relatedness between two constraints $\mathbb{S}$ and $\mathbb{G}$, inputs for which the candidate set consists entirely of candidates that satisfy $\mathbb{S}$ or entirely of candidates that violate $\mathbb{S}$ are ignored. Two obvious questions emerge from this observation: are either of these scenarios even possible? and if so, what is the reason for ignoring them?

Let us first address the question of possibility. We can quickly dispense with scenarios in which the candidate set generated from some input uniformly violates $\mathbb{S}$: given a candidate γ that violates $\mathbb{S}$, we can always generate another candidate κ that is just like γ except that the violation of $\mathbb{S}$ is removed (likely adding violations of other constraints, of course, but this consequence is irrelevant here).

Given the standard inclusiveness assumption of OT noted above, every candidate set is bound to include candidates like κ. Alternative architectures for OT may of course differ on this point (see McCarthy 2002: 163ff); for example, stratal architectures (Kiparsky forthcoming; Bermúdez-Otero forthcoming) and specifically less inclusive candidate set generator models (Wilson 2000 et seq., McCarthy 2007b et seq.) both make it more likely that sensible constraints might not separate a given candidate set.[4] But this is by no means guaranteed: whether or not a given constraint separates a given candidate set must still be determined case by case. If there are scenarios in which 𝕊 applies vacuously to some input *i*, then, it is highly unlikely that it will be because all candidates in Gen(*i*) *violate* 𝕊.

It thus remains to be seen whether it is possible for all candidates in Gen(*i*) to *satisfy* 𝕊. Again, given inclusiveness, every one of a wide swath of constraint types is expected to separate virtually every possible candidate set, even if only trivially. This is especially obvious in the case of standard markedness constraints. For example, an inclusive candidate set for any input is bound to include candidates with syllable-final consonants and candidates without; for every input *i*, then, 𝕄:NO-CODA applies nonvacuously to Gen(*i*). The same is true of standard faithfulness constraints penalizing any kind of insertion — the 𝔽:DEP-*x* family of constraints (McCarthy and Prince 1995, 1999) — because an inclusive candidate set will always include candidates with insertions of various kinds. If 𝕊 is a member of one of these two significant classes of constraints, then, no inputs can be ignored for the purposes of establishing Pāṇinian relatedness with some 𝔾.

Standard markedness constraints and DEP-*x* faithfulness constraints share the fact that a violation of either type of constraint makes at most only trivial presuppositions about the input. Standard markedness constraints of course make no reference at all to the input. DEP-*x* constraints do refer to the input, but the only presupposition that a violation of DEP-*x* makes is a trivial one: that for every violation of the constraint by a candidate, there is one instance of *x* in that candidate that does not correspond to an *x* in the input. Candidates with violations of both of these constraint types can thus be added at will to any candidate set.

Violations of standard faithfulness constraints other than those that penalize insertion *do* make nontrivial presuppositions about the input, however, and these constraints thus behave differently. For example, consider constraints penalizing any kind of deletion (the 𝔽:MAX-*x* family) or constraints penalizing feature value changes (the 𝔽:IDENT(*f*) family): a violation of 𝔽:MAX-*x* presupposes that the input has at least one instance of *x* to delete, and a violation of 𝔽:IDENT(*f*) presupposes that the input has at least one instance of *f* to change.[5] A candidate set generated from any input that does not meet the violation presuppositions of one of these constraints, then, will uniformly satisfy the constraint.

More generally, any constraint that makes nontrivial violation presuppositions about the input will be VACUOUSLY SATISFIED by all candidates generated from inputs that do not meet those presuppositions. In fact, this is how the example that Prince and Smolensky (1993) discuss in depth under the rubric of PTC fits

4. See now also Blaho et al. (2007) for challenges to inclusiveness (*a.k.a.* 'freedom of analysis').
5. If featural faithfulness involves 𝔽:MAX-*f* and 𝔽:DEP-*f* constraints, then these will naturally have the same kinds of violation presuppositions as 𝔽:MAX-*x* and 𝔽:DEP-*x* constraints, respectively.

the definition of Pāṇinian relatedness in (6.2). The 𝕊 constraint in that case is the nonstandard markedness constraint 𝕄:FREE-V, "[w]ord-final vowels must not be parsed (in the nominative)" (Prince and Smolensky 1993: 111).[6] 𝕄:FREE-V is vacuously satisfied by all candidates generated from inputs that are not nominatives as well as those generated from inputs with final consonants, and so those inputs must be ignored for the purposes of establishing Pāṇinian relatedness between 𝕄:FREE-V and the more general anti-deletion constraint 𝔽:PARSE.

We've thus answered the question of possibility in the affirmative: there are some inputs the candidates sets of which are not separated by at least some constraints; specifically, constraints for which violation makes nontrivial presuppositions about the input, and inputs that do not meet those presuppositions. These constraints are vacuously satisfied by all candidates generated from those inputs. The remaining question then is: what is the reason for ignoring such inputs for the purposes of establishing Pāṇinian relatedness? The answer is now simple: if such inputs are *not* ignored, then the fact that every one of the candidates in the set vacuously satisfies 𝕊 means that they would all have to violate 𝔾 in order for 𝕊 to stand to 𝔾 as specific to general in a Pāṇinian relation — but as we've seen, uniform violation of *any* constraint by an entire candidate set is not possible!

6.2.2 Vacuous and irrelevant satisfaction

So it may be necessary to ignore candidate sets made up entirely of candidates that vacuously satisfy 𝕊 — but if so, is this *sufficient* for the purposes of establishing 𝕊-to-𝔾 relatedness? The answer is no, for the simple reason that even constraints that make trivial violation presuppositions can be satisfied vacuously by some candidates. More specifically: even if 𝕊 applies nonvacuously to some input *i*, it may still be the case that Gen(*i*) contains some candidates that vacuously satisfy both 𝕊 and 𝔾 because of a (shared) nontrivial presupposition that each of the constraints makes *about output candidates*. By the definition in (6.2), a Pāṇinian relation cannot be established between 𝕊 and 𝔾 under this scenario — which is common enough given otherwise obvious contenders for 𝕊 and 𝔾 that it requires redefining the conditions for establishing the relevant relation between 𝕊 and 𝔾.

Consider, for example, 𝕄:NO-CODA and 𝕄:YES-CODA. As noted in §6.1.1, these constraints stand in a Pāṇinian relation regardless of which is considered 𝕊 and which is considered 𝔾, because *nonvacuous satisfaction* of either constraint (= 𝕊) entails violation of the other (= 𝔾). The reason why satisfaction of 𝕊 must be nonvacuous is because 𝕄:NO-CODA and 𝕄:YES-CODA share a nontrivial presupposition about output candidates: *a candidate must contain a syllable* in order for it to be determined that it ends in a consonant (and thus violating 𝕄:NO-CODA) or that it ends in a vowel (and thus violating 𝕄:YES-CODA). Candidates without syllables thus vacuously satisfy both constraints, flying in the face of their supposed (and desired) Pāṇinian relatedness. There are countless situations in which two constraints 𝕊 and 𝔾 that might otherwise stand as specific to general in a Pāṇinian relation fail to do so simply due to the existence of candid-

6. I classify this constraint as a nonstandard markedness constraint in the text, but it might be more accurately classified as an *antifaithfulness* constraint (Alderete 2001; Horwood 2001).

ates that vacuously satisfy both $\mathbb{S}$ and $\mathbb{G}$ in this way. In the case at hand we could perhaps point to the presumed absurdity of candidates lacking syllables, and this strategy may work in many other such cases. But the problem is more general, going beyond the immediate issue of purely vacuous satisfaction.

This can be appreciated by recalling the $\mathbb{S}$/$\mathbb{G}$ pair of constraints discussed in §4.2, $\mathbb{M}$:NO-VbV (= $\mathbb{S}$) and $\mathbb{M}$:NO-β (= $\mathbb{G}$). The problem in this case is that candidate sets are bound to include candidates with no voiced obstruents whatsoever, even if there are voiced obstruents in the inputs to those candidate sets — for instance, due to deletion or devoicing. Such candidates are not at all absurd, and they are guaranteed to satisfy both $\mathbb{M}$:NO-VbV and $\mathbb{M}$:NO-β. Significantly, neither of these instances of constraint satisfaction is vacuous. However, there is an important sense in which they are both IRRELEVANT, given the *a priori* constraint rankings that must hold in order to describe each of the mappings driven by $\mathbb{M}$:NO-VbV and $\mathbb{M}$:NO-β. Specifically, it is already given that the demands of $\mathbb{M}$:NO-VbV and $\mathbb{M}$:NO-β are best satisfied by changes in [±cont] in the grammar in question; that is, that $\mathbb{M}$:NO-VbV, $\mathbb{M}$:NO-β, $\mathbb{F}$:MAX-C (penalizing deletion) and $\mathbb{F}$:IDENT(voi) (penalizing changes in voicing) all outrank $\mathbb{F}$:IDENT(cont).[7]

Requiring nonvacuous application of $\mathbb{S}$ on i is thus not sufficient for establishing $\mathbb{S}$-to-$\mathbb{G}$ relatedness between many desired instances of $\mathbb{S}$ and $\mathbb{G}$. First, the problem of vacuous satisfaction makes clear that satisfaction of $\mathbb{S}$ needn't entail violation of $\mathbb{G}$, and so the problem is in the antecedent requirement of the definition of Pāṇinian relatedness that $\mathbb{S}$ be satisfied. Second, the problem of irrelevant satisfaction makes clear that the interaction between individual markedness constraints $\mathbb{S}$ and $\mathbb{G}$ is secondary to the interaction between the relevant *mappings* that are preferred by those markedness constraints within the grammar. This of course brings us closer to a direct comparison with the EC, which aims to describe the necessary interaction between two rules (= preferred mappings) $\mathcal{S}$ and $\mathcal{G}$.

6.2.3 Allowance

This is where we need the definition of *allowance*, introduced briefly in §4.1.5. Very loosely speaking, a candidate is allowed by an $[\![\mathbb{M} \gg \mathbb{F}]\!]$ ranking if it is not distinct from the structural change defined by the rule that corresponds to the $[\![\mathbb{M} \gg \mathbb{F}]\!]$ ranking. In order to guarantee this, reference must be made not only to the $[\![\mathbb{M} \gg \mathbb{F}]\!]$ ranking but also to other conflicting faithfulness constraints that might prefer distinct structural changes. Allowance is thus defined as follows.[8]

7. A parallel point can of course be made with the BCD $\mathbb{S}$/$\mathbb{G}$ constraint pair discussed in §4.3, $\mathbb{M}$:CIV (= $\mathbb{S}$) and $\mathbb{M}$:TROCH (= $\mathbb{G}$). Candidate sets are bound to include candidates with no branching feet whatsoever; such candidates are not at all absurd, they satisfy both constraints nonvacuously, and the demands of these constraints are best satisfied by changes in vowel length via violation of IDENT(long). Other ways of satisfying these markedness constraints are thus also irrelevant.
8. I continue to assume here that (i) candidates may violate constraints at most once each (see §6.4), and (ii) any other constraints conflicting with $\mathbb{M}$ are ranked in such a way that they coincide with the independently established preferences of the conflicting faithfulness constraints $\mathbb{F}$ and $\mathbb{F}'$.

(6.4) Dfn. **Allowance**

Let $\mathbb{M}$ be a markedness constraint that conflicts with a faithfulness constraint $\mathbb{F}$, let $\mathbb{F}'$ be all other faithfulness constraints that conflict with both $\mathbb{M}$ and $\mathbb{F}$, and let i be an input and Gen(i) its associated candidate set. A candidate $\Sigma \in$ Gen(i) is *allowed* by $[\![\{\mathbb{M}, \mathbb{F}'\} \gg \mathbb{F}]\!]$ iff

a. $\mathbb{M}(\Sigma) = \varnothing$ (i.e., Σ satisfies $\mathbb{M}$), and

b. $\forall \Sigma' \in \text{Gen}(i)$ s.t. $\mathbb{F}(\Sigma') \neq \mathbb{F}(\Sigma)$ and $\mathbb{F}'(\Sigma') = \mathbb{F}'(\Sigma)$, $\mathbb{M}(\Sigma') \neq \mathbb{M}(\Sigma)$.

This definition identifies a specific subset of candidates that satisfy $\mathbb{M}$ (6.4a): those that do so *by virtue of* their performance on $\mathbb{F}$ (6.4b), thus establishing nondistinctness with the corresponding rule's structural change. This latter part of the definition compares the candidate of interest, Σ, with every other candidate Σ' that differs minimally from Σ. Σ' is defined by three comparisons with Σ. The first comparison establishes a difference in terms of $\mathbb{F}$-violation profiles: if Σ violates $\mathbb{F}$ then Σ' satisfies $\mathbb{F}$ and if Σ satisfies $\mathbb{F}$ then Σ' violates $\mathbb{F}$. The second comparison ensures that this difference is minimal in terms of $\mathbb{F}'$-violation profiles: if Σ violates $\mathbb{F}'$ then Σ' also violates $\mathbb{F}'$ and if Σ satisfies $\mathbb{F}'$ then Σ' also satisfies $\mathbb{F}'$. Finally, every such Σ' must also differ from Σ in terms of its $\mathbb{M}$-violation profile; since (6.4a) already states that Σ satisfies $\mathbb{M}$, then Σ' must violate $\mathbb{M}$.

The main purpose of this condition is to ensure that Σ's satisfaction of $\mathbb{M}$ is not irrelevant — loosely speaking again, that it is not distinct from the structural change defined by the rule that corresponds to $[\![\mathbb{M} \gg \mathbb{F}]\!]$. If Σ satisfies $\mathbb{M}$ and violates $\mathbb{F}$, then Σ is allowed only if any attempt to minimally remove the violation of $\mathbb{F}$ from Σ would result in a candidate Σ' that violates $\mathbb{M}$.[9] A schematic example may help at this point. Consider the ranking $[\![\{\mathbb{M}$:No-β, $\mathbb{F}'$:Ident(voi)$\}$ $\gg \mathbb{F}$:Ident(cont)$]\!]$ in (6.5). Given the input /β/, the third candidate *b* is allowed (as indicated by '★') because any attempt to remove its violation of $\mathbb{F}$:Ident(cont) leads either to violation $\mathbb{M}$:No-β (the first candidate, *β*) or to a nonminimal change involving violation of $\mathbb{F}'$:Ident(voi) (the second candidate, *p*).

(6.5) Unfaithful allowance illustrated

/β/	$\mathbb{M}$:No-β	$\mathbb{F}'$:Ident(voi)	$\mathbb{F}$:Ident(cont)
β	* !		
p		* !	
★ b			*

This exemplifies a situation where the candidate allowed by $[\![\mathbb{M} \gg \mathbb{F}]\!]$ involves violation of $\mathbb{F}$. But allowance by $[\![\mathbb{M} \gg \mathbb{F}]\!]$ can also involve satisfaction of $\mathbb{F}$: in such a case, Σ is allowed by $[\![\mathbb{M} \gg \mathbb{F}]\!]$ only if any attempt to minimally *add* a violation of $\mathbb{F}$ to Σ would result in a candidate Σ' that violates $\mathbb{M}$. This is illustrated in the tableau in (6.6) below. Given the input /b/, $\mathbb{M}$:No-β is still satisfied by *b*,

9. This condition thus makes use of the *Method of Mark Eliminability* (Prince and Smolensky 1993: 127): "To show that a particular analysis is optimal, consider each of its marks *m*, and show that any way of changing the analysis to eliminate *m* results in at least one worse mark."

but this candidate in this case also satisfies 𝔽:IDENT(cont). Now this candidate is allowed because any attempt to add a violation of 𝔽:IDENT(cont) either violates 𝕄:NO-β or is nonminimal, violating 𝔽′:IDENT(voi).

(6.6) Faithful allowance illustrated

/b/	𝕄:NO-β	𝔽′:IDENT(voi)	𝔽:IDENT(cont)
β	* !		*
p		* !	*
★ b			

Defining allowance in terms of both unfaithful (6.5) and faithful (6.6) mappings is thus necessary because the path to optimal 𝕄-satisfaction may or may not involve 𝔽-deviation. The fact that blocking is circumstantial as opposed to applicational (recall §5.6) is of course related to this fact: blocking of an ⟦𝕄 ≫ 𝔽⟧ ranking entails ruling out candidates allowed by ⟦𝕄 ≫ 𝔽⟧, a state of affairs that can be achieved regardless of whether 𝔽 is violated or satisfied.[10]

There is in fact one more idealization made in the definition of allowance in (6.4) that must be addressed here, if only briefly. The definition presupposes that the candidates being compared differ only in terms of strictly binary feature specifications (whether +/– or present/absent), but this is of course not the only way in which relevant candidates may differ. I put aside here the possibility that features may have more than two values — a possibility that has not been particularly relevant to any of the examples discussed in this book — and focus instead on the fact that relevant candidates may also differ in terms of deletion and insertion.

Another schematic example constructed along the lines of the example above will clarify the limits of this idealization. Consider the ranking ⟦{𝕄:NO-CODA, 𝔽′:DEP-V} ≫ 𝔽:MAX-C⟧ in (6.7) below. Given the input /CVC/, the third candidate *CV* is allowed because any attempt to remove its violation of 𝔽:MAX-C leads either to violation of 𝕄:NO-CODA (the first candidate, *CVC*) or to a nonminimal change involving violation of 𝔽′:DEP-V (the second candidate, *CV.CV*).

(6.7) Unfaithful deletion allowance illustrated

/CVC/	𝕄:NO-CODA	𝔽′:DEP-V	𝔽:MAX-C
CVC	* !		
CV.CV		* !	
★ CV			*

Now consider the input /CV/ in (6.8). 𝕄:NO-CODA is still satisfied by *CV*, but in this case there is no deletion; 𝔽:MAX-C is also satisfied. This candidate

10. Blocking of ⟦𝕄 ≫ 𝔽⟧ can also be achieved regardless of whether 𝕄 is violated or satisfied by the ultimately optimal candidate. If 𝕄 is violated, then we have blocking of ⟦𝕄 ≫ 𝔽⟧ *tout court*; if 𝕄 is violated, then we have blocking of ⟦𝕄 ≫ 𝔽⟧ and triggering of another, ⟦𝕄 ≫ 𝔽′⟧ ranking instead. This is how the analysis of a conspiracy works in OT (see e.g. McCarthy 2002: 95ff).

should also be allowed in this case, but there can be no relevant attempt to *add* a violation of 𝔽:MAX-C such that the result will either violate 𝕄:NO-CODA or be nonminimal. In order to bring this type of case under the fold of allowance, then, we must somehow pair each 𝔽:MAX-*x* with its 𝔽:DEP-*x* counterpart such that a violation is added to the latter constraint for the purposes of faithful allowance.

(6.8) Faithful deletion allowance illustrated

/CV/	𝕄:NO-CODA	𝔽′:DEP-V	𝔽:MAX-C	𝔽:DEP-C
CVC	*!			*
CV.CV		*!		*
★ CV				

The definition of allowance must be amended to accommodate deletion and insertion and their corresponding faithfulness constraints. Rather than pursuing this more accurate definition here, however, we simply acknowledge the issue and move on to consider how allowance is used to establish Elsewhere relatedness.

6.2.4 Elsewhere mapping relation

The definition of allowance just established makes it possible to address our two remaining problems with the definition of Pāṇinian relatedness. One is the vacuous satisfaction problem, that satisfaction of 𝕊 isn't guaranteed to entail violation of 𝔾. The other is the one-sidedness insufficiency problem noted at the outset of this section: 𝕊 and 𝔾 can in principle both be violated by a given candidate.

These problems are both resolved in the definition of Elsewhere relatedness in (6.9) below. First, the excessively inclusive set of candidates that satisfy 𝕊 is replaced by the more appropriately restricted set of candidates that are allowed by the mapping-defining ranking ⟦𝕊 ≫ $\mathbb{F}_{\mathbb{S}}$⟧, thus avoiding the vacuous satisfaction problem. Second, the restrictiveness of the set of candidates defined by allowance permits a symmetrical definition whereby a candidate cannot violate both 𝕊 and 𝔾, thus avoiding the one-sidedness insufficiency problem.

(6.9) Dfn. **Elsewhere mapping relation**

Let ⟦𝕊 ≫ $\mathbb{F}_{\mathbb{S}}$⟧ and ⟦𝔾 ≫ $\mathbb{F}_{\mathbb{G}}$⟧ be two ⟦𝕄 ≫ 𝔽⟧ rankings. ⟦𝕊 ≫ $\mathbb{F}_{\mathbb{S}}$⟧ stands to ⟦𝔾 ≫ $\mathbb{F}_{\mathbb{G}}$⟧ as specific to general in an Elsewhere relation iff

a. any candidate which is allowed by ⟦𝕊 ≫ $\mathbb{F}_{\mathbb{S}}$⟧ violates 𝔾, and
b. any candidate which violates 𝕊 is allowed by ⟦𝔾 ≫ $\mathbb{F}_{\mathbb{G}}$⟧.

Again, a schematic example will help to clarify. Suppose 𝕊 = 𝕄:NO-VbV, 𝔾 = 𝕄:NO-β, and $\mathbb{F}_{\mathbb{S}}$ = $\mathbb{F}_{\mathbb{G}}$ = 𝔽:IDENT(cont). ⟦𝕄:NO-VbV ≫ 𝔽:IDENT(cont)⟧ stands to ⟦𝕄:NO-β ≫ 𝔽:IDENT(cont)⟧ as specific to general in an Elsewhere relation because they meet the two conditions in (6.9): (a) any candidate which violates 𝕄:NO-VbV is allowed by ⟦𝕄:NO-β ≫ 𝔽:IDENT(cont)⟧ — *VbV* violates 𝕄:NO-VbV, and as we saw in (6.5) and (6.6), all candidates with *b* are allowed by ⟦𝕄:NO-β ≫ 𝔽:IDENT(cont)⟧ — and (b) any candidate which is allowed by ⟦𝕄:NO-VbV ≫ 𝔽:IDENT(cont)⟧ — namely, *VβV* — violates 𝕄:NO-β.

6.3 The Elsewhere Theorem on Constraint-ranking

We are now almost in a position to state and prove the theorem that guarantees that in order for the mappings defined by $[\![\mathbb{G} \gg \mathbb{F}_{\mathbb{G}}]\!]$ and $[\![\mathbb{S} \gg \mathbb{F}_{\mathbb{S}}]\!]$ to coexist in a grammar, it must be the case that $[\![\mathbb{S} \gg \mathbb{G}]\!]$. The final piece of the puzzle is to define the 'existence' of an $[\![\mathbb{M} \gg \mathbb{F}]\!]$ ranking in a grammar as its OPERATIVENESS.

(6.10) Dfn. **Operativeness**

Let $[\![\mathbb{M} \gg \mathbb{F}]\!]$ be a ranking in a constraint hierarchy $\mathbb{CH}$ and let $\mathbb{CH}(i)$ be the optimal candidate of Gen(i) given $\mathbb{CH}$. $[\![\mathbb{M} \gg \mathbb{F}]\!]$ is operative on i iff $\mathbb{M}$ is active on i and $\mathbb{CH}(i)$ is allowed by $[\![\mathbb{M} \gg \mathbb{F}]\!]$.

The operativeness of an $[\![\mathbb{M} \gg \mathbb{F}]\!]$ ranking on a given input depends both on $\mathbb{M}$ being active on that input — that is, on the fact that $\mathbb{M}$ separates the set of candidates filtered down by higher-ranked constraints — as well as on the allowance of $[\![\mathbb{M} \gg \mathbb{F}]\!]$ — specifically, that the optimal candidate $\mathbb{CH}(i)$ be allowed by this ranking. This establishes that $[\![\mathbb{M} \gg \mathbb{F}]\!]$ is (at least partly) *responsible* for selecting $\mathbb{CH}(i)$ as optimal, and is for our purposes equivalent to the application of the rule corresponding to $[\![\mathbb{M} \gg \mathbb{F}]\!]$ in the corresponding derivation.

The theorem may now be stated as follows.

(6.11) **The Elsewhere Theorem on Constraint-ranking** (ETC)

Let $[\![\mathbb{S} \gg \mathbb{F}_{\mathbb{S}}]\!]$ and $[\![\mathbb{G} \gg \mathbb{F}_{\mathbb{G}}]\!]$ stand as specific to general in an Elsewhere relation. If $[\![\mathbb{G} \gg \mathbb{S}]\!]$, then $[\![\mathbb{S} \gg \mathbb{F}_{\mathbb{S}}]\!]$ is not operative on any input.

The proof of ETC is relatively straightforward. By part (b) of the definition of Elsewhere relatedness in (6.9), any candidate which is allowed by $[\![\mathbb{S} \gg \mathbb{F}_{\mathbb{S}}]\!]$ violates $\mathbb{G}$. Thus if $[\![\mathbb{G} \gg \mathbb{S}]\!]$, then any candidate allowed by $[\![\mathbb{S} \gg \mathbb{F}_{\mathbb{S}}]\!]$ is already ruled out by $\mathbb{G}$. $\mathbb{S}$ thus cannot be operative on any input. □

6.4 Multiple violation

Recall the idealization made in the foregoing, following the implicit lead of the literature on the EC and the explicit lead of Prince and Smolensky (1993: 89), that a given candidate violates a given constraint at most once. The more complex reality is that a candidate may result in more than one violation of a constraint due to there being more than one proper substructure of the candidate — one *locus* — that meets the violation conditions defined by the constraint.[11] In order to truly establish a Pāṇinian constraint relation between two constraints $\mathbb{S}$ and $\mathbb{G}$ or an Elsewhere mapping relation between two rankings $[\![\mathbb{S} \gg \mathbb{F}_{\mathbb{S}}]\!]$ and $[\![\mathbb{G} \gg \mathbb{F}_{\mathbb{G}}]\!]$, then, the potential for multiple violation must be taken into account.

For example, candidates with more than one syllable might violate either $\mathbb{M}$:NO-CODA or $\mathbb{M}$:YES-CODA (or both) multiple times, once for each (missing) syllable-final consonant. In order to establish a Pāṇinian relation between

11. I set aside here the independent problem of so-called 'gradient' constraints, such as alignment constraints, that can be violated multiple times by a single locus. See McCarthy (2003b).

these constraints, then — setting aside the independent vacuous satisfaction issue discussed in §6.2.2 — the final clause of the definition of Pāṇinian relatedness in (6.2), "any parse of i which satisfies $\mathbb{S}$ violates $\mathbb{G}$", should be more accurately rephrased as "any parse γ of i which performs better than another parse κ on $\mathbb{S}$ performs worse than κ on $\mathbb{G}$". Returning to our example: a polysyllabic candidate γ with fewer syllable-final consonants than another candidate κ performs better than κ on $\mathbb{M}$:NO-CODA, but κ must thereby of course also have fewer syllable-final vowels than γ and so γ performs worse than κ on $\mathbb{M}$:YES-CODA.

This alternative statement of the relevant clause may be more accurate, but it isn't strictly necessary because it in fact already follows from the original statement of the clause in (6.2) by cancellation of common marks in accordance with Prince and Smolensky's (1993: 152, 241) Cancellation Lemma.[12]

(6.12) **Cancellation Lemma**

Suppose two structures S_1 and S_2 both incur the same mark *m. Then to determine whether $S_1 \succ S_2$ [= *S_1 performs better than S_2*], we can omit *m from the list of marks of both S_1 and S_2 ('cancel the common mark') and compare S_1 and S_2 solely on the basis of the remaining marks. Applied iteratively, this means we can cancel *all* common marks and assess S_1 and S_2 by comparing only their unshared marks.

Common mark cancellation guarantees that the more accurate "any parse γ of i which performs better than another parse κ on $\mathbb{S}$ performs worse than κ on $\mathbb{G}$" reduces to the original "any parse of i which satisfies $\mathbb{S}$ violates $\mathbb{G}$" clause in the definition of Pāṇinian relatedness in (6.2). Given that $\gamma \succ \kappa$ with respect to $\mathbb{S}$ and $\kappa \succ \gamma$ with respect to $\mathbb{G}$, then iterative cancellation of the $\mathbb{S}$ and $\mathbb{G}$ marks common to γ and κ will result in γ having no marks for $\mathbb{S}$ (= γ satisfies $\mathbb{S}$) and some marks for $\mathbb{G}$ (= γ violates $\mathbb{G}$), just as the original clause of the definition states. □

The definition of allowance and other definitions that depend on it are quite a bit more complicated and appear to require a different approach. It is useful at this point to consider an example illustrating why the issue is important. Recall the interaction between Assimilation and Neutralization in Spanish discussed in §5.5, used as an illustration of the local (as opposed to global) nature of blocking. The rules are repeated here, with suitable $[\![\mathbb{M} \gg \mathbb{F}]\!]$ ranking translations.

(6.13) Rules affecting nasal place in Spanish, repeated from (5.17)

a. Assimilation

$[+\text{nas}] \longrightarrow [\alpha\text{pl}] \,/\, \text{—}\,]_\sigma\, [\alpha\text{pl}] \quad \approx [\![\mathbb{M}\text{:AGRNC(pl)} \gg \mathbb{F}\text{:IDENT(pl)}]\!]$

b. Neutralization

$[+\text{nas}] \longrightarrow [+\text{cor}] \,/\, \text{—}\,]_\sigma \quad \approx [\![\mathbb{M}\text{:CODN=COR} \gg \mathbb{F}\text{:IDENT(pl)}]\!]$

The surface form *riŋ'kon* 'corner (of a room)' illustrates the application and interaction of both rules. Assimilation applies to the first nasal and Neutralization applies to the second, but Neutralization is applicable to both nasals and does not

12. An extensive proof of this lemma is provided by Prince and Smolensky (2004: 258ff).

apply to the first due to blocking by Assimilation. As illustrated in (6.14), local blocking of Neutralization is an inevitable consequence of the minimal violation property of OT: blocking only happens at a locus of constraint conflict.[13]

(6.14) Local blocking due to minimal violation

/rimkom/	𝕄:AGRNC(pl)	𝕄:CODN=COR	𝔽:IDENT(pl)
rinˈkon	* !		**
☞ riŋˈkon		*	**
riŋˈkom		** !	*

The optimal candidate *riŋˈkon* necessarily violates the markedness constraint 𝕄:CODN=COR responsible for Neutralization and this candidate is therefore not allowed by the ranking ⟦𝕄:CODN=COR ≫ 𝔽:IDENT(pl)⟧ according to the first condition specified in the definition of allowance, requiring *satisfaction* of 𝕄.

(6.15) Dfn. **Allowance**, repeated from (6.4)

Let 𝕄 be a markedness constraint that conflicts with a faithfulness constraint 𝔽, let 𝔽′ be all other faithfulness constraints that conflict with both 𝕄 and 𝔽, and let *i* be an input and Gen(*i*) its associated candidate set. A candidate $\Sigma \in$ Gen(*i*) is *allowed* by ⟦{𝕄, 𝔽′} ≫ 𝔽⟧ iff

a. $\mathbb{M}(\Sigma) = \varnothing$ (i.e., Σ satisfies 𝕄), and

b. $\forall \Sigma' \in \mathrm{Gen}(i)$ s.t. $\mathbb{F}(\Sigma') \neq \mathbb{F}(\Sigma)$ and $\mathbb{F}'(\Sigma') = \mathbb{F}'(\Sigma)$, $\mathbb{M}(\Sigma') \neq \mathbb{M}(\Sigma)$.

But clearly, we want to be able to say that ⟦𝕄:AGRNC(pl) ≫ 𝔽:IDENT(pl)⟧ stands to ⟦𝕄:CODN=COR ≫ 𝔽:IDENT(pl)⟧ as specific to general in an Elsewhere mapping relation, because it is undoubtedly the case that (by the ETC) if ⟦𝕄:CODN=COR ≫ 𝕄:AGRNC(pl)⟧ then ⟦𝕄:AGRNC(pl) ≫ 𝔽:IDENT(pl)⟧ is not operative on any input. The solution to this definitional dilemma is to define Σ and Σ′ such that they refer not to entire candidates but to CORRESPONDING LOCI. The necessary notions are already defined in McCarthy (2003a), from which I thus borrow and quote rather liberally here. First, the notion *locus of violation*.

(6.16) Locus of violation (McCarthy 2003a: 6–8)

Every markedness constraint M_i is defined in terms of its locus-of-violation function Loc_i. Loc_i is a function from a candidate form to a set (strictly speaking, a multi-set) of loci of violation, which are segments in that candidate. … The result of applying M_i to [a candidate] *cand* is a number of violation-marks equal to the cardinality of the set obtained by applying Loc_i to *cand*.

For example, the Loc function of 𝕄:AGRNC(pl), $\mathrm{LOC}_{\mathbb{M}:\mathrm{AGRNC(pl)}}$, is "return every NC sequence, where N is a syllable-final and N-place ≠ C-place"; the

13. In these representations, the labial nasal *m* arbitrarily represents any nasal that does not satisfy the markedness constraint(s) applicable to it.

Loc function of $\mathbb{M}$:CODN=COR, $\text{LOC}_{\mathbb{M}:\text{CODN=COR}}$, is "return every N, where N is syllable-final and N-place ≠ [+cor]". Applied to *riŋ'kon*, $\text{LOC}_{\mathbb{M}:\text{AGRNC(pl)}}$ returns the empty set because N-place = C-place in the only NC sequence in this candidate, and so $\mathbb{M}$:AGRNC(pl) has no violations. $\text{LOC}_{\mathbb{M}:\text{CODN=COR}}$ returns a singleton set because only one of the two syllable-final Ns in this candidate is not [+cor], and so $\mathbb{M}$:CODN=COR has one violation.

The other notion is *t-correspondence*, necessary for establishing correspondence between the elements of different candidates within a candidate set.

(6.17) T-correspondence (McCarthy 2003a: 8)

> Let *cand1* and *cand2* be two [*different—EB*] candidates from input *inp*. Let *s1* be a segment . . . in *cand1* and *s2* be a segment in *cand2*. Then *s1* t-corresponds to *s2* iff *s1* corresponds to some segment *s-inp* in *inp* and *s2* also corresponds to *s-inp*. We say then that $s1\ \Re_t\ s2$, with $\Re_t$ standing for the correspondence relation obtained through transitivity.

McCarthy (2003a: 7) tentatively assumes that "loci are individual segments, not strings; and constraints on structures usually return the heads of those structures as loci", but I also assume that we can refer to t-corresponding *strings*, or sequences of t-corresponding segments.[14] The definition of allowance can now be amended so that Σ and Σ' are defined as relevant t-corresponding strings.

(6.18) Dfn. **Allowance**, locus of violation version

> A substring Σ of a candidate in Gen(*i*) is *allowed* by $[\![\{\mathbb{M}, \mathbb{F}'\} \gg \mathbb{F}]\!]$ iff
>
> a. for all substrings Σ' of candidates in Gen(*i*) such that (i) $\Sigma' \in \text{LOC}_{\mathbb{M}}$, (ii) $\Sigma'\ \Re_t\ \Sigma$, (iii) $\mathbb{F}(\Sigma') \neq \mathbb{F}(\Sigma)$, and (iv) $\mathbb{F}'(\Sigma') = \mathbb{F}'(\Sigma)$,
>
> b. $\mathbb{M}(\Sigma) = \varnothing$.

Note that the two conditions are reversed, with satisfaction of $\mathbb{M}$ by Σ now being a consequence of its relation to Σ'. Every Σ' is defined as (i) belonging to the set of $\mathbb{M}$-violating loci, (ii) a t-correspondent of Σ, (iii) differing from Σ in its $\mathbb{F}$-violation profile, and (iv) identical to Σ in its $\mathbb{F}'$-violation profile. If Σ satisfies $\mathbb{M}$ for all such instances of Σ', then Σ is allowed by $[\![\{\mathbb{M}, \mathbb{F}'\} \gg \mathbb{F}]\!]$.

With this definition of allowance in hand we can turn to the crucial definition of an Elsewhere mapping relation. In this case the amendment is relatively simple: instead of referring to *candidates* allowed by one $[\![\mathbb{M} \gg \mathbb{F}]\!]$ ranking and that *violate* the other $\mathbb{M}$-constraint, we refer to all *substrings* allowed by $[\![\mathbb{M} \gg \mathbb{F}]\!]$ that are members of the set returned by the Loc function of the other $\mathbb{M}$-constraint.

(6.19) Dfn. **Elsewhere mapping relation**, locus of violation version

> Let $[\![\mathbb{S} \gg \mathbb{F}_{\mathbb{S}}]\!]$ and $[\![\mathbb{G} \gg \mathbb{F}_{\mathbb{G}}]\!]$ be two $[\![\mathbb{M} \gg \mathbb{F}]\!]$ rankings. $[\![\mathbb{S} \gg \mathbb{F}_{\mathbb{S}}]\!]$ stands to $[\![\mathbb{G} \gg \mathbb{F}_{\mathbb{G}}]\!]$ as specific to general in an Elsewhere relation iff
>
> a. for any substring $\Sigma_{*\mathbb{G}}$ allowed by $[\![\mathbb{S} \gg \mathbb{F}_{\mathbb{S}}]\!]$, $\Sigma_{*\mathbb{G}} \in \text{LOC}_{\mathbb{G}}$, and
>
> b. for any substring $\Sigma_{*\mathbb{S}} \in \text{LOC}_{\mathbb{S}}$, $\Sigma_{*\mathbb{S}}$ is allowed by $[\![\mathbb{G} \gg \mathbb{F}_{\mathbb{G}}]\!]$.

---

14. Such sequences are generally contiguous unless deletion or insertion is involved. I set aside the details of accomodating deletion and insertion, as I did in §6.2.3.

Finally, we turn to the definition of operativeness. In this case, we still want to refer to an $[\![\mathbb{M} \gg \mathbb{F}]\!]$ being operative on an input given the candidate from that input selected as optimal, but the path to the optimal candidate must be mediated by a substring in that candidate that is allowed by $[\![\mathbb{M} \gg \mathbb{F}]\!]$. To now ensure that $[\![\mathbb{M} \gg \mathbb{F}]\!]$ is (at least partly) responsible for the optimality of this candidate, however, it must be the case that the candidate had at least one relevant competitor: namely, an alternative candidate that also survived the filter above $\mathbb{M}$ but containing a substring that violates $\mathbb{M}$ that t-corresponds to the substring in the optimal candidate allowed by $[\![\mathbb{M} \gg \mathbb{F}]\!]$. Operativeness is thus now amended as follows.

(6.20) Dfn. **Operativeness**, locus of violation version

Let $[\![\mathbb{M} \gg \mathbb{F}]\!]$ be a ranking in a constraint hierarchy $\mathbb{CH}$, let $\mathbb{CH}_{\gg\mathbb{M}}$ be the portion of $\mathbb{CH}$ ranked above $\mathbb{M}$, let $\mathbb{CH}_{\gg\mathbb{M}}(i)$ be the subset of Gen(i) that survives the $\mathbb{CH}_{\gg\mathbb{M}}$ filter, and let $\mathbb{CH}(i)$ be the optimal candidate of Gen(i) given $\mathbb{CH}$. $[\![\mathbb{M} \gg \mathbb{F}]\!]$ is operative on i iff

a. at least one substring $\Sigma \subseteq \mathbb{CH}(i)$ is allowed by $[\![\mathbb{M} \gg \mathbb{F}]\!]$, and
b. at least one candidate in $\mathbb{CH}_{\gg\mathbb{M}}(i)$ contains a substring Σ' such that $\Sigma' \, \Re_t \, \Sigma$ and $\Sigma' \in \text{Loc}_{\mathbb{M}}$.

6.5 Reflective remarks

In the course of thinking about and writing up the content of this particular chapter — from its early and entirely insufficient beginnings as a section of Baković (2006) until now — I have more than once run up against a brick wall of mistaken definitions or a tangled web of complicatedness. Each of those times, I have thought that there is little point in writing the chapter at all. Somehow I persevered, and I am at least not displeased with the result.

But I still have two big fears. The first is that some readers may see the many complex definitions here, and in some cases the not-much-simpler explanations of them, as undermining my argument that disjunctive application simply follows from the basic assumptions of OT. Indeed, who can deny that the EC does seem simpler to understand by comparison? But it must be remembered that what I have done in this chapter is attempt to prove relevant theorems following from the basic assumptions of OT, not to create novel principles like the EC. If that point is still missed, then there is little more I can say.

My second fear is that despite my best efforts, I've left some important stones unturned. The epigraph that introduces this chapter may as well also end it.

> (This is an oversimplified first cut at the true result; such claims must be stated carefully.)
>
> *Prince and Smolensky (1993: 88–89)*

Chapter 7

Conclusion

Why go elsewhere to be cheated? Come here first!

misleading used car advertisement

THE MAIN CONCLUSIONS OF THIS BOOK can be summarized as follows. *SPE* was built as a conjunctive-application machine, and so disjunctive application requires the postulation of an auxiliary principle like the EC which is at best an approximation of a synthesis of the relevant facts. OT, on the other hand, was built as a conflict-resolution machine, and so disjunctive application requires no auxiliary statement. Disjunctive application is a necessary consequence of run-of-the-mill OT constraint conflict resolution, but must be stipulated, bit by unexplanatory bit, in the precarious definition of the EC. In response to Halle's (1995) defense of the EC, Prince (1997a) makes the same point:

> Observe that the [EC] determines which one of two or more competing processes will apply in a given environment, blocking the expected derivational relationship between them. [Halle's] aim, then, is to argue from the failure of serial derivation to the conclusion that serial derivation is necessary: the logic is not going to be straightforward. By contrast, [OT] is thoroughly in the business of selecting which (of many) competing input-output maps will prevail and needs no [EC] to guide it. ... [EC] disjunctivity is a sub-case of the general mode of constraint interaction in OT. (Prince 1997a: 2)

One must conclude, as I have, that the amount of attention paid to the EC in the literature is due entirely to the intuitive correctness of its premise and the logical consequence of that premise. The premise is that elsewhere effects are not about serially ordered rule interactions but rather about comparisons between competing candidate outputs; its consequence is that elsewhere effects are not about the happenstantial undoing of earlier-ordered general rules but rather about the forced violation of lower-ranked general constraints.

Rather than elaborate further on these conclusions — that's what all of the preceding pages were for — I take the opportunity in this final chapter to briefly address three further matters of interest. First, in §7.1, I discuss the use of the EC (or an EC-like blocking principle) in the domains of linguistic theory aside from phonology where it has received considerable attention, morphology and morphosyntax. Second, in §7.2, I discuss the distinction between elsewhere interactions and other specific-general interactions in OT. And finally, in §7.3, I discuss the limits of invoking opacity in arguments for *SPE* (and against OT) as well as the limits of invoking blocking in arguments for OT (and against *SPE*).

7.1 Morphological blocking

The view that blocking (or "preemption"; Levin 1972) plays a significant role in morphology and morphosyntax has been held by many researchers; see e.g. Matthews (1972), Sanders (1974), Aronoff (1976), Anderson (1977, 1982, 1986), Andrews (1982, 1990), Aronoff and Sridhar (1983), Morin (1988), Calder (1989), Stump (1989, 2002), and Zeevat (1995).[1] A great many of the examples that have been argued to involve blocking can be described in 'elsewhere' terms, where a more specific morphological rule (or the specific listing of a particular lexical item) blocks a more general one. These examples are believed by many morphologists to result from a principle akin to the EC.

There are various types of examples that have been argued to fall under the scope of morphological blocking, but I only discuss here what appears to me to be the least controversial of these types. The key observation is that regular and irregular word forms tend not to coexist; this is often argued to involve blocking of the otherwise expected regular form by the existence of the irregular form. Thus the regular plural **mans* is blocked by irregular *men*, or the regular agentive **cooker* (in the sense of 'person who cooks') is blocked by irregular *cook*, or the regular comparative **gooder* is blocked by the irregular suppletive *better*.

The guiding intuition behind the blocking analysis of such examples is that (the rules responsible for) the irregular forms are more specific than the rules responsible for the regular forms; for example, the minor ablaut rule responsible for *men* applies only to a restricted subset of nouns, while the regular plural suffixation rule is presumably unrestricted in its application. This proper subset relation between these rules, coupled with the entirely reasonable assumption that their outputs are incompatible (i.e., that the doubly marked **mens* is independently impossible), naturally leads one to suspect a principle much like the EC.

My sense from a taste of the relevant literature is that even when a seemingly independent principle is formalized to account for morphological blocking, it is more often than not implicitly (if not explicitly) understood to be the other side of the EC coin; that is, that the morphological blocking principle and the EC are *not* separate principles that just so happen to share the specific-blocks-general idea. Either way, of course, one expects that many if not all of the criticisms leveled against the EC in this book apply equally to whatever principle is held to be responsible for morphological blocking: the fact that anything must be stated at all is the problem. An OT analysis would thus be preferable to one in terms of some morphological blocking principle (whether it's the EC or not), for all the

1. This is by no means an exhaustive list of relevant citations, nor is the discussion here meant to be definitive. Much of what I say here builds on conclusions by Janda and Sandoval (1984).

same reasons that have been discussed in this book: constraint conflict resolution explains blocking; a separate principle would simply stipulate it.

In their comprehensive survey of the relevant evidence to date, Janda and Sandoval (1984) claim that blocking of more general forms by more specific, lexically listed ones — or of more general rules by more specific, lexically restricted ones — may be the only predictable form of blocking in morphology.[2] Based on their review of evidence and counterevidence for an EC-like principle pertaining to "lexically-free" rules of morphology, Janda and Sandoval (1984: 35) conclude "that language-particular specifications of disjunctivity between lexically-free morphological rules are often necessary and so must be permitted by morphological theory". The authors cite Anderson (1977, 1982) and Matthews (1972) as precedent for the idea that morphological blocking may be stipulated on a case-by-case basis, whether or not the rules are related as special-to-general.

It is worth noting that there is a significant difference between virtually all types of morphological blocking and most types of phonological blocking. In the case of morphological blocking, a conjunctive ordering solution by which the more specific rule overwrites the prior effect of the more general rule is generally not possible. Consider the case of irregular *men* blocking regular **mans*: the more general regular plural affixation rule cannot be overwritten by the more specific irregular ablaut rule; at best, the effect of applying both rules would be additive (**mens*).[3] This all relates to a point also made by Prince and Smolensky (1993).

> [The EC] is sometimes said to entail that a given morphological category should have only one marking; double marking of e.g. plural by two different affixes, one specialized, the other of more general applicability, is then held to be an "exception" to the [EC] (Stump 1989). Here again, it should be clear that what's really at issue is a substantive matter: how morphological categories are expressed. A morphosyntactic feature [+PL] typically has one morpheme in a string devoted to it . . .; thus, different plural morphemes are incompatible. This allows for a special-case/general-case system, in which the logic of PTC determines the ranking that yields the observed facts. What double marking challenges is the assumption of incompatibility, without which the PTC is irrelevant. (Prince and Smolensky 1993: 120)

7.2 Elsewhere conflict vs. stringency

Recall that PTC defines conditions under which the more specific of two *conflicting* constraints is deactivated. Recall also that in order to render the more specific of two $[\![\mathbb{M} \gg \mathbb{F}]\!]$ rankings inoperative, the ETC also requires conflict. But there are also constraints that stand in a specific-to-general relation but that do not conflict: constraints related by STRINGENCY (Prince 1997b, c, 2000, 2001).

---

2. See also Embick (2007, 2010), and Embick and Marantz (2008) for opposition to the notion of blocking in these and other cases altogether.
3. But an ordering solution is possible if we assume something akin to the underspecification + feature-filling rule analysis of §3.1.2: the more specific irregular ablaut rule can render plural *men*, to which the more general regular suffixation rule is no longer applicable because the form is already marked as a plural.

Three prominent examples of constraint types that are related by stringency are (i) positional faithfulness constraints and their general faithfulness counterparts (Beckman 1995, 1997, 1998), (ii) local conjunctions and their conjuncts (Smolensky 1993, 1995, 1997, 2006, Smolensky et al. 2006), and (iii) markedness constraints penalizing sets of elements in proper inclusion relationships (Prince 1997b, c, 2000, 2001; de Lacy 2002, 2006). The more general constraint is the more stringent: it penalizes everything that the more specific constraint penalizes but not vice versa. For example, general $\mathbb{F}$:IDENT(voi) is more stringent than positional $\mathbb{F}$:IDENT(voi)$_{\text{Onset}}$ because everything that violates $\mathbb{F}$:IDENT(voi)$_{\text{Onset}}$ also violates $\mathbb{F}$:IDENT(voi) but not vice versa. Likewise, each of the conjuncts of a local conjunction is more stringent than the conjunction because everything that violates the conjunction also violates each of the conjuncts but not vice versa. Finally, a markedness constraint penalizing a more inclusive set of elements is more stringent than one penalizing a less inclusive set because everything that violates the latter also violates the former but not vice versa.

Two constraints related by stringency obviously do not conflict directly with one another, because any violation of the less stringent (= more specific) constraint simply entails a violation of the more stringent (= more general) constraint. This is illustrated with the case of the positional and general faithfulness constraints $\mathbb{F}$:IDENT(voi) and $\mathbb{F}$:IDENT(voi)$_{\text{Onset}}$ in (7.1) below. The hypothetical input under consideration is /*bad*/, with two voiced obstruents: initial /*b*/, the candidate output correspondents of which are in onset position, and final /*d*/, the candidate output correspondents of which are not in onset position.[4]

(7.1) Stringency relations: positional and general faithfulness

/bad/	$\mathbb{F}$:IDENT(voi)$_{\text{Onset}}$	$\mathbb{F}$:IDENT(voi)
☞ bad		
bat		*
pad	*	*
pat	*	**

Despite this lack of conflict, Beckman proposes that positional faithfulness constraints universally dominate their general faithfulness counterparts. In similar fashion, Smolensky proposes that local conjunctions universally dominate their conjuncts. Neither of these ranking metaconditions has been demonstrated to be empirically necessary.[5] More relevant to present concerns, the more specific of two constraints in a stringency relation is not necessarily deactivated when ranked below the more general, as discussed at length by Prince (1997b, c, 2000, 2001).

For example, Lombardi (1999: 285ff) presents an analysis of voicing assimilation in Swedish (following the description in Hellberg 1974) that demonstrates

4. Whether "onset position" is defined strictly as a syllabic position or as consonant released into a tautosyllabic sonorant (Lombardi 1991, 1999) is entirely irrelevant here.

5. Some work (e.g. Baković 2000, 2001; Baertsch 2002; Baertsch and Davis 2003) has made empirically crucial use of the ranking metacondition proposed by Smolensky for local conjunctions and their conjuncts, but these don't count as 'demonstrations' in the strict sense intended here.

— albeit indirectly — that 𝔽:IDENT(voi)$_{\text{Onset}}$ is crucially active on some inputs under some ranking conditions, even when dominated by 𝔽:IDENT(voi). The following ranking conditions hold for Lombardi's analysis of Swedish.[6]

(7.2) Crucially subordinated positional faithfulness

a. ⟦𝕄:AGREE(voi) ≫ 𝔽:IDENT(voi)⟧
Obstruent clusters agree in voicing at the expense of faithfulness.

b. ⟦𝔽:IDENT(voi) ≫ 𝕄:NO-VCDOBS⟧
Voiced obstruents are faithfully realized, modulo assimilation.

c. ⟦𝕄:NO-VCDOBS ≫ 𝔽:IDENT(voi)$_{\text{Onset}}$⟧
Assimilation is to [–voi] at the expense of onset faithfulness.

The combined effect of these rankings is to faithfully realize voicing distinctions except in obstruent clusters that underlyingly disagree in voicing, where the result is assimilation to voicelessness regardless of the position of the obstruent that undergoes the change. In order to be inactive, then, 𝔽:IDENT(voi)$_{\text{Onset}}$ must be subordinated to 𝕄:NO-VCDOBS (7.2c) — if the positional faithfulness constraint were any higher in the ranking, even if just below its general counterpart 𝔽:IDENT(voi), it would decide in favor of assimilation to the onset.

Independent problems with some aspects of this analysis notwithstanding (see Lombardi 1999: 294ff; Baković 1999a, Baković 2000: 24ff), what it makes clear is that positional faithfulness is not guaranteed to be inactive if it is simply subordinated to more stringent general faithfulness. Lombardi (1999: 287) speculates that the Swedish pattern is rare and that this rarity is perhaps due to some sort of bias toward rankings in which positional faithfulness dominates general faithfulness; this is of course an empirical matter, not one that can be decided on some principled grounds based on specific-to-general relations.

7.3 Opacity and blocking

Recall from Chapter 1 these two broadly conceived empirical arguments: that blocking is best handled by OT's basic assumptions of constraint ranking and candidate comparison, and that opacity is best handled by *SPE*'s basic assumptions of rule ordering and serial derivation. To uphold the basic assumptions of *SPE* while still having a descriptively adequate account of blocking, one argument goes, you need the intervention of constraints that are able to override the otherwise expected conjunctive operation of rules. To uphold the basic assumptions of OT while still having a descriptively adequate account of opacity, the other argument goes, you need some kind of serial architecture to break up the otherwise expected par-

6. The constraint names have been modified here, but they are assumed to have the same interpretation as Lombardi's. Also, Lombardi (1999: 286) does not specify the ranking in (7.2a) but her tableaux and discussion make it clear that it is necessary for the account to go through.

allel evaluation of candidates into steps that can be referenced by constraints.[7] Each of these arguments has its problems, as I discuss here in this final section.

The introduction of serialism into OT is often characterized by proponents of *SPE* as a complete capitulation, a denial of the basic tenets of the theory. Proponents of *SPE* rarely if ever even rhetorically acknowledge that the mixture of rules and constraints that most if not all of them advocate is at least as much a denial of the basic tenets of the theory as the introduction of serialism into OT is.[8] OT was originally built on the promise of a solution to "a conceptual crisis at the center of phonological thought" (Prince and Smolensky 1993: 1); opacity was (in retrospect, at least) a predictable major stumbling block to this promise, and the introduction of serialism, however limited, seems to have been as inevitable as the introduction of constraints into *SPE* was.

Although "inevitable" may be too strong a word here, I believe it highlights something common to the evolution of *SPE* and the evolution of OT in their respective literatures. Both theories began with strong rhetoric about the necessity and near-sufficiency of their most basic assumptions, but also acknowledging the necessity of some deviations from those assumptions and building them into the larger framework. In the case of *SPE*, these deviations included the transformational cycle, boundaries, and disjunctive application (Chomsky et al. 1956; Chomsky 1967; Chomsky and Halle 1968), while in OT they included alignment, level ordering, and particular assumptions about the theory of faithfulness (Prince and Smolensky 1993; McCarthy and Prince 1993a, b). The set of deviations evolved and grew in both cases and each theory was dragged, sometimes kicking and screaming, to the place it is now: a combination of ordered rules and interacting constraints in the case of *SPE* (e.g. Paradis 1988; Calabrese 1995, 2005) and a combination of ranked constraints and serial derivation in the case of OT (e.g. McCarthy 2007b; Kiparsky forthcoming; Bermúdez-Otero forthcoming).

All of this would be interesting enough if it were even the case that (i) the most basic assumptions of *SPE* had a lock on opacity and that the introduction of constraints were only necessary for blocking, or (ii) that the most basic assumptions of OT had a lock on blocking and that the introduction of serialism were only necessary for opacity. The reason that neither of these is the case is that instances of blocking are also instances of (non-surface-true) opacity (Baković 2011: 47ff). For example, nonderived environment blocking is problematic for *SPE* because

7. Other methods for analyzing blocking in *SPE* and opacity within OT have also been proposed, of course, but it is widely acknowledged that these methods only go so far in providing an adequate account of all types of blocking or opacity. Within *SPE*, probably the most successful of these alternative methods is the general method of underspecification + feature-filling rule application discussed in §3.1.2. Within OT, the most successful alternative methods are arguably representational solutions making crucial use of the resources of the 'containment' theory of faithfulness (e.g. van Oostendorp 2003, 2007a, b) or 'turbid' representations (Goldrick and Smolensky 1999; Goldrick 2001), even though local conjunction solutions (Kirchner 1996; Łubowicz 2002; Ito and Mester 2003a) appear to have gained more traction. Still other alternatives include sympathy theory (McCarthy 1999b), targeted constraints (Wilson 2000, 2001; Baković and Wilson 2000), comparative markedness (McCarthy 2003a), and contrast preservation theory (Łubowicz 2003).

8. For example, consider the claim that "the phonological component must be serial and rule-based" but that rules "are subject to the cycle, Structure Preservation, the Derived Environment Condition, and inviolable constraints on underlying and surface representations" (Vaux 2008: 29).

it involves blocking (recall §2.5.1), but it's also problematic for OT because it involves opacity (recall §4.1.3). Other examples tip the scales one way or the other: counterfeeding involves blocking but is unproblematic for *SPE* (§2.1.2), but it also involves opacity and so is problematic for OT (§4.1.3); do-something-except-when blocking involves opacity but is unproblematic for OT (§4.1.4), but it also involves blocking and so is problematic for *SPE* (§2.5.2) — and, of course, disjunctive application is the same, being little more than a special case of do-something-except-when blocking (§4.1.5).

It seems to me that all phonologists should devote substantially more energy and resources toward achieving a better understanding than we currently have of what the range and nature of phonological phenomena to be accounted for really are, given descriptions of those phenomena by theoretical assumptions that we share in common. For example, we all appear to agree that phonology involves inputs, outputs, and mappings between them, and that some aspects of phonology appear mapping-oriented while others appear output-oriented. Given this, then neither a fully mapping-oriented theory (as I've characterized *SPE* in this book) nor a fully output-oriented theory (as I've characterized OT) is likely to be entirely right. Pursuing what is to be described as well as what our theories are able to describe (Prince 2007), we can forge a more fruitful (though perhaps not incrementally monotonic) path of progress toward the right theory.

References

Alderete, J. (2001) Dominance effects as transderivational anti-faithfulness. *Phonology 18*: 201–253.

Alonso, A. (1945) Una ley fonológica del español; variabilidad de las consonantes en la tensión y distensión de la sílaba. *Hispanic Review 13*: 91–101.

Anderson, S. R. (1969) *West Scandinavian Vowel Systems and the Ordering of Phonological Rules*. Doctoral dissertation, MIT, Cambridge, MA.

Anderson, S. R. (1974) *The Organization of Phonology*. New York: Academic Press.

Anderson, S. R. (1977) On the formal description of inflection. In W. A. Beach, S. E. Fox and S. Philosoph (eds.) *Papers from the Thirteenth Regional Meeting*. Chicago, IL: Chicago Linguistic Society, 15–44.

Anderson, S. R. (1982) Where's morphology? *Linguistic Inquiry 13*: 571–612.

Anderson, S. R. (1986) Disjunctive ordering in inflectional morphology. *Natural Language and Linguistic Theory 4*: 1–31.

Anderson, S. R. and Browne, W. (1973) On keeping exchange rules in Czech. *Papers in Linguistics 6*: 445–482.

Andrews, A. D. (1982) The representation of case in Modern Icelandic. In J. Bresnan (ed.) *The Mental Representation of Grammatical Relations*. Cambridge, MA: MIT Press, 427–503.

Andrews, A. D. (1990) Unification and morphological blocking. *Natural Language and Linguistic Theory 8*: 507–557.

Archangeli, D. (1988) Aspects of underspecification theory. *Phonology 5*: 183–207.

Archangeli, D. and Pulleyblank, D. (1994) *Grounded Phonology*. Cambridge, MA: MIT Press.

Aronoff, M. (1976) *Word Formation in Generative Grammar*. Cambridge, MA: MIT Press.

Aronoff, M. and Sridhar, S. N. (1983) Morphological levels in English and Kannada, or atarizing Reagan. In J. F. Richardson, M. Marks and A. Chukerman (eds.) *Papers from the Parasession on the Interplay of Phonology, Morphology, and Syntax*. Chicago, IL: Chicago Linguistic Society, 3–16.

Baertsch, K. (2002) *An Optimality Theoretic Approach to Syllable Structure: The Split Margin Hierarchy*. Doctoral dissertation, Indiana University, Bloomington, IN.

Baertsch, K. and Davis, S. (2003) The split margin approach to syllable structure. *ZAS Papers in Linguistics 32*: 1–14.

Baković, E. (1994) Strong onsets and Spanish fortition. In C. Giordano and D. Ardron (eds.) *Proceedings of the 6th Student Conference in Linguistics*. Cambridge, MA: MIT Working Papers in Linguistics, 21–39. ROA-96, Rutgers Optimality Archive, http://roa.rutgers.edu.

Baković, E. (1996) Foot harmony and quantitative adjustments. ROA-96, Rutgers Optimality Archive, http://roa.rutgers.edu.

Baković, E. (1999a) Assimilation to the unmarked. In J. Alexander, N.-R. Han and M. Minnick Fox (eds.) *Proceedings of the 23rd Annual Penn Linguistics Colloquium, University of Pennsylvania Working Papers in Linguistics*, volume 6. Philadelphia, PA: University of Pennsylvania, 1–16.

Baković, E. (1999b) Deletion, insertion, and symmetrical identity. In B. Vaux and S. Kuno (eds.) *Harvard Working Papers in Linguistics*, volume 7. Department of Linguistics, Harvard University, 27–38.

Baković, E. (2000) *Harmony, Dominance and Control*. Doctoral dissertation, Rutgers University, New Brunswick, NJ.

Baković, E. (2001) Nasal place neutralization in Spanish. In M. M. Fox, A. Williams and E. Kaiser (eds.) *Proceedings of the 24th Annual Penn Linguistics Colloquium, University of Pennsylvania Working Papers in Linguistics*, volume 7. Philadelphia, PA: University of Pennsylvania, 1–12. ROA-386, Rutgers Optimality Archive, http://roa.rutgers.edu.

Baković, E. (2006) Elsewhere effects in Optimality Theory. In E. Baković, J. Ito and J. McCarthy (eds.) *Wondering at the Natural Fecundity of Things: Essays in Honor of Alan Prince*. Santa Cruz, CA: Linguistics Research Center, 23–70. http://repositories.cdlib.org/lrc/prince/4.

Baković, E. (2007) A revised typology of opaque generalisations. *Phonology 24*: 217–259. ROA-850, Rutgers Optimality Archive, http://roa.rutgers.edu.

Baković, E. (2009a) Abstractness and motivation in phonological theory. *Studies in Hispanic and Lusophone Linguistics 2*: 183–198.

Baković, E. (2009b) Local blocking and minimal violation. *Proceedings of the Chicago Linguistic Society 45*: 1–10. ROA-1042, Rutgers Optimality Archive, http://roa.rutgers.edu.

Baković, E. (2011) Opacity and ordering. In J. A. Goldsmith, J. Riggle and A. C. L. Yu (eds.) *The Handbook of Phonological Theory*. Oxford: Wiley-Blackwell, 2nd edition, 40–67.

Baković, E. (in preparation) Breaking down rule interactions. Manuscript.

Baković, E. and Wilson, C. (2000) Transparency, strict locality, and targeted constraints. *Proceedings of the West Coast Conference on Formal Linguistics 19*: 43–56.

Beckman, J. (1995) Shona height harmony: markedness and positional identity. In J. Beckman, L. Walsh Dickey and S. Urbanczyk (eds.) *Papers in Optimality Theory, University of Massachusetts Occasional Papers*, volume 18. Amherst, MA: GLSA, 53–75.

Beckman, J. (1997) Positional faithfulness, positional neutralization and Shona vowel harmony. *Phonology 14*: 1–46.

Beckman, J. (1998) *Positional Faithfulness*. Doctoral dissertation, University of Massachusetts, Amherst, MA. Published 1999, New York: Garland Press.

Beckman, J., Walsh Dickey, L. and Urbanczyk, S. (eds.) (1995) *Papers in Optimality Theory, University of Massachusetts Occasional Papers*, volume 18. Amherst, MA: GLSA Publications.

Benua, L. (1997) *Transderivational Identity: Phonological Relations Between Words*. Doctoral dissertation, University of Massachusetts, Amherst, MA. Published 2000, New York: Garland.

Bermúdez-Otero, R. (forthcoming) *Stratal Optimality Theory*. Oxford: Oxford University Press.

Bever, T. (1967) *Leonard Bloomfield and the Phonology of the Menomini Language*. Doctoral dissertation, MIT, Cambridge, MA.

Blaho, S., Bye, P. and Krämer, M. (eds.) (2007) *Freedom of Analysis?* Number 95 in Studies in Generative Grammar, Berlin: Mouton de Gruyter.

Blevins, J. (1997) Rules in Optimality Theory: two case studies. In I. Roca (ed.) *Derivations and Constraints in Phonology*. Oxford: Clarendon Press, 227–260.

Blumenfeld, L. (2006) Tone domains in Tonga. ROA-805, Rutgers Optimality Archive, http://roa.rutgers.edu.

Blust, R. (2004) Austronesian nasal substitution: a survey. *Oceanic Linguistics 43*: 73–148.

Bonet, E. and Mascaró, J. (1997) On the representation of contrasting rhotics. In F. Martínez-Gil and A. Morales-Front (eds.) *Issues in the Phonology and Morphology of the Major Iberian Languages*. Washington, DC: Georgetown University Press, 103–126.

Borowsky, T. (1986) *Topics in the Lexical Phonology of English*. Doctoral dissertation, University of Massachusetts, Amherst, MA.

Bradley, T. (2001a) A typology of rhotic duration contrast and neutralization. *Proceedings of the North East Linguistics Society 31*: 79–97.

Bradley, T. (2001b) *The Phonetics and Phonology of Rhotic Duration Contrast and Neutralization*. Doctoral dissertation, The Pennsylvania State University, College Park. ROA-473, Rutgers Optimality Archive, http://roa.rutgers.edu.

Bradley, T. (2006) Spanish rhotics and Dominican hypercorrect /s/. *Probus 18*: 1–33.

Brame, M. (1974) The cycle in phonology: stress in Palestinian, Maltese and Spanish. *Linguistic Inquiry 5*: 39–60.

Bright, W. (1957) *The Karok Language*. (University of California Publications in Linguistics), Berkeley: University of California Press.

Broadbent, J. (1991) Linking and intrusive r in English. *UCL Working Papers in Linguistics 3*: 281–302.

Bromberger, S. and Halle, M. (1989) Why phonology is different. *Linguistic Inquiry 20*: 51–70.

Broselow, E. (1995) Skeletal positions and moras. In J. Goldsmith (ed.) *The Handbook of Phonological Theory*. Oxford: Blackwell.

Burzio, L. (1993) English stress, vowel length and modularity. *Journal of Linguistics 29*: 359–418.

Burzio, L. (1994) *Principles of English Stress*. Cambridge: Cambridge University Press.

Burzio, L. (1996) Surface constraints versus underlying representation. In J. Durand and B. Laks (eds.) *Current Trends in Phonology: Models and Methods*. European Studies Research Institute: University of Salford Publications, 97–122.

Burzio, L. (2000) Cycles, non-derived-environment blocking, and correspondence. In J. Dekkers, F. van der Leeuw and J. van de Weijer (eds.) *Optimality Theory: Phonology, Syntax, and Acquisition*. Oxford: Oxford University Press, 47–87.

Burzio, L. (2011) Derived environment effects. In M. van Oostendorp, C. Ewen, B. Hume and K. Rice (eds.) *The Blackwell Companion to Phonology*. Oxford: Wiley-Blackwell.

Bye, P. (2006) Eliminating exchange rules in Dholuo. Unpublished manuscript, http://www.hum.uit.no/a/bye/Papers/dholuo-squib.pdf.

Calabrese, A. (1988) *Towards a Theory of Phonological Alphabets*. Doctoral dissertation, MIT, Cambridge, MA.

Calabrese, A. (1995) A constraint-based theory of phonological markedness and simplification procedures. *Linguistic Inquiry 26*: 373–463.

Calabrese, A. (2005) *Markedness and Economy in a Derivational Model of Phonology*. Number 80 in Studies in Generative Grammar, Berlin: Mouton de Gruyter.

Calder, J. (1989) Paradigmatic morphology. *EACL '89 Proceedings of the fourth conference on European chapter of the Association for Computational Linguistics*, 58–65 .

Campbell, L. (1973) Extrinsic order lives. Distributed by the Indiana University Linguistics Club.

Casali, R. (1996) *Resolving Hiatus*. Doctoral dissertation, University of California, Los Angeles. Published 1998, New York: Garland.

Casali, R. (1997) Vowel elision in hiatus contexts: Which vowel goes? *Language 73*: 493–533.

Chomsky, N. (1965) *Aspects of the Theory of Syntax*. Cambridge, MA: MIT Press.

Chomsky, N. (1967) Some general properties of phonological rules. *Language 43*: 102–128.

Chomsky, N. (1968) *Language and Mind*. New York: Harcourt Brace Jovanovich.

Chomsky, N. (1995) *The Minimalist Program*. Cambridge, MA: MIT Press.

Chomsky, N. and Halle, M. (1968) *The Sound Pattern of English*. New York: Harper and Row.

Chomsky, N., Halle, M. and Lukoff, F. (1956) On accent and juncture in English. In M. Halle (ed.) *For Roman Jakobson: Essays on the Occasion of His Sixtieth Birthday*. The Hague: Mouton, 65–80.

Clements, G. N. (1981) Akan vowel harmony: A nonlinear analysis. In *Harvard Studies in Phonology*, volume II. 108–177. Reproduced by the Indiana University Linguistics Club.

Clements, G. N. and Keyser, S. J. (1983) *CV Phonology*. Cambridge, MA: MIT Press.

Cohn, A. (1989) Stress in Indonesian and bracketing paradoxes. *Natural Language and Linguistic Theory 7*: 167–216.

Cohn, A. and McCarthy, J. J. (1998) Alignment and parallelism in Indonesian phonology. *Working Papers of the Cornell Phonetics Laboratory 12*: 53–137.

Colina, S. (2010) Rhotics in Spanish: A new look at an old problem. In C. Borgonovo, M. Español Echevarría and P. Prévost (eds.) *Selected Proceedings of the 12th Hispanic Linguistics Symposium*. Somerville, MA: Cascadilla Press, 75–86.

Davis, S. (1995) Emphasis spread in Arabic and Grounded Phonology. *Linguistic Inquiry 26*: 465–498.

Dobson, E. J. (1962) Middle English lengthening in open syllables. *Transactions of the Philological Society 61*: 124–148.

Doke, C. M. (1938) *Textbook of Lamba Grammar*. Johannesburg: Witswatersrand University Press.

Embick, D. (2007) Blocking effects and analytic/synthetic alternations. *Natural Language and Linguistic Theory 25*: 1–37.

Embick, D. (2010) *Localism versus Globalism in Morphology and Phonology*. Cambridge, MA: MIT Press.

Embick, D. and Marantz, A. (2008) Architecture and blocking. *Linguistic Inquiry 39*: 1–53.

Giegerich, H. J. (1988) Strict cyclicity and elsewhere. *Lingua 75*: 125–134.

Goldrick, M. (2001) Turbid output representations and the unity of opacity. *Proceedings of the North East Linguistics Society 30*: 231–245. http://faculty.wcas.northwestern.edu/matt-goldrick/nels30.pdf.

Goldrick, M. and Smolensky, P. (1999) Opacity and turbid representations in Optimality Theory. Paper presented at the 35th Annual Meeting of the Chicago Linguistic Society.

Goldsmith, J. (1981) Towards an autosegmental theory of accent: the case of Tonga. Distributed by the Indiana University Linguistics Club.

Goldsmith, J. (1984a) Meeussen's rule. In M. Aronoff and R. T. Oehrle (eds.) *Language Sound Structure*. Cambridge, MA: MIT Press, 245–259.

Goldsmith, J. (1984b) Tone and accent in Tonga. In G. N. Clements and J. Goldsmith (eds.) *Autosegmental Studies in Bantu Tone*. Cinnaminson, NJ: Foris, 19–51.

Goldsmith, J. and Laks, B. (forthcoming) Generative phonology: its origins, its principles, and its successors. In L. R. Waugh, J. E. Joseph and M. Monville-Burston (eds.) *The Cambridge History of Linguistics*. Cambridge: Cambridge University Press. http://hum.uchicago.edu/~jagoldsm/Papers/GenerativePhonology.pdf.

Gouskova, M. (2003) *Deriving Economy: Syncope in Optimality Theory*. Doctoral dissertation, University of Massachusetts, Amherst, MA. ROA-610, Rutgers Optimality Archive, http://roa.rutgers.edu.

Green, A. D. (1996) Some effects of the Weight-to-Stress Principle and Grouping Harmony in the Goidelic languages. *Working Papers of the Cornell Phonetics Laboratory 11*: 117–155. ROA-153, Rutgers Optimality Archive, http://roa.rutgers.edu.

Grimshaw, J. (1997) Projection, heads, and optimality. *Linguistic Inquiry 28*: 373–422.

Guerssel, M. (1978) A condition on assimilation rules. *Linguistic Analysis 4*: 225–254.

Haas, M. (1940) *Tunica*. Extract from the Handbook of American Indian Languages, vol. 4. New York: J. J. Augustin.

Haiman, J. (1972) Phonological targets and unmarked structures. *Language 48*: 365–377.

Hale, K. (1973) Deep-surface canonical disparities in relation to analysis and change: an Australian example. In T. Sebeok (ed.) *Current Trends in Linguistics*. The Hague: Mouton, 401–458.

Halle, M. (1977) Tenseness, vowel shift, and the phonology of back vowels in Modern English. *Linguistic Inquiry 8*: 611–625.

Halle, M. (1978) Formal vs. functional considerations in phonology. *Studies in the Linguistic Sciences 8*: 123–134. Also in B. Brogyanyi (ed.), *Studies in Diachronic, Synchronic, and Typological Linguistics: Festschrift for Oswald Szemerényi on the Occasion of his 65th Birthday*, 325–341. Amsterdam: John Benjamins, 1979.

Halle, M. (1995) Comments on Burzio (1995). *GLOT International 1*(9/10): 27–28.

Halle, M. (2002) *From Memory to Speech and Back: Papers on Phonetics and Phonology 1954-2002*. Berlin: Mouton de Gruyter.

Halle, M. and Clements, G. N. (1983) *Problem Book in Phonology*. Cambridge, MA: MIT Press.

Halle, M. and Idsardi, W. J. (1997) *r*, hypercorrection, and the Elsewhere Condition. In I. Roca (ed.) *Derivations and Constraints in Phonology*. Oxford: Clarendon Press, 331–348.

Halle, M. and Idsardi, W. J. (1998) A response to Alan Prince's letter. *GLOT International 3*: 1 & 22.

Halle, M. and Kenstowicz, M. J. (1991) The Free Element Condition and cyclic vs. noncyclic stress. *Linguistic Inquiry 22*: 457–501.

Halle, M. and Keyser, S. J. (1971) *English Stress: Its Form, Its Growth, and Its Role in Verse*. New York: Harper and Row.

Halle, M. and Mohanan, K. P. (1985) Segmental phonology of Modern English. *Linguistic Inquiry 16*: 57–116.

Halle, M. and Vergnaud, J.-R. (1982) On the framework of Autosegmental Phonology. In H. van der Hulst and N. Smith (eds.) *The Structure of Phonological Representations, Pt. 1*. Dordrecht: Foris, 65–82.

Halle, M. and Vergnaud, J.-R. (1987) *An Essay on Stress*. Cambridge, MA: MIT Press.

Harris, J. (1994) *English Sound Structure*. Oxford: Oxford University Press.

Harris, J. W. (1969) *Spanish Phonology*. Cambridge, MA: MIT Press.

Harris, J. W. (1974) Evidence from Portuguese for the "Elsewhere Condition" in phonology. *Linguistic Inquiry 5*: 61–80.

Harris, J. W. (1983) *Syllable Structure and Stress in Spanish: A Nonlinear Analysis*. Cambridge, MA: MIT Press.

Harris, J. W. (1984) Autosegmental phonology, lexical phonology, and Spanish nasals. In M. Aronoff and R. T. Oehrle (eds.) *Language Sound Structure*. Cambridge, MA: MIT Press, 67–82.

Harris, J. W. (1992) Spanish stress: the extrametricality issue. Distributed by the Indiana University Linguistics Club.

Harris, J. W. (1999) Nasal depalatalization *no*, morphological wellformedness *sí*; the structure of Spanish word classes. In K. Arregi, B. Bruening, C. Krause and V. Lin (eds.) *Papers on Morphology and Syntax, Cycle One*, volume 33. MIT Working Papers in Linguistics, 47–82.

Harris, J. W. (2001) Reflections on *A Phonological Grammar of Spanish*. In J. Herschensohn, E. Mallen and K. Zagona (eds.) *Features and interfaces in Romance*. Amsterdam: Benjamins, 133–145.

Harris, J. W. (2002) Flaps, trills, and syllable structure in Spanish. *MIT Working Papers in Linguistics 42*: 81–108.

Hastings, A. J. (1974) Stifling. Distributed by the Indiana University Linguistics Club.

Hayes, B. (1980) *A Metrical Theory of Stress Rules*. Doctoral dissertation, MIT, Cambridge, MA. Distributed 1981, Bloomington: Indiana University Linguistics Club; published 1985, New York: Garland.

Hayes, B. (1982) Extrametricality and English stress. *Linguistic Inquiry 13*: 227–276.

Hayes, B. (1986) Inalterability in CV Phonology. *Language 62*: 321–351.

Hayes, B. (1989) Compensatory lengthening in moraic phonology. *Linguistic Inquiry 20*: 253–306.

Hayes, B. (1995) *Metrical Stress Theory: Principles and Case Studies*. Chicago, IL: The University of Chicago Press.

Hellberg, S. (1974) *Graphonomic Rules in Phonology: Studies in the Expression Component of Swedish*. Göteborg: Acta Universitatis Gothoburgensis.

Hill, J. H. (1970) A peeking rule in Cupeño. *Linguistic Inquiry 1*: 534–539.

Horwood, G. (2001) Anti-faithfulness and subtractive morphology. ROA-466, Rutgers Optimality Archive, http://roa.rutgers.edu.

Howard, I. (1972) *A Directional Theory of Rule Application*. Doctoral dissertation, MIT, Cambridge, MA.

Howard, I. (1975) Can the 'Elsewhere Condition' get anywhere? *Language 51*: 109–127.

Hualde, J. I. (1989) The strict cycle condition and noncyclic rules. *Linguistic Inquiry 20*: 675–680.

Hualde, J. I. (2004) Quasi-phonemic contrasts in Spanish. *Proceedings of the West Coast Conference on Formal Linguistics 23*: 374–398.

Hualde, J. I. (2005) *The Sounds of Spanish*. Cambridge: Cambridge University Press.

Hulstaert, G. (1961) *Grammaire du lomóngo*. Terveuren: Musée royale de l'Afrique centrale.

Hyman, L. (1985) *A Theory of Phonological Weight*. Dordrecht: Foris.

Inkelas, S. (1999) Phonotactic blocking through structural immunity. ROA-366, Rutgers Optimality Archive, http://roa.rutgers.edu.

Ito, J. (1986) *Syllable Theory in Prosodic Phonology*. Doctoral dissertation, University of Massachusetts, Amherst, MA. Published 1988, New York: Garland.

Ito, J. and Mester, A. (2003a) On the sources of opacity in OT: Coda processes in German. In C. Féry and R. van de Vijver (eds.) *The Syllable in Optimality Theory*. Cambridge: Cambridge University Press, 271–303.

Ito, J. and Mester, A. (2003b) Weak layering and word binarity. In T. Honma, M. Okazaki, T. Tabata and S.-i. Tanaka (eds.) *A New Century of Phonology and Phonological Theory: A Festschrift for Professor Shosuke Haraguchi on the Occasion of His Sixtieth Birthday*.

Tokyo: Kaitakusha, 26–65. Originally circulated in 1992 as working paper LRC-92-09, Linguistic Research Center, UC Santa Cruz.

Iverson, G. K. (1976) A guide to sanguine relationships. In A. Koutsoudas (ed.) *The Application and Ordering of Grammatical Rules*. The Hague: Mouton, 22–40.

Janda, R. and Sandoval, M. (1984) 'Elsewhere' in morphology. Bloomington, IN: Indiana University Linguistics Club.

Johnson, C. D. (1972) *Formal Aspects of Phonological Description*. Berlin: Mouton de Gruyter.

Kahn, D. (1976) *Syllable-based Generalizations in English Phonology*. Doctoral dissertation, MIT. Published 1980, New York: Garland Press.

Kavitskaya, D. and Staroverov, P. (2010) When an interaction is both opaque and transparent: the paradox of fed counterfeeding. *Phonology 27*: 255–288.

Kean, M.-L. (1974) The strict cycle in phonology. *Linguistic Inquiry 5*: 179–203.

Kenstowicz, M. and Pyle, C. (1973) On the phonological integrity of geminate clusters. In M. J. Kenstowicz and C. W. Kisseberth (eds.) *Issues in Phonological Theory*. The Hague: Mouton, 27–43.

Kenstowicz, M. J. (1994a) On metrical constituents: unbalanced trochees and degenerate feet. In J. Cole and C. W. Kisseberth (eds.) *Perspectives in Phonology*. Stanford, CA: CSLI Publications, 113–131.

Kenstowicz, M. J. (1994b) *Phonology in Generative Grammar*. Cambridge, MA: Blackwell.

Kenstowicz, M. J. and Kisseberth, C. W. (1977) *Topics in Phonological Theory*. New York: Academic Press.

Kenstowicz, M. J. and Kisseberth, C. W. (1979) *Generative Phonology: Description and Theory*. San Diego, CA: Academic Press.

Kielhorn, F. (1960) *The Paribhāsendusekhara of Nāgojībhaṭṭa*. Poona: Bhandarkar Institute.

Kiparsky, P. (1968a) Linguistic universals and linguistic change. In E. Bach and R. T. Harms (eds.) *Universals in Linguistic Theory*. New York: Holt, Reinhart, and Winston, 170–202. Reprinted in *Explanation in Phonology*, 13–55. Dordrecht: Foris, 1982.

Kiparsky, P. (1968b) Metrics and morphophonemics in the *Kalevala*. In C. E. Gribble (ed.) *Studies Presented to Roman Jakobson by his Students*. Cambridge, MA: Slavica Publishers, 137–148. Reprinted in D. C. Freeman (ed.), *Linguistics and Literary Style*, 1970. New York: Holt, Rinehart, and Winston.

Kiparsky, P. (1971) Historical linguistics. In W. O. Dingwall (ed.) *A Survey of Linguistic Science*. College Park: University of Maryland Linguistics Program, 576–642. Reprinted in *Explanation in Phonology*, 57–80. Dordrecht: Foris, 1982.

Kiparsky, P. (1972) Metrics and morphophonemics in the *Rigveda*. In M. Brame (ed.) *Contributions to Generative Phonology*. Austin: University of Texas Press, 171–200.

Kiparsky, P. (1973a) Abstractness, opacity, and global rules. In O. Fujimura (ed.) *Three Dimensions of Linguistic Theory*, chapter 2 of Part I, *Phonological Representations*. Tokyo: TEC, 57–86.

Kiparsky, P. (1973b) "Elsewhere" in phonology. In S. R. Anderson and P. Kiparsky (eds.) *A Festschrift for Morris Halle*. New York: Holt, Reinhart, and Winston, 93–106.

Kiparsky, P. (1981a) Remarks on the metrical structure of the syllable. In W. U. Dressler, O. E. Pfeiffer and J. E. Rennison (eds.) *Phonologica 1980*. Institut für Sprachwissenschaft der Universität Innsbruck, 245–256.

Kiparsky, P. (1981b) Vowel harmony. Unpublished manuscript, MIT.

Kiparsky, P. (1982) From cyclic phonology to lexical phonology. In H. van der Hulst and N. Smith (eds.) *The Structure of Phonological Representations, Pt. 1*. Dordrecht: Foris, 131–175.

Kiparsky, P. (1984) On the lexical phonology of Icelandic. In C.-C. Elert, I. Johansson and E. Stangert (eds.) *Nordic Prosody III*. Stockholm: Almquist & Wiksell, 135–163.

Kiparsky, P. (1985) Some consequences of Lexical Phonology. *Phonology Yearbook 2*: 85–138.

Kiparsky, P. (1993) Blocking in nonderived environments. In S. Hargus and E. M. Kaisse (eds.) *Studies in Lexical Phonology, Phonetics and Phonology*, volume 4. San Diego, CA: Academic Press, 277–313.

Kiparsky, P. (forthcoming) *Paradigms and Opacity*. Stanford: CSLI.

Kirchner, R. (1996) Synchronic chain shifts in Optimality Theory. *Linguistic Inquiry 27*: 341–350.

Kisseberth, C. W. (1969) *Theoretical Implications of Yawelmani Phonology*. Doctoral dissertation, University of Illinois, Champaign-Urbana, IL.

Kisseberth, C. W. (1970a) On the functional unity of phonological rules. *Linguistic Inquiry 1*: 291–306.

Kisseberth, C. W. (1970b) The Tunica stress conspiracy. Unpublished manuscript, University of Illinois, Urbana.

Kisseberth, C. W. (1972) On derivative properties of phonological rules. In M. Brame (ed.) *Contributions to Generative Phonology*. University of Texas Press, 201–228.

Kisseberth, C. W. (1973) Is rule ordering necessary in phonology? In B. Kachru, R. Lees and Y. Malkiel (eds.) *Issues in Linguistics: Papers in Honor of Henry and Renée Kahane*. University of Illinois Press.

Koutsoudas, A., Sanders, G. and Noll, C. (1974) On the application of phonological rules. *Language 50*: 1–28.

Krämer, M. (2005) English schwa insertion before liquids and phonological opacity. *Proceedings of the Chicago Linguistic Society 41*: 267–282.

Kula, N. C. (2006) Derived environment effects in GP. *SOAS Working Papers in Linguistics 14*: 95–108.

Kula, N. C. (2008) Derived environment effects: A representational approach. *Lingua 118*: 1328–1343.

Kuroda, S.-Y. (1967) *Yawelmani Phonology*. Cambridge, MA: MIT Press.

de Lacy, P. (2002) *The Formal Expression of Markedness*. Doctoral dissertation, University of Massachusetts, Amherst, MA.

de Lacy, P. (2006) *Markedness: Reduction and Preservation in Phonology*. Cambridge: Cambridge University Press.

Lahiri, A. and Fikkert, P. (1999) Trisyllabic shortening in English: past and present. *English Language and Linguistics 3*: 229–267.

Lakoff, G. (1970) Global rules. *Language 46*: 627–639.

Levin, S. (1972) Non-paradigmatic forms: suppletion or preemption? *Foundations of Language 8*: 346–359.

Liberman, M. and Prince, A. (1977) On stress and linguistic rhythm. *Linguistic Inquiry 8*: 249–336.

Lieber, R. (1979) On Middle English lengthening in open syllables. *Linguistic Analysis 5*: 1–27.

Lipski, J. M. (1990) Spanish taps and trills: phonological structure of an isolated opposition. *Folia Linguistica 24*: 153–174.

Lloret, M.-R. and Mascaró, J. (2007) Depalatalization in Spanish revisited. In F. Martínez-Gil and S. Colina (eds.) *Optimality-Theoretic Studies in Spanish Phonology, Linguistik*

Aktuell/Linguistics Today, volume 99. Amsterdam: John Benjamins, 74–98. ROA-708, Rutgers Optimality Archive, http://roa.rutgers.edu.

Lombardi, L. (1991) *Laryngeal Features and Laryngeal Neutralization*. Doctoral dissertation, University of Massachusetts, Amherst, MA.

Lombardi, L. (1999) Positional faithfulness and voicing assimilation in Optimality Theory. *Natural Language and Linguistic Theory 17*: 267–302.

Lozano, M. d. C. (1979) *Stop and Spirant Alternations: Fortition and Spirantization Processes in Spanish Phonology*. Doctoral dissertation, Ohio State University, Columbus, OH. Distributed by the Indiana University Linguistics Club, Bloomington.

Łubowicz, A. (2002) Derived environment effects in Optimality Theory. *Lingua 112*: 243–280.

Łubowicz, A. (2003) *Contrast Preservation in Phonological Mappings*. Doctoral dissertation, University of Massachusetts, Amherst, MA. ROA-554, Rutgers Optimality Archive, http://roa.rutgers.edu.

Luick, K. (1898) Beiträge zur Englischen Grammatik III: Die quantitätsveränderungen im laufe der englischen sprachentwicklung. *Anglia 20*: 335–362.

Luick, K. (1964) *Historische Grammatik der englischen Sprache*, volume 1. Oxford and Stuttgart: Bernhard Tauchnitz. Fotomechanisher Nachdruck der ersten Auflage 1914.

Malouf, R. (2005a) Disjunctive rule ordering in finite state morphology. Paper presented at the 41st Meeting of the Chicago Linguistics Society. http://bulba.sdsu.edu/~malouf/papers/cls05-slides.pdf.

Malouf, R. (2005b) Realizational morphology by disjunctive composition. Paper presented at the Alpino Workshop, University of Groningen. http://bulba.sdsu.edu/~malouf/papers/mgreek.pdf.

Mascaró, J. (1976) *Catalan Phonology and the Phonological Cycle*. Doctoral dissertation, MIT, Cambridge, MA.

Matthews, P. H. (1972) *Inflectional Morphology*. Number 6 in Cambridge Studies in Linguistics, Cambridge: Cambridge University Press.

McCarthy, J. J. (1979) *Formal Problems in Semitic Phonology and Morphology*. Doctoral dissertation, MIT, Cambridge, MA.

McCarthy, J. J. (1981) A prosodic theory of nonconcatenative morphology. *Linguistic Inquiry 12*: 373–418.

McCarthy, J. J. (1991) Synchronic rule inversion. *Proceedings of the Berkeley Linguistics Society 17*: 192–207.

McCarthy, J. J. (1993) A case of surface constraint violation. *Canadian Journal of Linguistics 38*: 169–195. Special issue: Constraint-Based Theories in Multilinear Phonology.

McCarthy, J. J. (1997) Process-specific constraints in Optimality Theory. *Linguistic Inquiry 28*: 231–251.

McCarthy, J. J. (1999a) Appendix: A note on Boston *r* and the Elsewhere Condition. Appendix to Review of *Derivations and Constraints in Phonology* by Iggy Roca, *Phonology* 16(2), 265–271. http://people.umass.edu/jjmccart/appendix.pdf.

McCarthy, J. J. (1999b) Sympathy and phonological opacity. *Phonology 16*: 331–399.

McCarthy, J. J. (2002) *A Thematic Guide to Optimality Theory*. Cambridge: Cambridge University Press.

McCarthy, J. J. (2003a) Comparative markedness. *Theoretical Linguistics 29*: 1–51.

McCarthy, J. J. (2003b) OT constraints are categorical. *Phonology 20*: 75–138.

McCarthy, J. J. (2003c) Sympathy, cumulativity, and the Duke-of-York gambit. In C. Féry and R. van de Vijver (eds.) *The Syllable in Optimality Theory*. Cambridge: Cambridge University Press, 23–76.

McCarthy, J. J. (2007a) Derivations and levels of representation. In P. de Lacy (ed.) *The Cambridge Handbook of Phonology*. Cambridge: Cambridge University Press, 99–117.

McCarthy, J. J. (2007b) *Hidden Generalizations: Phonological Opacity in Optimality Theory*. London: Equinox.

McCarthy, J. J. (2008a) The gradual path to cluster simplification. *Phonology 25*: 271–319.

McCarthy, J. J. (2008b) The serial interaction of stress and syncope. *Natural Language and Linguistic Theory 26*: 499–546.

McCarthy, J. J. (2009) Harmony in Harmonic Serialism. ROA-1009, Rutgers Optimality Archive, http://roa.rutgers.edu.

McCarthy, J. J. and Prince, A. (1993a) Generalized alignment. In G. Booij and J. van Marle (eds.) *Yearbook of Morphology*. Dordrecht: Kluwer, 79–153. ROA-7, Rutgers Optimality Archive, http://roa.rutgers.edu.

McCarthy, J. J. and Prince, A. (1993b) *Prosodic Morphology: Constraint Interaction and Satisfaction*. RuCCS-TR-3, Rutgers University Center for Cognitive Science. ROA-482, Rutgers Optimality Archive, http://roa.rutgers.edu.

McCarthy, J. J. and Prince, A. (1995) Faithfulness and reduplicative identity. In J. Beckman, L. Walsh Dickey and S. Urbanczyk (eds.) *Papers in Optimality Theory, University of Massachusetts Occasional Papers*, volume 18. Amherst, MA: GLSA, 249–384. ROA-60, Rutgers Optimality Archive, http://roa.rutgers.edu.

McCarthy, J. J. and Prince, A. (1999) Faithfulness and identity in prosodic morphology. In R. Kager, H. van der Hulst and W. Zonneveld (eds.) *The Prosody-Morphology Interface*. Cambridge: Cambridge University Press, 218–309. ROA-216, Rutgers Optimality Archive, http://roa.rutgers.edu.

McCawley, J. D. (1968) *The Phonological Component of a Grammar of Japanese*. The Hague: Mouton.

Mester, R. A. (1994) The quantitative trochee in Latin. *Natural Language and Linguistic Theory 12*: 1–61.

Mohanan, K. P. (1991) On the bases of radical underspecification. *Natural Language and Linguistic Theory 9*: 285–325.

Moreton, E. (2004) Non-computable functions in Optimality Theory. In J. J. McCarthy (ed.) *Optimality Theory in Phonology: A Reader*. Oxford: Blackwell, 141–163.

Morin, Y.-C. (1988) Disjunctive ordering and French morphology. *Natural Language and Linguistic Theory 6*: 271–282.

Myers, S. (1985) The long and the short of it: a metrical theory of English vowel quantity. *CLS 21*: 275–288.

Myers, S. (1987) Vowel shortening in English. *Natural Language and Linguistic Theory 5*: 485–518.

Myers, S. (1991a) Persistent rules. *Linguistic Inquiry 22*: 315–344.

Myers, S. (1991b) Structure Preservation and the Strong Domain Hypothesis. *Linguistic Inquiry 22*: 379–385.

Newman, S. (1944) *Yokuts Language of California*. 2, New York: Viking Fund Publications in Anthropology.

Norton, R. J. (2003) *Derivational Phonology and Optimality Phonology: Formal Comparison and Synthesis*. Doctoral dissertation, University of Essex, Colchester, UK.

Odden, D. (2005) *Introducing Phonology*. Cambridge: Cambridge University Press.

O'Keefe, M. (2003) *Akan Vowel Harmony*. Undergraduate thesis, Swarthmore College.

van Oostendorp, M. (2003) Comparative markedness and containment. *Theoretical Linguistics 29*: 65–75.

van Oostendorp, M. (2007a) Derived environment effects and consistency of exponence. In S. Blaho, P. Bye and M. Krämer (eds.) *Freedom of Analysis?* Berlin: Mouton de Gruyter, 123–148.

van Oostendorp, M. (2007b) Restricting repairs. Unpublished manuscript, http://www.vanoostendorp.nl/pdf/toomanyrepairs.pdf.

Orgun, C. O. (2001) English *r*-insertion in Optimality Theory. *Natural Language and Linguistic Theory 19*: 737–749.

Padgett, J. (1991) *Stricture in Feature Geometry*. Doctoral dissertation, University of Massachusetts, Amherst, MA.

Padgett, J. (1994) Stricture and nasal place assimilation. *Natural Language and Linguistic Theory 12*: 465–513.

Paradis, C. (1988) On constraints and repair strategies. *The Linguistic Review 6*: 71–97.

Pater, J. (1999) Austronesian nasal substitution and other NC̥ effects. In R. Kager, H. van der Hulst and W. Zonneveld (eds.) *The Prosody-Morphology Interface*. Cambridge: Cambridge University Press, 310–343. ROA-160, Rutgers Optimality Archive, http://roa.rutgers.edu.

Pater, J. (2001) Austronesian nasal substitution revisited. In L. Lombardi (ed.) *Segmental Phonology in Optimality Theory: Constraints and Representations*. Cambridge: Cambridge University Press, 159–182.

Penny, R. (2002) *A History of the Spanish Language*. Cambridge: Cambridge University Press, 2nd edition.

Pensado, C. (1997) On the Spanish depalatalization of /ɲ/ and /ʎ/ in rhymes. In F. Martínez-Gil and A. Morales-Front (eds.) *Issues in the Phonology and Morphology of the Major Iberian Languages*. Washington, DC: Georgetown University Press, 595–618.

Perlmutter, D. (1995) Phonological quantity and multiple association. In J. Goldsmith (ed.) *The Handbook of Phonological Theory*. Oxford: Blackwell.

Poser, W. J. (1993) Are strict cycle effects derivable? In S. Hargus and E. M. Kaisse (eds.) *Studies in Lexical Phonology, Phonetics and Phonology*, volume 4. San Diego, CA: Academic Press, 315–321.

Prince, A. (1980) A metrical theory for Estonian quantity. *Linguistic Inquiry 11*.

Prince, A. (1985) Improving tree theory. *Proceedings of the Berkeley Linguistics Society 11*: 471–490.

Prince, A. (1991) Quantitative consequences of rhythmic organization. Linguistics & Cognitive Science Program and Center for Complex Systems, Brandeis University.

Prince, A. (1993) Minimal violation. Handout from *Rutgers Optimality Workshop* (ROW-1) talk.

Prince, A. (1997a) Elsewhere & otherwise. *GLOT International 2*: 1, 23–24. Expanded and reformatted as ROA-217, Rutgers Optimality Archive, http://roa.rutgers.edu. Page references are to the ROA version.

Prince, A. (1997b) Paninian relations. Handout from UMass Amherst colloquium talk. http://equinox.rutgers.edu/gamma/talks/umass1997.pdf.

Prince, A. (1997c) Stringency and anti-paninian hierarchies. LSA Linguistic Institute handout, Cornell University. http://equinox.rutgers.edu/gamma/talks/insthdt2.pdf.

Prince, A. (1998) Two lectures on Optimality Theory. Handouts from 1998 Phonology Forum talks, Kobe University.

Prince, A. (2000) The Special and the General. Handout from Penn Linguistics Colloquium talk. http://equinox.rutgers.edu/gamma/talks/plc-hdt.pdf.

Prince, A. (2001) Invariance under re-ranking. Handout from WCCFL talk. http://equinox.rutgers.edu/gamma/talks/WCCFL2001.pdf.

Prince, A. (2002) Arguing optimality. In A. Carpenter, A. W. Coetzee and P. de Lacy (eds.) *Papers in Optimality Theory II, University of Massachusetts Occasional Papers*, volume 26. Amherst, MA: GLSA, 269–304.

Prince, A. (2007) In pursuit of theory. In P. de Lacy (ed.) *The Cambridge Handbook of Phonology*. Cambridge: Cambridge University Press, 33–60.

Prince, A. and Smolensky, P. (1993) *Optimality Theory: Constraint Interaction in Generative Grammar.* Rutgers University Center for Cognitive Science: Technical Report RuCCS-TR-2. ROA-537, Rutgers Optimality Archive, http://roa.rutgers.edu. Page references are to the 2002 ROA version.

Prince, A. and Smolensky, P. (2004) *Optimality Theory: Constraint Interaction in Generative Grammar.* Malden, MA: Blackwell.

Pulleyblank, D. (1996) Neutral vowels in Optimality Theory: A comparison of Yoruba and Wolof. *Canadian Journal of Linguistics 41*: 295–347.

Pulleyblank, D., Jiang-King, P., Leitch, M. and Ọlanikẹ Ọla (1995) Typological variation through constraint rankings: Low vowels in tongue root harmony. In *Proceedings of South Western Optimality Theory Workshop*. The University of Arizona Coyote Papers, 184–208.

Pullum, G. K. (1976) The Duke of York gambit. *Journal of Linguistics 12*: 83–102.

Rubach, J. (1996) Shortening and ambisyllabicity in English. *Phonology 13*: 197–237.

Sanders, G. A. (1974) Precedence relations in language. *Foundations of Language 11*: 361–400.

Sapir, D. (1965) *A Grammar of Diola-Fogny*. Cambridge: Cambridge University Press.

Sapir, E. and Swadesh, M. (1978) *Nootka Texts: Tales and Ethnological Narratives, with Grammatical Notes and Lexical Material.* New York: AMS Press.

Saporta, S. (1965) Ordered rules, dialect differences, and historical processes. *Language 41*: 218–224.

Schein, B. and Steriade, D. (1986) On geminates. *Linguistic Inquiry 17*: 691–744.

Selkirk, E. O. (1984) *Phonology and Syntax: The Relation between Sound and Structure.* Cambridge, MA: MIT Press.

Singh, R. (1987) Well-formedness conditions and phonological theory. In W. U. Dressler (ed.) *Phonologica 1984*. Cambridge: Cambridge University Press, 273–286.

Smolensky, P. (1993) Harmony, markedness, and phonological activity. Handout from *Rutgers Optimality Workshop* (ROW-1) talk; ROA-87, Rutgers Optimality Archive, http://roa.rutgers.edu.

Smolensky, P. (1995) On the internal structure of the constraint component *Con* of UG. Handout from talk presented at the UCLA Linguistics Department; ROA-86, Rutgers Optimality Archive, http://roa.rutgers.edu.

Smolensky, P. (1996) The initial state and 'richness of the base' in Optimality Theory. Technical Report JHU-CogSci-96-4, Department of Cognitive Science, Johns Hopkins University. ROA-154, Rutgers Optimality Archive, http://roa.rutgers.edu.

Smolensky, P. (1997) Constraint interaction in generative grammar II: Local conjunction (or, Random rules in Universal Grammar). Handout from talk presented at the Hopkins Optimality Theory Conference.

Smolensky, P. (2006) Optimality in phonology II: harmonic completeness, local constraint conjunction, and feature domain markedness. In P. Smolensky and G. Legendre (eds.) *The Harmonic Mind: From Neural Computation to Optimality-Theoretic Grammar*, volume II: Linguistic and Philosophical Implications, chapter 14. Cambridge, MA: MIT Press, 27–160.

Smolensky, P., Legendre, G. and Tesar, B. (2006) Optimality Theory: the structure, use, and acquisition of phonological knowledge. In P. Smolensky and G. Legendre (eds.) *The*

Harmonic Mind: From Neural Computation to Optimality-Theoretic Grammar, volume I: Cognitive Architectures, chapter 12. Cambridge, MA: MIT Press, 453–544.

Sommerstein, A. (1974) On phonotactically motivated rules. *Journal of Linguistics 10*: 71–94.

Stampe, D. (1979) *A Dissertation on Natural Phonology*. Outstanding Dissertations in Linguistics, New York: Garland Publishing. Doctoral dissertation, University of Chicago, 1973 (originally titled 'How I spent my summer vacation').

Steriade, D. (1982) *Greek Prosodies and the Nature of Syllabification*. Doctoral dissertation, MIT, Cambridge, MA.

Steriade, D. (1987) Redundant values. In A. Bosch, B. Need and E. Schiller (eds.) *Papers from the Parasession on Autosegmental and Metrical Phonology*. Chicago, IL: Chicago Linguistic Society, 339–362.

Steriade, D. (1995) Underspecification and markedness. In J. Goldsmith (ed.) *The Handbook of Phonological Theory*. Oxford: Blackwell, 114–174.

Stewart, J. M. (1967) Tongue root position in Akan vowel harmony. *Phonetica 16*: 185–204.

Stockwell, R. and Minkova, D. (2002) Interpreting the Old and Middle English close vowels. *Language Sciences 24*: 447–457.

Stump, G. (1989) A note on Breton pluralization and the Elsewhere Condition. *Natural Language and Linguistic Theory 7*: 261–273.

Stump, G. (2002) Morphological blocking and Pāṇini's principle. Papers from the *Periphrasis and Paradigms Workshop*, UC San Diego, April 12–13, 2002. http://www.cs.uky.edu/~gstump/periphrasispapers/malto.pdf.

Uffmann, C. (2007) Intrusive [r] and optimal epenthetic consonants. *Language Sciences 29*: 451–476.

Vaux, B. (2008) Why the phonological component must be serial and rule-based. In B. Vaux and A. Nevins (eds.) *Rules, Constraints, and Phonological Phenomena*. Oxford: Oxford University Press, 20–60.

Vennemann, T. (1972) Rule inversion. *Lingua 29*: 209–242.

van de Vijver, R. (2003) The CiV-generalization in Dutch: what *petunia*, *mafia*, and *sovjet* tell us about Dutch syllable structure. In C. Féry and R. van de Vijver (eds.) *The Syllable in Optimality Theory*. Cambridge: Cambridge University Press, 338–355.

Whitley, M. S. (2003) Rhotic representation: problems and proposals. *Journal of the International Phonetic Association 33*: 81–86.

Whorf, B. L. (1943) Phonemic analysis of the English of Eastern Massachusetts. *Studies in Linguistics 2*: 21–40.

Wilkinson, K. (1988) Prosodic structure and Lardil phonology. *Linguistic Inquiry 19*: 325–334.

Wilson, C. (2000) *Targeted constraints: An approach to contextual neutralization in Optimality Theory*. Doctoral dissertation, Johns Hopkins University, Baltimore, MD.

Wilson, C. (2001) Consonant cluster neutralisation and targeted constraints. *Phonology 18*: 147–197.

Wilson, C. (2003) Unbounded spreading in OT (or, Unbounded spreading is local spreading iterated unboundedly). Paper presented at *SWOT 8*, Tucson, AZ.

Wilson, C. (2004) Analyzing unbounded spreading with constraints: Marks, targets, and derivations. Manuscript, UCLA.

Wilson, C. (2006) Unbounded spreading is myopic. Paper presented at *PhonologyFest 2006*, Bloomington, IN. http://www.linguistics.ucla.edu/people/wilson/Myopia2006.pdf.

Wright, J. and Wright, E. M. (1923) *An Elementary Middle English Grammar.* London: Oxford University Press.

Yip, M. (1987) English vowel epenthesis. *Natural Language and Linguistic Theory 5*: 463–484.

Zeevat, H. (1995) Idiomatic blocking and the Elsewhere Principle. In M. Everaert, E.-J. van der Linden, A. Schenk and R. Schreuder (eds.) *Idioms: Structural and Psychological Perspectives.* Hillsdale, NJ: Lawrence Erlbaum Associates, Inc., 301–316.

Index

www.ingramcontent.com/pod-product-compliance
Lightning Source LLC
LaVergne TN
LVHW011204090826
844660LV00058B/267

* 9 7 8 1 8 4 5 5 3 3 3 6 6 *